T0398188

Europe Managing the Crisis

Studies of the recent financial crisis have been largely dominated by economists, but the similarities and differences between European countries' response reflect both economic and political perspectives that have resulted in considerable differences in their decisions.

Drawing on uniquely comprehensive research data, this book presents an in-depth comparative analysis of how fourteen European governments tackled the challenge of fiscal consolidation, and analyses the political decision-making behind these measures. By exploring national responses not just in fiscal terms, but also from a political perspective, it reveals that decision-making has been driven by political factors with profound effects on public administration and management.

This ground-breaking book fills an important gap in the research literature for scholars of Public Management, Public Administration and Policy, and will be a benchmark for future work on the global economic crisis.

Walter J. M. Kickert is Professor of Public Management at Erasmus University Rotterdam, the Netherlands.

Tiina Randma-Liiv is Professor of Public Management and Public Policy at Tallinn University of Technology, Estonia.

The strength of the book is in the transparent analytical framework and the full coverage of aspects: cuts, expenditures, revenues, investments. The focus on decision making (or non-decision making) turns the book into a supremely useful embedded case for teaching in leadership, decision making, political economy, governance and administration. For this reason, the book becomes relevant for political science, economists, public administration, management, and even lawyers. Finally, the book is crucial since it is not just analyzing and discussing process but also effects. For all these reasons, this book will become a standard volume in crisis governance.

Geert Bouckaert, President of the International Institute of Administrative Sciences

Drawing on a wealth of original research, comparing the response of a range of countries to the economic crisis, this book delivers valuable insight into the issues raised by the recent near collapse of much of the world's economy. The strength of the book is that it places political considerations, decisions and institutions in their rightful place – at the center of its analysis.

Andrew Massey, Professor, University of Exeter, UK and Editor of International Review of Administrative Sciences and Public Money and Management

This is a much-needed book. Kickert and Randma-Liiv tackle the crucial issue of understanding the responses adopted by national governments across Europe to the financial, economic and fiscal crises. They map decision-making patterns and delve into the explanations and the effects of them, by bringing political and administrative factors to the foreground. Decision-makers and scholars alike will benefit greatly from this major study.

Edoardo Ongaro, Professor, Northumbria University, UK and President of the European Group for Public Administration

The global financial crisis has been the subject of an immense amount of scholarly and popular attention. This book is one of the very best treatments available on the reactions of European governments to the crisis and the effects of their policy choices. Kickert and Randma-Liiv combine generalisations about government actions with insightful examinations of the policy choices of individual countries.

B. Guy Peters, Professor, University of Pittsburgh, USA and President of the International Public Policy Association

Europe Managing the Crisis

The politics of fiscal consolidation

Walter J. M. Kickert and Tiina Randma-Liiv

Routledge
Taylor & Francis Group

LONDON AND NEW YORK

First published 2015
by Routledge
2 Park Square, Milton Park, Abingdon, Oxon OX14 4RN

Simultaneously published in the USA and Canada
by Routledge
711 Third Avenue, New York, NY 10017

Routledge is an imprint of the Taylor & Francis Group, an informa business

British Library Cataloguing in Publication Data
A catalogue record for this book is available from the British Library

Library of Congress Cataloging in Publication Data
Kickert, Walter J. M. (Walter Julius Michael)
 Europe managing the crisis: the politics of fiscal consolidation/
 Walter J. M. Kickert and Tiina Randma-Liiv.
 pages cm
 Includes bibliographical references and index.
 1. Public administration – Europe – Cost control. 2. Budget deficits –
 Europe. 3. Government spending policy – Europe. 4. Financial crises –
 Europe. I. Randma-Liiv, Tiina. II. Title.
 JN94.A58K53 2015
 330.94′05611 – dc23
 2014040828

ISBN: 978-1-138-85362-1 (hbk)
ISBN: 978-1-315-72268-9 (ebk)

Typeset in Berling and Futura
by Florence Production Ltd, Stoodleigh, Devon, UK

Contents

Figures

Tables

Foreword

Geert Bouckaert

President of the International Institute of
Administrative Sciences

In reading this book, I made three reflections on managing crises: one on the cultures of managing crises, another on understanding managing crises through disciplines, and a final one on the capacity of comparing and learning from others.

Managing crises or muddling through

There is an expression in Dutch that weak healers make stinking wounds. There also seems to be a tension between the direct and unambiguous word 'crisis', and labelling almost euphemistically its response as 'consolidation'. Not only risks, but also responses to catastrophes, revolutions, or crises are culturally determined, as Mary Douglas clearly demonstrated. There could be a culture of determinism, but also of voluntarism expressed in statements that one never should waste a crisis. The fiscal crisis has shown several levels and its management seems not always to have been proportional.

There are single-loop crises within a financial system that could be solved within that system by respecting, for example, standards of deficits, or levels of debt. There are double-loop crises where the rationality of the system itself is affected. The debates on volumes of money in a system, or the stop-go investment policies, or the failing efficiency of markets (see the controversy of the 2013 Nobel Prize winners Fama, Shiller and Hansen) are expressions of a failing rationality of a fiscal system. Finally, there are deutero-crises, where there is a crisis of the concept 'crisis' itself. The concept of crisis itself shifts. If there is a conviction that systems are 'too big to fail', then the concept of 'crisis' shifts. This may move into a 'state of exception' (Agamben 2005), unprecedented, where 'exceptions' suddenly become 'normality' and 'standard operating procedures'. It is also a situation where weak or even 'hollow states' (Frederickson and Frederickson 2006) emerge and crises become a relative reality.

Handling single-loop crises assumes that known causes lead to known consequences. Double-loop crises need to adjust the systemic key characteristics and the rationality of these systems. OECD (2009) has emphasised the need to have independent authorities that also can enforce certain logics. Cangiano *et al.* (2013) demonstrated the need for a new macro-governance architecture with new logics and rationalities. Deutero-crises have all the features of wickedness and could be unmanageable if there is no time and authority to establish a new system with a new rationality.

Different disciplines for different purposes

If this exercise would be reduced to the field of accounting, perhaps the only conclusion would be at the level of balance sheets: 'what is left is right, and what is right has left.' However, solid and reliable monitoring, surveillance and oversight are indispensable for financial and non-financial information. Historically, public-sector budgeting accumulated macro-economic issues, policy allocation and managerial functions. As a consequence, different disciplines (economics, policy and political sciences, and management) are involved for different purposes, also in a crises modus.

All these approaches are also legally framed. In several countries, there were appeals up to the highest courts to fight 'solutions' of the crises. Common-law countries do have different legal frames and degrees of freedom compared to civil-law countries. Finally, anthropology and cultural theory certainly provide context to avoid blind copy pasting of 'solutions'.

The field of Public Administration, as a consolidating scientific platform of different disciplines, should use this crisis as an opportunity to promote not only multidisciplinary research, but certainly to develop seriously interdisciplinary research.

International comparative research on 'political decision-making capabilities of governments'

The ultimate purpose of this international comparative research is to better understand the nature and mechanisms of crises, and to learn how to cope with this crisis and the next crises. The level of describing, explaining and even predicting depends on the levels of the crises themselves. Single-loop will be easier than double-loop, which will be less difficult than deutero-crises.

The capacity of governments to solve problems will be one of the essential challenges of the next decades to keep trust and legitimacy of populations in our systems. For this reason, this book contributes significantly to this European agenda, and beyond. One could only wish that all the 'evidence' available in this book will influence the leadership to tackle all future crises effectively.

This Kickert/Randma-Liiv book: a guide and survival kit for solutions

This book is written by two top scholars in the field. They give a very well-documented description of the fiscal crisis. It is one of the best available texts on the mechanisms, the scope and the consequences of the crisis. The value added is that it is based on a lot of types of information, including interviews with key officials, and that it puts the crisis in a political context. The crucial question suddenly becomes: Does politics matter if economics gives the impression to have taken over?

The strength of the book is in the transparent analytical framework and the full coverage of aspects: cuts, expenditures, revenues, investments. The focus on decision-making (or non-decision-making) turns the book into a supremely useful embedded case for teaching in leadership, decision-making, political economy, governance and administration. For this reason, the book becomes relevant for political science, economists, Public Administration, management and even lawyers. Finally, the book is crucial since it is not just analysing and discussing process, but also effects. For all these reasons, this book will become a standard volume in crisis governance.

It is my conviction that this book is teaching us a lot of lessons, even if the scientific conclusions seem more ambiguous and the meaning of 'solution' is part of this ambiguity. The major lesson for the futures of our democratic systems is ultimately how to handle crises and ambiguity. This book is a guide and survival kit for all of us.

References

Agamben, Giorgio (2005) *State of Exception* (Trans. Kevin Attell). Chicago, IL: University of Chicago Press.

Cangiano, Marco, Curristine, Teresa and Lazare, Michel (eds) (2013) *Public Financial Management and its Emerging Architecture*. Washington, DC: IMF.

Frederickson, David G. and Frederickson, H. George (2006) *Measuring the Performance of the Hollow State*. Washington, DC: Georgetown University Press.

OECD (2009) *OECD Strategic Response to the Financial and Economic Crisis: Contributions to the Global Effort*. Paris: OECD.

Part one

Introduction

Chapter 1

Introduction

For much of the recent past, the main occupation of European governments has been to make cutbacks. That is, to ensure the restoration of sound public finances via the reduction of excessive budget deficits through cuts to public expenditures and rises in tax revenues. Politicians, governments and administrations have been repeatedly confronted with the unpleasant necessity of this thankless task.

Since the outbreak of the global financial crisis in 2008 and the following economic crisis, public finances have come under enormous pressure. The worldwide financial system suddenly, unexpectedly, and completely collapsed. While initially many continental European governments hoped this US-originated crisis would not spread to their economies, European domestic economies were soon infected by the effects of the crisis on the international financial markets. Economies deteriorated, business declined and unemployment rose. Despite governments immediately launching economic recovery measures, European economies continued to slow, and in many countries they have only recently, and slowly, recovered. This has led to mounting public budget deficits, which, by necessity, have had to be reduced – whether governments and politicians have liked that thankless task or not.

At first, politicians in most countries tried to avoid unpopular cutbacks, primarily by disputing the necessity and strictness of budget deficit ceilings, such as the EU norm of 3 per cent. Alternatively, politicians tried to postpone budget cutbacks, leaving them for the next administration to cope with. But whatever their tactics to buy time, sooner or later cuts became inevitable, and unfortunately not just once, but in many successive rounds. Economies continued to perform disappointingly, and economic recovery took more time than expected. National public finances repeatedly turned out to be less optimistic than hoped for, and a next round of cutbacks had to be made. Political authorities faced sometimes massive protests and social interest, and hard decisions about where and when to cut. This has been the reality for many European countries for several years. Governments and politicians are constantly employed with, and often overwhelmed by, making decisions about cutbacks. And although the early signals of fragile economic recovery now seem more than just wishful thinking, the task is not yet over by some long way.

In this book, we will describe, analyse and explain how European governments handled the crisis, from a political and administrative science perspective. Much of our international, predominantly English-speaking, audience will be acquainted with how the United States and the United Kingdom handled the crisis, and probably the German and French cases, to some extent. Most other European countries are, however, less known to the international audience. Who is knowledgeable about the smaller Western European countries, such as Belgium, Ireland and the Netherlands? Who knows how the crisis impacted the Central and Eastern European countries of Estonia, Hungary and Lithuania? And although a larger international audience is aware of the depth of the crisis in Southern Europe, very little is known about what exactly happened in countries such as Italy and Spain.

In this book, we consider how fourteen large and small countries in Western, Southern and Eastern Europe – Belgium, Estonia, France, Germany, Hungary, Iceland, Ireland, Italy, Lithuania, the Netherlands, Norway, Slovenia, Spain and the United Kingdom – have managed the fiscal crisis. This range and scope makes this book highly informative to the international audience, not only to the academic audience, but also to practitioners and policy-makers who will be interested in the many country examples. We hope these provide helpful insights into how the complex problems they face have been addressed elsewhere.

This book seeks to introduce to an Anglo American audience various European approaches to managing the crisis, as well as informing Europeans about the way the crisis was handled by their neighbours. It encourages readers to view national distinctiveness in an international comparative perspective. And in the final discussion section, when we are less hindered by methodological and empirical limitations from making statements about countries outside Europe, we tentatively compare the European experience with other parts of the world – the United States, Japan, India, and the upcoming economic superpower, China.

The first question addressed in this book is how fourteen countries in Western, Southern and Eastern Europe managed in the period 2008–2012. How did European governments respond to the fiscal crisis? What fiscal consolidation and cutback measures were undertaken by governments to reduce the increasing budget deficits? How did the political decision-making leading up to these measures take place?

The attentive reader may have noticed that we employed the terms 'describe, analyse and explain' in the above formulation of our book's objective. The book is not only descriptive and informative, but also analytical and explanatory. In this book, we analyse and explain, primarily from an administrative and political science perspective, how European governments responded to the crisis. Although both authors are scholars in politics and administration, rather than economics and public finances, this by no means makes the economic perspective less relevant. On the contrary, it is obvious that fiscal consolidation and cutbacks are, first and foremost, concerned with decisions about budgets, about economic facts and figures. Naturally, the economic perspective on how governments managed the financial and economic crisis is paramount is reflected in the many publications on the subject from this perspective; a review of twenty-one books about the financial crisis written by academics, journalists and a practitioner (Lo 2011) reveals that, despite the many different and often contradictory perspectives used, all are written from an economic point of view.

This book pays attention not only to the economic aspects of the fiscal consolidation measures taken by governments, but also pays particular attention to the political aspects of the decision-making processes leading up to these measures. Did politics matter in managing the crisis? Studies by political and administrative scholars are only beginning to appear, and there are only a limited number of publications on the current fiscal crisis and cutbacks in the fields from the perspective of political, administrative and public management sciences. So, the second question addressed in this book is how the fiscal consolidation measures that were taken by European governments can be analysed and explained from both an economic and a political perspective.

After elaborating the political perspective in the next chapter, we adopt an analytical framework that focuses on both the contents of the cutback measures and the political decision-making processes. We pay special attention to the characteristics of decision-making – the distinction between across-the-board (cheese-slicing) cuts, on the one hand, and targeted (selective) cuts based on political priorities, on the other. Moreover, attention focuses on the typical political characteristics of cutback decision-making, that is, that it takes place in a series of stages, usually beginning with denial of the gravity and duration of the crisis, gradually leading to compliance with the need for cutbacks, and only ultimately resulting in targeted cuts and political priority-setting.

In its comparative analysis of how fourteen European countries managed the fiscal crisis, the book focuses on key questions. What were the similarities and differences between the countries? How can the similarities and differences between the countries be explained? The individual country studies are framed in an internationally comparative perspective with the aim of comparing the similarities and differences between countries, from both an economic and a political perspective. What financial-economic factors explain the variation in the fiscal consolidation measures of the various governments? What political-administrative factors have explanatory power? And what other factors have a significant influence on fiscal consolidation?

It is self-evident that economic factors play a principal role in explaining fiscal consolidation measures. After all, fiscal consolidation is aimed at reducing the budget deficit and rise of state debt, so the financial and economic 'size' of the fiscal crisis evidently influences the 'size' of the consolidation measures.

The size of fiscal consolidation will depend on the economic and budgetary situation in a country prior to the crisis, and our comparative analysis, of course, confirms this.

Did politics also matter in fiscal consolidation? While the economic size of fiscal consolidation is chiefly explained by the prior economic and budgetary circumstances, we may yet expect political decision-making to be influenced by political-administrative factors as well. The in-depth country case examples make it clear that political factors play a role in explaining how governments handled the crisis. In the countries hit most severely by the crisis, the political aspects seem to dominate cutback decision-making. From an international comparative perspective, however, the explanatory evidence becomes less clear. How did the type of state structure affect decisions? How did the type of government affect decisions? Were single-party governments better able to take hard cutback decisions than multi-party coalitions? Were grand majority coalitions better able than coalitions with merely parliamentary minority? Did the political orientation of governments play a role? The common assumption is that right-wing parties in government tend to take swifter and harder cutback decisions than left-wing parties. How did the electoral cycle affect cutback decisions? Were politically unpopular cutback decisions postponed when general elections approached?

And finally, how did it work out? For academic scientists, an international comparative analysis per se may be interesting enough, but our guess is that practitioners, politicians and policy-makers are, above all, interested in the question of how it worked. Was fiscal consolidation successful? Which country did better, and why? What were the success and failure factors?

We have to admit that we cannot possibly answer such questions, for a number of reasons. First, it is much too early to evaluate the success of fiscal consolidation now. In many European countries, the first cutback measures were only taken in 2010. And in many countries, that was the mere beginning of subsequent rounds of cutbacks. The fiscal crisis is not yet over by some long way. New cutbacks repeatedly appear to be necessary. There is no way that one could currently assess successfulness. Second, a normative evaluation study of fiscal consolidation runs the danger of serious methodological pitfalls. What are the criteria for success? Only deficit reduction and economic recovery, or also social and political aspects? Economic recovery is dependent on more than domestic consolidation efforts alone.

Rather than running away from the methodological risks and completely giving up, we carry out the more neutral exercise of effect measurement. So, the final question addressed in this book is what the effects were of the fiscal consolidations and cutback measures taken by European governments, again in terms of economics, politics and administration. In this way, we hope to perhaps somewhat mollify the interests of the practitioners.

After this introductory prelude to the substance of this book, we now turn to the relevance of the subject. Though we expect that the international audience reading this book is well aware of the utmost relevance of the current global financial, economic and fiscal crisis, we nevertheless consider it sensible and useful to give a brief and hopefully convincing indication why the crisis is a most important and urgent challenge for many Western countries. We therefore present a brief overview of the severity and scale of the global crisis, and of the measures that governments took in response, amply illustrated with country examples.

Severity of the crisis

On 15 September 2008, the American investment bank Lehman Brothers collapsed. Immediately, the financial markets panicked. Worldwide, bank stock prices plummeted. Many large banks glided to the fringe of bankruptcy and were about to collapse. The mutual trust between banks fell away, and therewith the interbank money market. The international financial markets suddenly came to a standstill. Governments were obligated to rescue their vital 'systemic banks' in order to prevent a total collapse of domestic finances and economy. The costs were enormous.

Initially in Western Europe, the hopeful idea prevailed that the problem of the 'subprime mortgages' and banking crisis in the United States would not spread over to the continent. The French (conservative) president Sarkozy at the time declared that this was merely a crisis of 'Anglo-Saxon (read British and American) capitalism'. The house price bubble in the United States and Britain supposedly did not exist on the continent. The banks there did not sell insecure mortgages (so-called 'subprime mortgages') with short-term loans from the 'low-rent, easy-credit' money market. It soon turned out that the European banks *did* possess such 'toxic assets', and the banking crisis also spread to continental Europe. The worldwide dry up of interbank loans caused an

Banking crisis in the United States

On 8 September 2008, the government of the United States was forced to save Fannie Mae and Freddie Mac, which together possessed about half of the mortgages in the United States. The weekend before Monday 15 September, the United States government had, in vain, attempted to have Lehman Brothers taken over by the British bank Barclays. On 16 September, the United States government had to rescue the largest insurance company in the world, AIB, for $85 billion.

Banking crisis in Great Britain

On 18 September 2008, the British government had HBOS bank taken over by Lloyds. Bradford & Bingley threatened to go bankrupt and was nationalised by the British government. After 'meltdown Monday' on 6 October, when the London stock exchange completely wiped away the stock prices of the largest British companies and banks, the government was obliged to further interfere. On 8 October, a package of £50 billion capital injections into banks was announced, plus £200 billion to buy up 'toxic assets', as well as a guarantee on interbank loans. This amounted to the nationalisation of the Royal Bank of Scotland (RBS), HBOS and Lloyds.

Source: Treasury Committee (2009a)

Banking crisis in the Netherlands

The Dutch state took over the Dutch part of the bankrupt Fortis bank for €16.8 billion and therewith became the owner of the Dutch Fortis part of ABN AMRO bank, which was taken over in 2007 by an international consortium of the British RBS, the Spanish Santander and the Belgian Fortis bank. Including later credits and guarantees, the costs for the rescue of ABN AMRO amounted €29.4 billion. Furthermore, a €20 billion fund was established for banks' capital injections, of which ING bank received €10 billion, AEGON Insurances €3 billion, and SNS real €750 million in exchange for stocks. The Dutch state also created a €200 billion guarantee fund.

Source: Algemene Rekenkamer (2009) and De Nederlandse Bank (2009)

international financial crisis, leading to bank collapses in many European countries, and subsequent government rescue operations.

Decision-making during the banking crisis was urgent crisis management. In virtually all countries, a small group of key players (Prime Minister, Finance Minister and President of the National Bank) took swift and far-reaching decisions without much interference from parliament. Time was pressing, the crisis was urgent and huge, and enormous amounts were at stake. Nightly and weekend crisis consultation took place. Bank take-overs had to be hurriedly realised before the financial markets reopened.

Though in the course of 2008 the recognition had grown that the 'subprime mortgage' problem and its highly complex financial derivates were a worldwide problem not confined to the United States, nobody had foreseen such a sudden and severe worldwide crisis. Ministries of Finance and National Banks were caught out in surprise. The financial authorities were completely surprised and unprepared for the gigantic banking and financial crisis. The blow hit hard and the misery was not yet over by some long way, as it led to an economic crisis.

In the autumn of 2008, some governments still hoped that the crisis would remain contained to the banking sector and not blow over to the 'real economy'. That hope soon evaporated into an illusion as the financial crisis was followed by an economic one. Signs of an upcoming economic crisis, such as a decline in company turnovers and a rise in lay-offs, surfaced in the autumn of 2008. The economic crisis forced many governments to take considerable economic recovery measures.

Decision-making during the economic crisis was not urgent crisis management. In this second phase, governmental decision-making about economic recovery plans involved politics and parliament or extensive deliberations with

---

Economic crisis in Great Britain

In the April 2009 budget, the British government announced a recovery plan for economic growth, welfare and prosperity for all. The Bank of England decreased the interest rate. The government undertook stimulus measures such as lowering VAT, forwarding investments of £3 billion and increasing public expenditures, all together amounting to a value of 4 per cent of GDP.

Source: Treasury Committee (2009b)

Economic crisis in Germany

The German government conceived an economic recovery package (Konjunkturpaket) in two rounds in October 2008 and January 2009 to secure employment and stability, and enhance economic growth and modernisation. The October 2008 package announced an extra €31 billion public expenditures and was relatively small, as Chancellor Merkel wanted to remain thrifty as to ensure long-term sustainability. New alarming economic forecasts, international (American and European) pressure to take more action and the electoral competition with the Social Democrats (September 2009 general elections) led to a second 'Konjunkturpaket' in January 2009, where extra expenditures were raised to €80 billion. Moreover, a €115 billion economic fund (Wirtschaftsfonds) was created for guarantees and credits for firms.

Source: Bundesministerium der Finanzen (bmf.bund.de): Konjunkturpaket and Kickert (2013b)

Economic crisis in China

In November 2008, the Chinese central government announced an economic stimulus package of 4 trillion Yuan (about €568 billion, some 14 per cent of GDP) to be spent on infrastructure, energy and environment, and reconstruction works in the Sichuan earthquake area. China's leaders' prime objective is economic growth. As long as hundreds of millions of Chinese each year escape poverty and increase their incomes and material prosperity, the Communist Party will continue to receive popular support. Decline of economic growth, let alone economic deterioration, would threaten the party's prime legitimacy.

Source: International Herald Tribune (2008)

trade unions and employer organisations. Normal and regular procedures of political decision-making and social partners' consultation were restored.

After 2009, the crisis was still not over. The banking crisis and economic crisis were followed by a fiscal crisis. After state debts and deficits had augmented due to the massive bank rescue measures, and after economic recovery plans had led to a further increase of budget deficits, the inevitable next phase was a fiscal crisis. The rising debt and deficits were somehow to be compensated by public expenditure cutbacks and revenue increases – what economists call 'fiscal consolidation' measures, and the core subject of this book.

Virtually all European governments were obliged to take consolidation measures, though in varying degrees and speed. Generally, the higher the size of the fiscal crisis in a country, the higher and swifter the fiscal consolidation measures. However, political considerations also played an important role.

In the single-party state of China, political considerations made it impossible for central government to carry out public expenditure cutbacks and tax revenue

Cutbacks in Great Britain

The cutback measures taken in Britain in 2010 were huge and unprecedented. The budget deficit was 12 per cent of GDP and an annual £43 billion interest had to be paid on the state debt. After the May 2010 general elections, which for the first time in thirty-six years did not yield a single party absolute majority, a coalition was formed with Cameron (Conservatives) as Prime Minister and Clegg (Liberal Democrats) as deputy Prime Minister. Draconic cutback measures were announced of £81 (some €100 billion). Public expenditures were to be cut by 25 per cent and a loss of 490,000 public-sector jobs was announced.

Source: Treasury Committee (2010)

Cutbacks in Germany

In July 2010, the German government, in the presentation of its annual budget, announced a savings package (Sparpaket) to reduce its national debt by €82 billion in 2014 by decreasing subsidies and participation in firms, cutting the costs of administration and adjusting the social security system. The 'Sparpaket' consisted first of tax revenue increases by decreasing subsidies and ecological adjustment of taxes (energy subsidies reduction, eco-tax on aeroplane tickets); second of increased costs for firms (nuclear energy tax, banks' contributions); third a restructuring of the system of social benefits and allowances (labour market measures, parents' allowances, house-heating allowances); fourth of a reform of the army (Bundeswehr) by cutting 40,000 soldiers; fifth of cutbacks in administrative expenditures (salary reduction and cutting 10,000 jobs); and some other minor savings.

Source: Bundesministerium der Finanzen (bmf.bund.de): Sparpaket and Kickert (2013b)

Cutbacks in the Netherlands

The decision-making on cutbacks was lifted over the June 2010 general elections (like in many other European countries). In October 2010, a new (minority) coalition was formed with Rutte (Conservative Liberals) as Prime Minister and Verhagen (Christian Democrats) as deputy Prime Minister, with parliamentary support of the right-populist 'anti-Muslim' Freedom Party of Wilders. In the coalition agreement, the new cabinet announced a retrenchment program of up to €18 billion in 2015. The largest cuts were in (national, provincial and local) administration (€6.1 billion out of the €18 billion). The pension age was to be increased. Reforms in youth unemployment and benefits were announced, as well as in social security. The innovation budget of the Ministry of Economic Affairs was abolished. The budget for international development was cut from 0.8 to 0.7 per cent of GDP. And nuclear energy was no longer taboo.

Source: Kickert (2012d)

increases, as that might jeopardise the Communist Party's prime, and maybe only, legitimacy to its population. Another well-known, and widely deemed outrageous, example of political deadlock is the United States, where the polarised Republicans and Democrats held each other hostage over fiscal consolidation.

Cutbacks in Estonia

Estonia did not face a banking crisis (its banking sector being almost completely dominated by Nordic banks) and did not engage in costly economic recovery measures. Instead, it decided for immediate and drastic fiscal consolidation, already in 2008 and 2009, much earlier than most European governments. The Estonian government imposed fiscal consolidation measures in three successive supplementary budgets, first in 2008 and two more in 2009, as well as several other one-off measures. In 2009, the volume of fiscal consolidation (about €1.2 billion) was about 9 per cent of GDP (which was relatively very high), declining to 6 per cent in 2010, and 3 per cent in both 2011 and 2012. The Estonian government front-loaded its largest fiscal consolidation in the first year, whereas in virtually all European countries, consolidation measures were back-loaded. So not only was its fiscal consolidation comparatively large, but it was also early, mainly due to the government's political priority to join the Eurozone.

Source: Savi and Randma-Liiv (2013)

Cutbacks in the United States

In 2010, a divided Congress decided to extend the tax cuts from the previous Bush administration for two years. In 2011, Congress passed a Budget Control Act, installed a 'Super Committee' with members of the House and Senate, and evenly divided between Democrats and Republicans, to reach an agreement about $1.2 trillion of spending cuts, which it failed to do, and decided for a cutback procedure called 'sequestration'. That means that spending cuts are automatically imposed on all expenditure categories by an equal percentage, the American synonym for 'across-the-board' and 'cheese-slicing'. In January 2013, this 'fiscal cliff' would lead to a simultaneous increase in tax rates and a decrease in expenditures. The 'fiscal cliff' was avoided at the very last minute by Congress convening on New Year's Eve and New Year's Day.

Source: Wikipedia: United States fiscal cliff; Budget sequestration, accessed 6 June 2013

As the examples illustrate, the decision-making by governments about the fiscal crisis was highly politicised. Cutbacks in social security, health, housing, education and welfare are politically sensitive and publicly unpopular. In the United States, tax revenue increases are widely considered political suicide, especially among Republicans. Politics, not only economics, certainly mattered in fiscal consolidation.

Furthermore, in 2010, the crisis described and illustrated above was followed by a new, and in future maybe even graver, financial and economic crisis, that is, the European sovereign debt crisis, or so-called 'Eurozone crisis'. In 2010, the Eurozone crisis erupted due to the insolvency of Greece, followed by Ireland and Portugal. These members of the European Union and Eurozone were no longer capable of financing their national state debts. The poor fiscal positions of the four Southern countries (particularly Greece, which was blamed for 'creative' public accounting) plus Ireland had led to a downgrading of international credit ratings, resulting in ever-increasing interest rates on their largely foreign-owned state bonds. In 2010, this resulted in the Greek default. As a member state default would be damaging to the credibility of the Euro as a whole, irrespective of whether it withdrew from the Eurozone or not, the European Union could do nothing but bail it out.

The previous brief and abundantly illustrated sketch gives a first impression of the severe nature and enormous size of the worldwide crisis that erupted in 2008, and has caused most Western governments serious problems and concerns during the past couple of years, and will continue to do so probably for years to come. Governments have been compelled to rescue domestic banks for gigantic amounts of money followed by the costly economic recovery plans, and then the harsh and significant cutback measures. The brief sketch made it absolutely clear that governments were indeed seriously and upset by the crisis, not only in the financial and economic sense, but also socially. In many countries, major cutbacks were introduced in social security, health, education, housing and more, thus seriously affecting the nature of the welfare states. A rise in pension age, a cut in unemployment duration and benefits, a rise in own health care contribution, introduction of market mechanisms in health care and so on

---

Eurozone crisis

In May 2010, the European Union and International Monetary Fund decided on a substantial rescue package for Greece (followed by a second package in February 2012). By the end of 2010, the crisis of Irish public finances and the collapse of Irish banks caused it to require a bail-out. In March 2011, Portugal followed suit with a request for a bail-out. As of 2011, the European Central Bank started to massively buy up endangered state bonds (also in Italy and Spain) to prevent further interest rate increases. In July 2012, the European Central Bank provided a loan to Spain in order to rescue and restructure the failing Spanish banking sector. In June 2012, Cyprus required a bail-out because its oversized banking sector had collapsed.

Source: European Central Bank: Timeline of the
Financial Crisis (www.ecb.europe.eu)

represent not only financial cutbacks in existing measures, but in the end amount to substantive changes in the nature of welfare arrangements, like the previous global crisis of the 1970s and 1980s, when a long period of incessant cutbacks ultimately led to a change of welfare state and administration. Here, we have a brief look at the past.

Previous global crisis in the 1970s and 1980s

The previous worldwide economic and fiscal crisis happened in the 1970s and 1980s. The first oil crisis of 1975, worsened by the second one in 1979, led to a worldwide economic crisis and stagnation, which, on its turn in many Western countries, caused excessive public budget deficits and state debts, forcing Western governments to fiscal consolidation and severe cutbacks that dominated Western societies for most of the 1980s. The Western welfare states threatened to become unaffordable. The states had to substantially withdraw from many societal policy sectors. Massive cutbacks occurred in social security, public health, housing, education and other welfare arrangements. It was no longer merely a question of finances and economics, but a substantive shift in the nature of Western welfare states, as reflected in the many publications by sociologists during the 1980s with titles including phrases such as the stagnating, the twilight, the retreat and the end of the welfare state. In the field of Public Administration, the main focus at the time was on retrenchments and cutbacks, as well as managing the fiscal crisis (Levine 1978, 1980).

In the end, the fiscal crisis of the 1980s had a major effect on states and administrations. In Europe, the governance relations between states and societies in some countries shifted to new-right neo-Liberalism, and in less ideologically preoccupied countries, such as the Scandinavian and North Western European ones, to a major drive for effectiveness, efficiency and management. In hindsight, this fiscal crisis in many Western countries has led to a dominant and common administrative reform trend, that is, the so-called 'new public management' reforms: marketisation, client orientation and the introduction of business-like management techniques in Western administrations. Public administration scholars in the early 1990s became aware of this major reform trend (Hood 1991). Public management became a dominant research subject (Bozeman and Straussman 1990; Flynn 1990; Hughes 1994; Lynn 1996; Pollitt 1990). Public management became the predominant reform trend all over the Western world (Pollitt and Bouckaert 2000).

In light of these experiences with the previous global crisis, the question arises as to what impact the current fiscal crisis and consolidation will have on Public Administration and management in the longer term. One apparent question is whether public management will once more become a worldwide reform trend.

The effects of the fiscal crisis on Public Administration and reforms are described in Chapter 7 of this book.

Scientific research on the crisis

The previous brief sketch of the severity of the global crisis leads to the conclusion that, from an empirical and practical viewpoint, it does indeed seem undeniably relevant to study how various European governments managed the current crisis, and to see what lessons can be drawn from an international analysis. After having evidenced the social relevance, we now turn to the scientific relevance of the subject.

The previous worldwide economic and fiscal crisis in the 1970s and 1980s led to major public management reforms in many Western states. The prominent response of governments on budget cutbacks was to take cost-efficiency measures in the form of public management reforms. This led to the boom of cutback literature, where, in the field of political and administrative sciences, numerous studies on 'the politics of retrenchment', 'managing the fiscal crisis' and 'cutback management' were published (e.g. Austin 1984; Behn 1980; Dunsire and Hood 1989; Hood and Wright 1981; Levine 1978, 1980; Levine *et al.* 1981; Rubin 1985; Schick 1980). We will partly base our analytical framework about political decision-making, as described in Chapter 3 of this book, on an extensive overview of the cutback management literature of the 1970s and 1980s (Raudla *et al.* 2013).

The current crisis and the subsequent government responses have by now been extensively studied by international organisations and scholars from an economic perspective (e.g. European Commission 2009a, 2009b; OECD 2011, 2012; World Bank 2008; World Health Organization 2009). There is an increasing literature in economics and political economy examining the causes and consequences of the different phases of the crisis (see, inter alia, Connolly 2012; Dabrowski 2009; Kattel and Raudla 2013; Krugman 2009; Marer 2010; Myant and Drahokoupil 2012; Posner and Sommerfeld 2013; Starke 2006; Stiglitz and Heymann 2014; van den Noord 2011).

The political and administrative sciences are well positioned to contribute to research on the crisis by bringing in the dimensions of cutback decision-making, the administration of cutback measures and ultimately the impact of the crisis on Public Administration itself. The existing scholarly research has already provided some insights about the implications and impact of the 2008 financial crisis on Public Administration. For instance, Pandey (2010) has focused on the paradox of 'publicness' in cutback management, and Bozeman (2010) explored the (ir)relevance of generic decline literature in studying the crisis. Several authors point out that the crisis has substantially redrawn the boundaries between public and private sectors (Thynne 2011) by empowering the former (Moulton and Wise 2010; see also opposing theorising by Pandey 2010). The fragility of public-private partnerships in the global financial crisis has been discussed by Agostino and Lapsley (2013). A number of studies conclude that the 2008 financial crisis resulted from coordination failures (Dabrowski 2009; Gieve and Provost 2012). Peters *et al.* (2011) offer hypotheses about the effects of the crisis on centralisation, politicisation and coordination. Lodge and Hood (2012) have theorised about the shifting competencies required from public servants and governments due to the crisis. Also, the implications of fiscal austerity on public management (Di Mascio and Natalini 2015) and local governments (Overmans and Noordegraaf 2014) have been investigated. In addition, the issue of citizens' (declined) trust, (heightened) expectations and general attitudes towards government and the role of public leadership have been addressed (Kattel and Raudla 2013; Massey 2011; Posner and Blöndal 2012; Van de Walle and Jilke 2014).

The existing academic studies show that until now, government responses to the crisis have been diverse. There have been 'as many responses as countries' (Peters 2011: 76), and in many cases the responses have been diverging (see Bideleux 2011; Kickert 2012b, 2012c, 2012d, 2013a, 2013b; Lodge and Hood 2012; Peters 2011; Peters *et al.* 2011; Pollitt 2010; Verick and Islam 2010). Although the number of publications in the fields of Public Administration and political science addressing the recent crisis has been markedly growing during the past couple of years, there is still a lack of comparative studies based on common methodology.

This book attempts to fill this gap in research. Here, an international comparative analysis is made of how fourteen European countries responded to the recent crisis. The countries included in the comparative study are Belgium, Estonia, France, Germany, Hungary, Iceland, Ireland, Italy, Lithuania, the Netherlands, Norway, Slovenia, Spain and the United Kingdom. These countries were studied as part of the EU Seventh Framework project 'Coordinating for Cohesion in the Public Sector of the Future' (COCOPS) in its seventh work package, titled 'The Global Financial Crisis in the Public Sector', which was coordinated by both authors of this book. Later on, in Table 1.2, we describe in more detail the empirical studies and the domestic authors of the country studies underlying the work package, and therefore this book, which is an extension and elaboration of the work package report (Kickert *et al.* 2013).

Research questions

This book describes and analyses the fiscal consolidation measures and the cutback decisions that have been taken in the European countries; therefore, it is first informative. The second objective is also to compare the countries and try to explain the similarities and differences in the fiscal consolidation measures taken in different countries. To this end, we not only consider the contents of the government measures, but also the political decision-making processes that led up to these measures. In addition to financial and economic explanatory factors, we also use political-administrative factors and supra-national influences that have affected the consolidation process. The third objective is to analyse what were the effects of the fiscal consolidation and cutback decisions on economics and politics, especially on Public Administration itself, and whether administrative and public management practices have been affected by the fiscal crisis and cutbacks. The following research questions are addressed in this book:

- How did the European governments respond to the fiscal crisis, what fiscal consolidation and cutback measures were undertaken, and how did the decision-making take place? What are the main similarities and differences between the countries?
- How can the similarities and differences in consolidation measures and decision-making processes be explained from both an economic and a political perspective?
- What were the fiscal and economic effects of fiscal consolidation, what were the political effects, and what were the effects on Public Administration and reform?

Outline of the book

After this introduction describing the relevance of the book and its research objectives, we turn to the nature of the crisis in Chapter 2. A distinction is made between four stages of the crisis: the banking, economic and fiscal crisis, plus the Eurozone crisis. The political decision-making in these four stages, not only the contents of the measures, strongly differed. In this book, we focus on the fiscal crisis. What was its nature, what was fiscal consolidation, and how did politics matter?

The analytical framework is outlined in Chapter 3. The economic perspective on fiscal consolidation in terms of expenditure cuts and revenue increases, and the political perspective in terms of governments' decision-making. Explanations of fiscal consolidation are distinguished into economic, political and supra-national ones, and the effects of fiscal consolidation into economic, political and administrative ones.

We then proceed with the application of the analytical framework to the country studies. First, in Chapter 4, the contents of the consolidation measures are considered, that is, the economic perspective on expenditures and revenues. We pay particular attention to the category of operational expenditures, that is, the costs of administration itself. In most countries, a major part of the cutbacks occurred in this category: hiring and pay freeze, salary cuts, lay-offs, efficiency cuts, reorganisations, etc.

Second, in Chapter 5, we consider the political decision-making of governments leading up to the cutbacks, that is, the political perspective in terms of states (federal, unitary), politics (majoritarian, consensus) and governments (one party or coalition, margin of majority, right wing/centre/left wing). The decision-making is considered along the distinction between across-the-board cuts versus targeted priority-setting, and is further developed into a more refined typology of characteristics of decision-making. Subsequently, a distinction is made into stages of decision-making. Fiscal consolidation was not a one-off event, but in most countries consisted of a series of rounds of cutbacks, beginning with small and temporary measures and evolving into serious cutbacks, and only ultimately resulting in targeted political priority-setting.

Chapter 6 is about the possible explanations of the consolidation measures and the decision-making. Explanations are offered of the similarities and differences in state responses, using not only financial-economical explanatory factors (prior economic situation, economic recovery, state debt and budget deficit), but also political-administrative ones (political system, government, administration, budget procedure). It turns out that the economic size of fiscal consolidation is primarily explained by the size of the economic and fiscal crisis, but the contents of the measures and the decision-making are affected by political factors such as, for example, the political colour of the government (right/centre/left) and its margin of parliamentary majority (minority/grand).

After this chapter on the causes of fiscal consolidation, we proceed, in Chapter 7, with its effects. Restoring the domestic public finances and the economy depends on more factors than the domestic cutback measures alone. The international economic developments have a major influence. After considering the fiscal and economic effects, we turn to the political-electoral effects of the consolidation and cutbacks, and their effects on Public Administration and management. How did the cutbacks affect the administrations in the various countries? Did they lead to administrative reform programs, and were these similar to the public management reforms of the 1980s and 1990s?

Finally, in Chapter 8, we reach some conclusions from the international analysis, such as a clustering of countries as to their responses to the crisis, and we reflect about the cutbacks, the causes and the effects. What really explains for success or failure? What are the methodological pitfalls? Does politics matter? We reflect upon the basic dilemma between the apparent incapability of governments to set fundamental political priorities and the ever-increasing necessity to do so.

Outline of the book

Part 1: Introduction

1   Introduction

Severity of crisis – scientific research – research questions – empirical sources

2   Fiscal crisis and consolidation

Different stages of crisis – does politics matter? – political efforts of government

3   Analytical framework

Fiscal consolidation: contents of measures – political decision-making

Explanations of fiscal consolidation: economical – political – supra-national

Effects of fiscal consolidation: economical – political – administration

Part 2: Fiscal consolidation

4   Fiscal consolidation: Content of measures

Overview of measures – cutbacks in administration

5   Fiscal consolidation: Decision-making

Characteristics of decision-making – stages of decision-making

Part 3: Causes and effects of fiscal consolidation

6   Explanations of fiscal consolidation

Economic – political – supra-national

7   Effects of fiscal consolidation

Economy and public finances – politics – administration and management

Part 4: Conclusions and discussion

8   Conclusions and discussion

Consolidation – explanations – effects – clusters of countries – discussion

Three empirical sources

The research underlying this book was carried out by the partners and affiliated researchers involved in the EU Seventh Framework project COCOPS seventh work package 'global financial crisis in the public sector'. Researchers within the COCOPS project conducted the primary research on the fiscal crisis and consolidation in their respective countries (see tables below). The empirical sources used in this book are the country reports and country case studies conducted by the COCOPS WP7 research partners, for which we express our profound gratitude.

The countries included in the COCOPS seventh work package were the following: Belgium, Estonia, France, Germany, Hungary, Iceland, Ireland, Italy, Lithuania, the Netherlands, Norway, Slovenia, Spain and the United Kingdom. (Denmark was not included in the COCOPS project; references to that country are based on an earlier country study by Kickert 2013a). These countries varied as to their financial-economic characteristics, as some countries had moderate budget deficits but high debt, some others had high deficits and moderate debts, and still others both high deficits and debts. The political-administrative characteristics also varied between the countries, including both majoritarian and consensus democracies, single-party governments and multi-party coalitions, and so forth. This makes them a good country choice for an international comparative investigation.

This book draws on the information and findings from three different empirical sources.

First, *ten short country reports* providing analytical descriptions of the national governments' main responses to the crisis in a particular country following a common framework. These country reports were based on the country data collection by the partners, analysis of the COCOPS survey findings and in-depth interviews with national decision-makers. Table 1.1 provides an overview of the country reports.

Second, *eleven academic country case studies* focusing on analysing consolidation measures and the impact of the crisis on Public Administration. These case studies integrated the information and analysis prepared for the short country reports, provided more in-depth analysis of the national responses to the crisis and linked the empirical analysis to the theoretical literature. Table 1.2 offers an overview of country case studies.

All references in this book to country examples are derived from the aforementioned country reports and case studies unless another explicit reference is made.

Third, for *twelve countries* the relevant findings of the COCOPS third work package *Executive Survey on Public Sector Reform in Europe* have been utilised (Hammerschmidt *et al.* 2013). The survey explored the senior executives'

TABLE 1.1 Country reports

Country	Title	Authors
Belgium	The global financial crisis in the public sector as an emerging coordination challenge: Short country report for Belgium	Trui Steen, Steve Troupin, Jesse Stroobants (Catholic University Leuven)
Estonia	Country note: Estonia	Riin Savi (Tallinn University of Technology)
France	Country note: France	Vanessa Albert, Philippe Bezes, Patrick Le Lidec (National Centre for Scientific Research, Sciences Po)
Germany	Country report: Germany	Jobst Fiedler, Gerhard Hammerschmidt, Max Osterheld (Hertie School Governance)
Hungary	Country data sheet: Hungary	György Hajnal (Corvinius University)
Italy	Country report: Italy	Edoardo Ongaro (Northumbria University), Fabrizio Di Mascio, Davide Galli, Alessandro Natalini, Francesco Stolfi (Bocconi University Milan)
Netherlands	Fiscal consolidations in the Netherlands	Walter Kickert (Erasmus University Rotterdam)
Norway	Impact of the global financial crisis that started in 2008 on Norway: No fiscal crises and cutback management	Per Laegreid (University of Bergen)
Spain	The global financial crisis in the public sector as an emerging coordination challenge: Spain	Judith Clifton and Jose M. Alonso (University of Cantabria)
United Kingdom	The global financial crisis in the public sector as an emerging coordination challenge. Short country report: the UK	Oliver James and Ayako Nakamura (University of Exeter)

TABLE 1.2 Case studies

Country	Title	Authors
Belgium	The impact of the fiscal crisis on Belgian federal government: Changes in the budget decision-making process and intra-governmental relations	Trui Steen, Steve Troupin and Jesse Stroobants (Catholic University Leuven)
Estonia	Public policy making in time of crisis: Cutback management in Estonia	Riin Savi and Tiina Randma-Liiv (Tallinn University of Technology)
France	The French politics of retrenchment à la carte (2007–2012): Ideational frames, interest groups and political cycles	Philippe Bezes and Patrick Le Lidec (National Centre for Scientific Research, Sciences Po)
Germany	Public sector cutback management in Germany: A substantial gap between a new tight fiscal governance framework and a weak capacity for administrative reform	Max Osterheld, Jobst Fiedler, Anja Görnitz and Gerhard Hammerschmid (Hertie School of Governance)
Hungary	Fiscal consolidations in Hungary	György Hajnal (Corvinius University)
Iceland	Iceland after the revolution: The impact of crisis on governance	Gunnar Helgi Kristinsson (University of Iceland)
Ireland	State retrenchment and fiscal consolidation in Ireland	Muiris MacCarthaigh (Queen's University Belfast) and Niamh Hardiman (University College Dublin)
Italy	The impact of the crisis on administrative reform in a 'context of motion': Italy 2007–2012	Edoardo Ongaro (Northumbria University), Fabrizio Di Mascio, Davide Galli, Alessandro Natalini and Francesco Stolfi (Bocconi University Milan)
Lithuania	Fiscal consolidation in Lithuania in the period 2008–2012: From grand ambitions to hectic fire-fighting	Vitalis Nakrošis, Ramūnas Vilpišauskas and Vytautas Kuokštis (Vilnius University)
Netherlands	Fiscal consolidation in the Netherlands	Walter Kickert (Erasmus University Rotterdam)
Slovenia	Fiscal balance and public sector downsizing in Slovenia	Primož Pevcin (University of Ljubljana)

opinions and experience with regard to public-sector reforms, and included a special section on the impact of the fiscal crisis on Public Administration. The survey targeted top-level decision-makers and civil servants in central government, and was sent to more than 21,000 European senior civil servants in 2012–2013. The results of the survey included answers by 3,397 executives from twelve countries of our sample. The overall response rate was 24 per cent, ranging from 35 per cent in Estonia and 34 per cent in Norway, to 18 per cent in Spain and 11 per cent in the United Kingdom. Although it is difficult to make representative conclusions because of the low response rate in some countries, the overall response rate is rather consistent with other existing executives' surveys in Public Administration. It is based on a full census of the defined target population, and represents by far the largest existing data set of this kind for European Public Administrations.

Table 1.3 summarises the empirical sources for the fourteen countries studied.

TABLE 1.3 Empirical sources

Country	Short country report	Country case study	COCOPS executive survey
Belgium (BEL)	+	+	–
Estonia (EST)	+	+	+
France (FRA)	+	+	+
Germany (GER)	+	+	+
Hungary (HUN)	+	+	+
Iceland (ISL)	–	+	+
Ireland (IRL)	–	+	+
Italy (ITA)	+	+	+
Lithuania (LTU)	–	+	+
Netherlands (NLD)	+	+	+
Norway (NOR)	+	–	+
Slovenia (SLO)	–	+	–
Spain (ESP)	+	–	+
United Kingdom (GBR)	+	–	+

Qualitative and quantitative methodology

In this book, ample illustrations with country examples are presented, as has already been detailed in this introduction. We continue to do so throughout the book. In view of the readily available wealth of the ten country reports and eleven country case studies, it would be a shame not to use these plentiful in-depth country materials. As mentioned before, it is likely that the average English-speaking reader of this book is not very well acquainted with the lesser-known and smaller European countries, so, first of all, many of the country examples are highly informative. Country case studies have the advantage of in-depth exploration of empirical evidence.

Qualitative case study methodology is highly suitable for initial exploration of still unknown empirical grounds. The way in which many of the European governments had managed the fiscal crisis, for us, typically represented the situation of 'terra incognita'. The many country reports and case studies did indeed yield an immense wealth of empirically relevant and practically useful information, and to some extent qualitative country case studies can also be presented in a comparative way, as in a couple of instances in this book.

The well-known disadvantage of qualitative case studies, however, is that they are, in essence, unique, and therefore hard to compare. So, we had to supplement the qualitative country cases with quantitative empirical materials to allow for statistical correlation analysis. In the chapters on causes and effects of fiscal consolidation, we employed three additional quantitative data sets. First, the facts and figures gathered by the OECD (2012) on how its member states had restored their public finances, that is, the quantitative data on fiscal consolidation plans provided by the various governments to the OECD Senior Budget Officials Group. Second, the World Bank (2012) database of political institutions, especially their figures about the political orientation of governments and their margin of parliamentary majority. Third, we employed the Eurostat data on economic growth and budget deficits. These data allowed us to carry out some quantitative international comparison by means of statistical analysis.

As mentioned before, we also utilised the COCOPS executive survey on public sector reform in Europe (Hammerschmidt *et al.* 2013). These responses from twelve countries provided an international comparison of the quantitative response data from the different countries on the various questions.

In our view, it makes little sense to debate qualitative and quantitative methodology in 'either/or' terms. Such dichotomous methodological debates have commonly been rather detrimental to the social sciences. We prefer the 'and/and' stance. The authors are aware that, particularly in the North American political sciences, the prevailing trend is to concentrate on quantitative statistics and mathematical modelling. One of the authors, having graduated in experimental physics (albeit forty years ago), is far from impressed and rather amused when mathematics is embraced by social scientists, so we rather prefer methodological variety. This book liberally employs both methodologies.

Acknowledgement

The research leading to these results received funding from the European Union's Seventh Framework Program under grant agreement No. 266887 (Project COCOPS), Socio-economic Sciences & Humanities, from the Estonian Research Council's institutional grant no. IUT19-13, from the Estonian Science Foundation grant no. 9435, and from a travel costs subsidy from the Dutch Ministry of Home Affairs. We are most grateful to Riin Savi for her help in collecting and analysing country data. The authors would also particularly like to convey their thanks to all the COCOPS core and affiliated partners who provided valuable empirical information on their particular countries.

Chapter 2

Fiscal crisis and consolidation

In this book, we investigate how European governments responded to the global crisis with a focus on the fiscal crisis and fiscal consolidation. In the introduction, we offered the reader a brief sample of the nature of the current worldwide crisis, showing that the fiscal crisis is only one of the various stages of what is widely called 'the global crisis'. In this chapter, we therefore considered it wise to further and deeper explore the nature of this crisis. What was it about? What exactly is the fiscal crisis? What is fiscal consolidation? In order to address the nature of the fiscal crisis, we must first examine the preceding stages of the crisis, that is, the banking and economic crisis. The nature of these different stages, the contents of the measures taken in the different stages and the political decision-making during the different stages were all dissimilar.

Different stages of the global crisis

Making statements about 'the' global crisis creates confusion. There was no one single crisis. The crisis consisted of different stages, which were different in their very nature. The problems were different; the solutions were different; everything was different. So, for the sake of conceptual clarity, the global crisis is to be distinguished into separate (sequential) stages (Kickert 2012a):

- The banking crisis, the first stage of the crisis, when banks and other financial institutions faced serious problems and bankruptcy. The total collapse of the financial institutions was averted by governments with bank rescue and support measures.
- The economic crisis, the second stage, when the worldwide break-down of the financial markets damaged the real economy. Severe economic decline and an alarming rise in unemployment followed. Governments undertook measures to stimulate economic recovery.
- The fiscal crisis, the third stage of the crisis. The gigantic bank rescue measures had resulted in significant increase in state debts and the economic

recovery plans resulted in further increases in budget deficit. In response, governments started consolidating budgets and undertaking cutbacks (Kickert 2012a; Posner and Blöndal 2012).

■ The Eurozone crisis. Since 2010, the fourth stage of the crisis erupted, the European sovereign debt crisis, also called the Eurozone crisis. Countries with excessive debt levels and budget deficits, and with ever-increasing interest rates on state bonds, became incapable of financing their state debts. They were bailed out by the European Union.

The problems differed in the four stages – collapsing banks, alarming economic decline, excessive budget deficit, insolvency of states. The measures that governments took to solve the problems differed in the four stages – saving banks, stimulating economic recovery, expenditure cutbacks and revenue increases, state bail-outs. And the political decision-making by governments to reach the solutions also differed considerably – urgent crisis-management, deliberation with political parties and social partners, coalition formation, joint EU decision-making. In almost all investigated countries, the global crisis could be differentiated between these four stages. The severity of the various crises varied per country. Some were confronted with a banking crisis of massive proportions, while a few countries in our sample missed this stage altogether. Economic deterioration varied per country. So did the level of budget deficit and state debt. And only few countries underwent a bail-out by the European Union, European Central Bank and International Monetary Fund. Nevertheless, the conceptual distinctions were clear.

This book concentrates on the stage of the fiscal crisis. In order to further clarify the distinctive nature and character of the fiscal crisis, in this chapter we first shed some additional light on the banking and economic crisis. What was the nature of these two crises, what measurements were undertaken by governments to solve them, and what was the political decision-making like? The two main aspects of fiscal consolidation that we concentrate upon in this book – the contents of consolidation measures and political decision-making – are thus placed in a broader context.

Eurozone crisis

The banking, economic and fiscal crises were all managed by national governments. The Eurozone crisis was not. The very nature of the Eurozone crisis was that a national government was no longer capable to finance its national state debt. Excessive state debt and deficit in the country, combined with negative economic prospects, led international credit rating agencies to downgrade them, leading to ever-increasing interest rates on largely foreign-owned state bonds. So they became insolvent. Supra-national instances and influences overpowered the national government. The resulting crisis was not managed domestically by the national government, but by the Troika of the European Union, European Central Bank and International Monetary Fund. In return for the loan programme, the Troika enforced hard conditions about fiscal consolidation and reform upon the national government, nothing much the national government had control of.

In this book, we investigate how national governments responded to the crisis. That is why we do not pay separate attention to the fourth stage of European sovereign debt crisis in this book. That would have required an investigation of the joint multi-national decision-making in the European Union, which is quite a different level of analysis, and hardly comparable to the national level, and actually a completely different type of study, from which we therefore abstained.

This absolutely does not mean that the influence of the Eurozone crisis on the way national governments domestically managed their national fiscal crises is to be neglected. On the contrary, that influence was markedly and directly present in the countries we studied that underwent a bail-out, that is, Iceland and Ireland. And in Italy, where the European Central Bank, as of 2011, started to massively buy up impaired state bonds to curb a further rise of interest rate. And in Spain, where the European Central Bank, in June 2012, provided a massive loan to rescue and reform the failing Spanish banking sector. The examples of these four countries provided throughout this book clearly reflect the vital importance of these supra-national influences. The Eurozone crisis also had an indirect significant influence on domestic governments' actions. The rising European Union scepticism due to the costly bail-outs of Southern European states, especially the repeatedly failing Greece, that had to be paid for by Western European tax-payers, clearly influenced governments in election times. Chancellor Merkel was punished in several regional elections for her stance towards Greece. German tax-payers wanted a thrifty government. However, despite the undeniable influence of the Eurozone crisis, the multi-national joint decision-making at the European level is not separately investigated here, but only considered as contextual information in analysing national governments' responses to the fiscal crisis.

Banking crisis

The worldwide banking crisis broke out after the collapse of Lehman Brothers in September 2008. There were earlier signs in the United States of banks getting into serious problems. In Britain, the Northern Rock bank got into serious problems in August 2007, had to ask for assistance, and finally had to be nationalised. By 2007, it became clear that the low interest rates, easy credit and short-term borrowing bubble was going to burst. The Bank of England raised interest rates and warned the banks. In 2007, Northern Rock was taken into public ownership, as was Bradford & Bingley. For some time, things seemed to return to normal, until the sudden collapse of Lehman Brothers in September 2008. All over the Western world, large and respected banks became insolvent and were about to go bankrupt. Mutual trust between banks fell away. The international financial markets came to a sudden and complete standstill. It became imperative to restore confidence in the banking sector. Governments were forced to rescue large and vital 'systemic banks'. The measures that governments took to rescue and support banks in order to restore the confidence in the financial world can roughly be divided into the following economic categories (European Commission 2009a, 2009b; OECD 2009):

Deposit guarantees. The main argument for governments to increase the guarantee on bank deposits was to avert 'bank runs'. In Britain in 2007, a 'bank run' had occurred on Northern Rock. When the news leaked that the bank was in serious problems and required emergency assistance, the next day, long queues formed of bank clients withdrawing their deposits. The queues and panic only died down after a 100 per cent deposit guarantee was promised by the government. When bank account holders suspect that a bank is going to fail and have no guarantee on their deposit, they will rush to withdraw their money from the bank as quickly as possible before all is gone.

Capital injections. Governments injected capital into banks in order to save them from bankruptcy. When governments as shareholders injected equity, that allowed the government, and thus the tax-payer, some control over the bank (to ensure operational restructuring) and possible future benefits from the recovery of the bank. Nationalisation occurred when a significant fraction of a bank became owned by the government, giving the state total control over the bank, usually with the intention of returning it into private enterprise again. Nationalisation is criticised in free-market economics for going against principles of efficiency and fair competition, and allowing for political interference.

Guarantees on bank liabilities. This measure was meant to increase the liquidity of the banking sector and to stimulate interbank lending. The measure was taken to restrain liquidity and credit problems that lead to insufficient lending to and from banks and to firms. In this way, the government encourages banks to safely lend to each other and to firms. However, the complaint of medium-sized and small firms was, and remained, that it became virtually impossible to receive any loan after the outbreak of the crisis.

Relief of toxic assets. The bad or toxic assets of a bank had to be isolated and put aside in special-purpose entities to let the sound part of the bank survive. Direct buying of 'toxic assets' by governments was complicated because at the time it was hardly possible to determine at which price the bad assets should be bought. Ring-fencing involved first isolating the impaired assets and dealing with the costs at a future time, thus postponing the complicated decision. Table 2.1 presents the European Commission's overview of the bank rescue and support measures officially approved by governments up until July 2009.

TABLE 2.1 Rescue and support measures per country, 2009 (per cent of GDP)

	Capital injections	Guarantees on bank liabilities	Relief of impaired assets	Liquidity support	Total all approved measures	Deposit guarantee
Belgium	5.3	76.6	10.1	n/a	92.0	€100,000
Denmark	6.1	253.0	0.0	0.3	259.4	100%
Estonia	0.0	0.0	0.0	0.0	0.0	€50,000
France	1.2	16.6	0.2	0.0	18.1	€70,000
Germany	4.4	18.6	1.4	0.0	24.4	100%
Hungary	1.1	5.9	0.0	0.0	7.1	100%
Ireland	6.6	225.2	0.0	0.0	231.8	100%
Italy	1.3	n/a	0.0	0.0	1.3	€103,000
Lithuania	0.0	0.0	0.0	0.0	0.0	€100,000
Netherlands	6.4	34.3	3.9	7.5	52.0	€100,000
Slovenia	0.0	32.8	0.0	0.0	32.8	100%
Spain	0.0	9.3	0.0	2.8	12.1	€100,000
United Kingdom	3.5	21.7	0.0	16.4	41.6	£50,000
Total EU	2.6	24.8	0.8	2.9	31.2	

Note: These figures were approved government measures up until July 2009. The figures for effectively applied measures were lower.

Source: European Commission (2009b)

From an economic perspective, the measures all followed the same pattern of the above-mentioned categories. The nature and volume of the banking and financial sectors, however, varied per country, as did the bank rescue measures. Let us now give a few country examples illustrating some of the differences.

Banking sector in Great Britain

In Great Britain, the financial sector was economically very large and had successfully contributed to economic growth in the past decade. Moreover, the position of London as the financial 'world capital' besides New York had to be preserved. The banking crisis was hard, deep and very costly. Another reason was that in Great Britain, the period before 2007 was characterised by low interest rates, easy credit and short-term borrowing. This easy credit, combined with poor housing supply, had caused a house-price bubble. Despite the attempt of the Bank of England to slow the overheated economy by fiscal tightening, the bubble burst.

Source: Treasury Committee (2009a)

Remarkably, the 'New Labour' government under Prime Minister Brown – who, together with Blair at the end of the 1990s, was the founder of 'New Labour' – at first was reluctant to nationalise banks for fear of being accused of returning to 'Old Labour' habits, an allegation they got from the Conservative Party anyway. In 2007, Brown was finally persuaded to let the Treasury take Northern Rock into 'temporary public ownership', wording that avoided the Old Labour stigma of nationalisation (Seldon and Lodge 2011).

In Germany, the banking sector was not as important as the industrial export sector, and its rescue was not that costly. Also, German banks supposedly were more solid. The German banking sector consisted of three types of banks: commercial banks, saving banks and banks that were connected to regional state governments (Landesbanken). The saving banks (Sparkassen) were solid indeed. But financial problems started with some regional 'Landesbanken', which were known to be politically influenced, and hence financially less trustworthy (see box below). The commercial banks Hypo Real and Commerzbank also got into financial trouble, thus forcing the federal government to undertake support and rescue measures. In October 2008, Germany established a €480 billion banking saving fund (Sonderfonds Finanzmarktstabilisierung, Soffin). Of this fund, €80 billion was to save system banks; the other €400 billion was for guarantees on bank loans.

Landesbanken

The 'Landesbanken' were notoriously known for the politicisation of their financial decisions due to their close ties with regional governments. They were a major financing instrument for regional economic development by the regional state governments (Landesregierungen). In these banks, professional financial management was less pronounced. When the bank threatened to collapse, the 'Landersregierung' would somehow save it in any case. Now the problems were so large, and some 'Länder' were in such bad financial state, that some 'Landesbanken' could not be rescued from bankruptcy. Now the federal government was asked to do so, which Chancellor Merkel of course had no intention to do. A restructuring seemed more apt.

Source: Kickert (2013b)

In Spain, a similar situation existed of regional saving banks (Cajas) that were strongly governed by local and regional governments, and got into serious problems during the global financial crisis. The 'Cajas' were required to carry out a restructuring and merger operation and were recapitalised.

Cajas

Spanish saving banks (Cajas) are public entities. Their general assembly and board of directors used to carry heavy representation of local and regional governments (up to 50 per cent). Traditionally, they had an important role in financing regional economies. 'Cajas' also substantially supported social welfare, health, education and cultural projects. 'Cajas' were not primarily profit maximising – they had no shareholders and were not noted on the stock market – but provided financial support to economic and social-cultural activities in the regions.

The 'Cajas' formed a major portion of the Spanish banking sector. They possessed about half of the market share for loans and deposits, and were strongly expanding since 1997 when the Spanish building and construction boom – the property bubble – began. Vast credit amounts were pumped into the 'brick economy', and when the property bubble burst in 2007–2008, the banks faced enormous bad assets and their creditworthiness plummeted.

In 2008, a restructuring operation was imposed by the National Bank of Spain. The 'Cajas' were urged to merge, and the political influence of regional governments was reduced. In June 2009, a fund for orderly bank restructuring (Spanish acronym 'FROB') was established with a capital of €9 billion to financially assist the restructuring. The restructuring resulted in mergers between banks within one single region. Integrations between banks across regions, however, were only 'virtual', with the entities continuing to operate separately and only their risk management being merged. Apparently, the regional governments did not lose all political clout.

Source: Ysa *et al.* (2012)

In May 2012, the large bank Bankia (a merger between several 'Cajas') was about to collapse and was nationalised with €26 billion credit. Moreover, in summer 2012, Spain was downgraded by international rating agencies such as Standard & Poor's to about junk status, leading to soaring bond interest rates and closing off Spain's access to international finance markets. The Spanish government was forced to request financial support from Europe. In June 2012, an EU-ECB-IMF rescue operation for the Spanish banking sector was launched with up to €100 billion credit for recapitalisation of banks. Another far more drastic restructuring and merger operation of Spanish banks ensued (Contijoch 2012).

In the Netherlands and Belgium, the financial sector was relatively large and important. The Dutch ABN AMRO bank found itself in special circumstances.

ABN AMRO

The year before the banking crisis, the Dutch ABN AMRO bank was taken over by the British Royal Bank of Scotland, the Spanish Santander bank and the (smaller) Belgian Fortis bank. This foreign sell-out of a crucial national enterprise was widely shamed and disgraced. When, in 2008, Fortis was on the verge of bankruptcy, the Dutch minister of Finance was able to buy back the Dutch Fortis part of ABN AMRO. This act of heroism was welcomed in the Netherlands. And the price at the time seemed very good, much less than Fortis itself had paid in 2007. Though, in 2012, the parliamentary enquiry committee headed by de Wit reached a critical conclusion about the take-over price.

Source: Kickert (2012d)

The Belgian banking rescue package was large, in relative size just behind Iceland, Ireland and Britain. Some Belgian banks were ambitious in international expansion and had become strongly dependent on foreign creditors. When the 'low-rent, easy-credit' bubble imploded, so did these banks.

Banking crisis in Belgium

In October 2008, the Federal Participation and Investment Company (FPIM) had to save several banks. Fortis received a capital injection of €9.4 billion and was (partly) sold to the French group BNP Paribas. Dexia was recapitalised for €6 billion by the Belgian federal and regional governments and the French state. KBC (a large Belgian insurance company) and Ethias received capital injections of €7 billion and €1.5 billion, respectively. Besides FPIM, the Flemish, Walloon and Brussels regional governments undertook capital injections. The government also issued hundreds of billions of credit guarantees to banks and insurance companies.

Source: Rekenhof (2009)

In Belgium, the impression was created that they were outwitted by the Dutch and French. The Dutch minister of Finance had triumphantly announced that he had purchased the 'sound parts' of Fortis for a 'favourable price'. Moreover, the Belgians believed they had paid more than the French for the rescue of Dexia. The Belgian part of Dexia was healthier than the French, but was not fenced off. Allegedly, the Belgian surpluses had compensated the French losses. A parliamentary enquiry committee did not reach clear conclusions. In 2011, Dexia once more got into trouble, this time due to the Eurozone crisis, and the Belgian part was bought up by the FPIM in October 2011 for €11 billion.

Denmark had already experienced a banking crisis during the late 1980s and early 1990s, and hoped to be able to continue with the strategy devised at that time.

Danish banking crisis in 1980–1990

The Danish banking sector had already endured a crisis during the late 1980s and early 1990s. This crisis had resulted from a strong expansion of loans, especially in the construction sector, and caused an economic recession. The Danish financial and banking sector consisted of a multitude of small local and medium-sized regional banks, plus a few large national banks. Between 1984 and 1994, forty-seven banks had collapsed and were either broken up or had merged with larger healthy banks. This banking crisis was solved largely without state support. The strategy was to merge failing banks with larger healthy banks and provide state guarantees if necessary, but the Danish government refused to become owner, not even partly.

Source: Carstensen (2011) and Kickert (2013a)

This strategy to have large banks take over smaller failing banks was once more applied in 2008. However, when in summer 2008 the medium-sized Roskilde bank threatened to collapse, the strategy did not work. Danish banks were not prepared to take over bad parts of failing banks. These had to be bought by the 'Financial Stability Enterprise'. Only then were banks prepared to take over the sound parts of failing banks. The decision-making by the Danish government took four successive rounds of bank rescue measures.

These Danish ideas of a guarantee fund financed by the banking sector itself, and of winding up of banks with 'haircuts' for creditors and large deposit holders,

---

Four Danish bank packages

October 2008 stability package

The first package contained an unlimited state guarantee on deposits. The state guarantee fund was to be funded by the banking sector itself, with the state coming in when losses would exceed 35 billion DKK. A separate private institution for winding up distressed banks was set up, the state-owned 'Financial Stability Company'.

January 2009 credit package

The Danish government injected 100 billion DKK into the financial sector. The measure was accompanied by stricter regulation of transparency, monitoring and executive payments.

October 2010 winding up distressed banks

A new model for the take-over of distressed banks was introduced. The winding up was to take place with customers continuing to conduct normal banking transactions. Distressed banks were to be closed down over a weekend. All creditors and deposits over 750,000 DKK were subject to a 'haircut' (proportion of loss).

September 2011 consolidation package

After the collapse of two banks, the new winding up rules of the third package were redressed. A new process was devised with compensation by the Danish sate and guarantee fund. The financing of the guarantee fund was changed into an insurance scheme with fixed annual payments.

Source: Kickert (2013a)

Danish currency crisis in 2008

Denmark did not belong to the Eurozone, but the Danish Krone was coupled to the Euro. In September 2008, the international financial markets – read currency speculators – opened an attack on the European fixed exchange rate of the Danish Krone and forced the Danish National Bank to take far-reaching rescue measures. The small and open Danish economy learned its lesson of being outside the Eurozone with a fixed exchange rate at the very height of the banking crisis.

Source: Bernstein (2010)

---

were reinvented at the time of the June 2012 Cyprus bail-out, and have since been worked out by the European Council of Finance Ministers.

Another salient circumstance was that Denmark also experienced a currency crisis at the same time the banking crisis raged.

Other countries hardly suffered any banking crisis. In Estonia, the banking sector was almost completely in the hands of Nordic banks, and therefore not harmed by the global banking crisis. Italian banks were relatively conservative and had refrained from getting involved in modern and complex financial products, such as the United States sub-prime mortgages derivatives, and therefore did not possess 'toxic assets', and so escaped the banking crisis.

Decision-making during the banking crisis

In all countries, the decision-making during the banking crisis was a matter of urgent crisis management. A small group of key role players, usually consisting of the Prime Minister, the Finance Minister and the President of the National Bank, assisted by the smallest possible number of top officials – the leaking of market-sensitive information about bank take-overs could cost the state billions extra – took swift and far-reaching decisions without much parliamentary interference. In evenings and weekends, multibillion decisions were taken by a handful of people.

Such highly centralised, drastic and swift decision-making may not be uncommon in the British government system, and the German Chancellor also possesses some central authorities. In consensus democracies, however, this sort of decision-making is exceptional. The huge and urgent crisis gave governments simply no alternative. Governments were completely surprised and unprepared. There was no time for the usual numerous consultations and deliberations with all parties concerned. Multibillion decisions had to be taken very hurriedly. Consensual politics had to wait a while and parliament grudgingly stood aside.

Although parliaments understood why they could not be consulted, they still responded critically. The German 'Bundestag' made it perfectly clear that this was a once and never again decision, and insisted that future financial rescue packages henceforth had to receive prior approval of parliament. The autonomy of the German Chancellor in making deals about later Eurozone rescue packages has consequently been clearly constrained. In the Netherlands, parliament responded by installing a parliamentary enquiry committee for the evaluation of the banking rescue operation, headed by the left-wing Socialist de Wit, which, not surprisingly, reached very critical conclusions about the course of affairs and the outcomes. In Belgium, a parliamentary enquiry committee was installed, which, for party-political reasons, did not succeed to reach clear and unanimous conclusions. Also, in Denmark, a parliamentary enquiry committee was established.

In Great Britain, Prime Minister Brown was 'Chancellor of the Exchequer' under Blair for a decade. Decision-making during the banking crisis was completely centralised in his hands. The role of 'Chancellor' Darling and his 'Treasury' was quite small. Brown installed his trustee minister Vadera as contact person to undertake secret negotiations with the banks. The 'Treasury', 'Financial Services Authority' (the British regulatory agency for the banking sector) and the 'Bank of England' were involved in making plans, but Brown and his small entourage of political assistants at 10 Downing Street made all decisions (Darling 2011; Seldon and Lodge 2011).

In Germany, decision-making was centralised as well. The Christian Democratic Chancellor Merkel and the Social Democratic Finance Minister Steinbrück enjoyed good cooperation (only later in the election campaign did they oppose each other). The cooperation with the president of the 'Bundesbank' was also good. Merkel was seconded by her economic top advisor in the Chancellery, Weidman (who, in 2011, became president of the 'Bundesbank'), and Steinbrück was seconded by his 'Staatssekretär' Asmussen (who, in 2011, became a board member of the European Central Bank). Weidman and Asmussen were friends and closely cooperated, which endorsed the cooperation between Merkel and Steinbrück.

In Belgium, the key role players were Prime Minister Leterme (Flemish Christian Democrat) and minister of Finance (and deputy Prime Minister) Reijnders (French Liberal), both experienced in financial-economic affairs. The next decision-making layer was the core cabinet, consisting of the five deputy Prime Ministers of the five coalition parties. The full cabinet only played a marginal role. The primary role in the Belgian banking crisis was played by the so-called 'pilotage comité' (steering committee).

During the banking crisis in all countries, external advisors and specialists were hired, such as investment bankers, lawyers and accountants, in order to assist in the take-over of banks, the checking of the bank accounts, the determination of the price of the banks' toxic assets and more. To conform with

---

Pilotage Comité

Each of the five coalition parties had appointed a financial expert in the 'pilotage comité'. Four of them were directors at the National Bank, and one was head of a ministerial cabinet but had formerly been a bank director. The other steering group members had previously been active in ministerial cabinets. Chairman of the steering group was the vice governor of the National Bank Coene (currently governor), who had been head of the ministerial cabinet of the Flemish Liberal Prime Minister Verhofstadt. This steering group fulfilled the multiple tasks of providing financial expertise for the urgent bank rescue decisions, keeping the coalition parties informed about the ins and outs of the crisis decisions and informally deliberating and consulting with them to prepare for the formal decision-making in the core cabinet. The 'pilotage comité' also functioned as liaison between government and the banks.

Source: Kickert (2012c)

---

the normal practice for commercial mergers and take-overs, these external specialists were normally paid for by the failing banks themselves.

Economic crisis

The banking crisis was followed by the second stage of the global crisis, that is, the economic crisis. The 'low-rent, easy-credit' economic bubble imploded. The international financial markets dried up. Banks hardly provided any credit anymore, neither to each other, nor to business firms. Despite the liquidity stimulus measures of the governments' bank rescue plans, it became nearly impossible for firms to receive loans. The collapse of the credit market soon resulted in economic stagnation. In late 2008 and early 2009, the early warning signs that business and employment were under heavy pressure became alarming. Governments were forced to take measures to support and recover the stagnating economies. The economic recovery measures that governments took can be distinguished into the following economic categories:

Revenue decrease measures. Tax revenue measures can further be distinguished into income tax, corporation tax and consumption tax. Examples of reductions in individual taxes were individual tax allowances, tax deductions, child allowances, housing insulation subsidies, etc. Examples of corporate taxes were tax advantages for companies, depreciation rules, etc. And examples of consumptive taxes were a decrease of VAT, levies on tobacco and alcohol, on aeroplane tickets, cars, etc.

Abwrackprämie

In Germany, the measure to subsidise the replacement of old cars with new ones had a major effect on car sales and was successful for the relatively large German car industry. In Great Britain and the Netherlands, the majority of new cars were imported. There, the effects of the car scrap measure on the domestic economy could be questioned.

Source: Kickert (2013b)

Part-time unemployment benefit

In the Netherlands and Belgium, the measure to enable sufficiently viable firms that were going through temporary problems, to retain employees that would otherwise be fired by paying the firms with temporary unemployment benefits turned out be highly effective in sustaining employment. When the economy again improved, these firms were able to swiftly increase their production.

Source: Kickert (2012d)

Extra public investments

In November 2008, the Socialist Zapatero government announced a 'Spanish plan for stimulating the economy and the employment', including an extra €8 billion for public investments by local governments, a doubling of the normal municipal investment budget. Municipalities were required to make plans that could quickly generate employment. Some 30,000 municipal building and construction projects were carried out all over Spain, and some 410,000 people were employed.

Source: Plan Español para el Estímulo de la Economía y el Empleo (Plan E), November 2008 and Kickert and Ysa (2014)

Expenditure increase measures. The measures governments took to stimulate the economy by increasing expenditures can further be distinguished into public expenditures, contributions to households and contributions to companies. Examples of public expenditures were public investments in infrastructure, schools, buildings, etc. Examples of household contributions were pensions, child allowances, support for low incomes, handicapped and chronically ill persons, etc. And examples of contributions to companies were innovation and R&D, part-time unemployment, etc.

From an economic viewpoint, the economic recovery measures all followed the pattern of these categories. The economic crisis, however, differed per country, and so did the nature and size of the recovery measures. The following country examples concisely illustrate some of the differences.

The Spanish economy was hit by the burst of the housing and construction bubble in 2007–2008. The Spanish economy suffered a double-dip. The first recession lasted from late 2008 until early 2010, and the second recession from early 2011 until late 2013. The virtually complete collapse of the 'brick economy' (the property bubble) resulted in sharply rising unemployment, especially massive youth unemployment (43 per cent in 2010). Moreover, the Eurozone crisis led to a downgrading of Spain's credit ratings and sharply rising bond interest rates, urging Spain to restore the trustworthiness of its public finances, that is, spending cuts, thus leaving little room for extra fiscal stimulus of the economy. The hesitant Spanish economic recovery in 2010 was soon followed by a second recession. Youth unemployment further rose to 52 per cent in 2012.

In Great Britain, the economic crisis was severe as the economy was highly dependent on the financial and housing sectors, which were both deeply affected. The economic recovery package was substantial. Nevertheless, the British economy hardly recuperated. Firms went broke, unemployment soared, and massive house expulsions were feared.

The open and export-oriented German economy was also hit. The first economic recovery package (Konjunkturpaket) the German government made in October 2008 was relatively modest. The continuing deterioration of the economy, the international pressure of the United States and Europe on Chancellor Merkel to act more firmly, and the upcoming general elections of September 2009 led to a second recovery package in January 2009 announcing €80 billion extra expenditures. The German government, however, remained cautious and thrifty with extra expenditures. The German economy recovered relatively quickly and well, mainly because of rising industrial exports to Asia, especially China. The economic recovery in the neighbouring countries Belgium, Denmark and the Netherlands, which are economically strongly connected to Germany, was thus partially due to German success.

In March 2009, the Dutch government announced the economic recovery plan 'Working on the Future', with an impressive list of stimulus measures. Yet, the government remained rather cautious. The recovery package actually did not contain much extra investment, but chiefly consisted of forwarding already planned investments and postponing planned retrenchments. The ministry of Finance's primary objective was to reduce the excessively mounting budget deficit. A future €3.2 billion cutback was part of the recovery package. Although the recovery measures were politically and publicly presented as economic stimulus measures, under the surface it was mainly about budget discipline.

In December 2008, economic recovery measures were taken by the Belgian federal and Flemish and Walloon regional governments. The measures were moderate. The Belgian budget deficit was, and remained, relatively low. Belgian politicians refrained from costly stimulus plans. The Prime Minister Van Rompuy prevented a second additional recovery plan. The Belgian state debt was very high (96 per cent of GDP), so there was not much room for additional expenditure.

Decision-making during the economic crisis

After the swift, drastic and centralised decision-making – the urgent crisis management – during the banking crisis, the decision-making during the economic crisis in countries with multi-party coalition cabinets regained its normal character of consultations, deliberations, compromises and consensus between the many parties concerned.

Politics and the Konkunkturpaket

The minister of Economic Affairs, Zu Guttenberg, of the Bavarian Christian Democrat coalition party (CSU) was a declared opponent of extra economic support and only wanted to support viable companies, contrary to the Social Democrats (SPD), who wanted to avoid an economic crisis like in the 1930s at all costs. The approaching general elections of September 2009 foreshadowed the decision-making. The Social Democrat minister of Finance, Steinbrück, and particularly the minister of Foreign Affairs, Steinmeier, who was SPD party leader and Candidate-Chancellor, dominated the debate, and, for example, proposed the 'Abwrackprämie' that came to be immensely popular. The CDU and CSU ministers were more passive and reactive in their approach. Chancellor Merkel took over many of the SPD proposals, and therewith 'neutralised' the party-political proposals. The minister of Foreign Affairs, Steinmeier, organised a meeting with trade unions to discuss the economic recovery plans, which brought Merkel to organise an 'economic summit' meeting with representatives of science, employers, trade unions and interest groups to discuss the plans. The relatively modest first 'Konjunkturpaket' of October 2008 was hurriedly devised under great time pressure. Merkel and Steinbrück initially opposed a second additional recovery package. SPD-minister Steinbrück, pressured by his party, agreed with the preparation of a second package, resulting in the January 2009 'Konjunkturpaket'.

Source: Kickert (2013b)

In Germany, Chancellor Merkel and Finance Minister Steinbrück remained the key role players, but German consensual politics resurfaced. Although the German 'Bundeskanzlerin' possesses certain central authorities, and ministers are obligated to jointly cooperate in the cabinet, individual ministers do retain a certain autonomy in their policy area. Even a minister who had nothing to do with finances and the economy, such as the minister of Foreign Affairs Steinmeier, in his role as Social Democrat (SPD) party leader during the election campaign, played a key role in the economic recovery package.

The German Christian-Social Democrat (CDU/CSU-SPD) grand coalition actively involved political parties in the decision-making through the normal parliamentary channels. In federal Germany, the federal government decisions are also influenced by the regional governments, represented in the 'Bundesrat' (Senate). In the past years, the 'Bundesrat' has become more and more influential, especially in budgetary affairs (right of consent), which gave non-coalition parties another indirect influence. In cases that drew much public attention, such as the rescue of the retailer Karstadt (also owner of KaDeWe, the Berlin equivalent of Harrods in London), or the large postal order company Quelle, and the refusal to save Arcandor, many politicians joined the debate. The German plan to rescue the car manufacturer Opel drew international attention and became so sensitive (unfair German competition against foreign Opel companies) that the decision was lifted over the elections.

In Great Britain, Prime Minister Brown was very concerned about the economic decline. Although he certainly did not want to be named the 'killer' of 'New Labour politics', he chose a Keynesian stimulus package. To the despair

National Economic Council

The National Economic Council (NEC) was chaired by the British Prime Minister and co-chaired by the Chancellor. Various ministries were members. Its secretariat was led by the Cabinet Office and the Treasury, and included staff from other government departments. The NEC was able to accelerate the decision-making in Whitehall by bringing in a sense of urgency and seriousness of the crisis. To reflect the urgency, its meetings were held in the secure 'Cobra' briefing room in the Cabinet Office basement. The Treasury disliked the idea of giving up its monopoly on economic policy-making, and so considerable tensions existed. In its initial most effective phase, the NEC became more important than the cabinet – hence its nickname 'economic war cabinet'. It was an effective way of bringing coherence into the departmentalised structure of Whitehall and speeding up decision-making in departments in the high days of the crisis.

Source: Corry (2011)

of the 'Treasury', he broke his own 'golden rule' of not borrowing more than 40 per cent of GDP. VAT was decreased, top income taxes were raised and billions of investments were forwarded. The Conservative media accused Brown of returning to the 'Old Labour' habit of high taxes, high debts and nationalising. The budget deficit rose, but the economy and employment kept falling. In October 2008, Prime Minister Brown installed a 'National Economic Council' to rapidly and coherently combat the economic crisis.

In the Netherlands, the decision-making was explicitly politicised. The 2009 economic recovery plan was an official addition to the 2007 coalition agreement. Prime Minister Balkenende and the deputy Prime Ministers decided to make a new (additional) coalition agreement, which involves an institutionalised procedure of political consultation of the parliamentary parties and deliberation between the coalition party leaders. Assistance was provided by officials seconded from the Ministry of General Affairs (the Prime Minister's office) and the ministry of Finance (the deputy Prime Minister's office), who worked in offices in the Senate building and did not have contact with their superiors in their home ministries. The Prime Minister had a prime and coordinating role.

In March 2009, the Danish government reached a political agreement with the populist Danish People's Party on an economic stimulus package. The cornerstone of the package was lowering marginal income taxes, especially the top rate. Tax freeze and relief had long been a political promise of the Liberal-Conservative government. After tax cuts in 2003 and 2007, the Social Democrats had suggested tax reforms, and in response the government installed a Tax Commission. As neither the Social Democrats nor the government were able to agree, the government instead reached an agreement with the populist Danish People's Party. The reform measures more or less followed the Tax Commission's proposals. Income taxes were reduced, while ecological 'green' taxes were increased.

Fiscal crisis and consolidation: political aspects

Here, we now have a look at the third stage of the global crisis, the main subject addressed in this book: the fiscal crisis and consolidation. After state debts had significantly mounted due to the massive bank rescue packages, and budget deficits had further mounted due to the economic recovery plans, in many countries governments realised they had ended up with a fiscal crisis. For the next stage of the global crisis, governments had to balance their public finances. The hard times of downsizing, cutbacks and retrenchments began, or, more neutrally, fiscal consolidation.

Just as the economic recovery measures could be categorised as expenditures and revenues, so could the fiscal consolidation measures. However, this time it was the other way around. Reducing the public budget deficit essentially consists of the two following economic categories:

Reducing expenditures. These can be distinguished into operational and programme expenditures (OECD 2011, 2012). Operational expenditures are the costs of the Public Administration itself, such as salaries, number of public employees, efficiency, etc. Programme expenditures are the costs of policy sectors and programs. As social security, public health and education largely were the highest spending posts, it was no surprise that cuts were largely aimed at pensions, health and welfare (OECD 2011, 2012). In many countries, education and research were less affected by cutback plans.

Increasing revenues. These generally consisted of increases in consumption taxes (tobacco and alcohol, VAT, environmental, etc.), as well as rising (top) income taxes and taxation of the financial sector (e.g. on bankers' bonuses).

In this section, we do not elaborate upon the economic aspects of the fiscal consolidation measures, but rather focus on the political aspects of fiscal decision-making. Economically, the decisions are clear. Governments either cut spending or raised incomes, or both simultaneously. This is the opposite of economic recovery measures when governments raised spending and cut taxes, which, of course, gives rise to a discussion that surfaces each time new rounds of cutbacks are again deemed necessary: Does fiscal consolidation not have the undesired side effects of economic deterioration? The disagreement among economists about the possible answers to this question nourished the reluctance of politicians to repeatedly take hard and unpopular cutback measures. Here,

---

Restoring public finances in Belgium

The Belgian budget deficit is relatively modest, but its state debt is enormous (98 per cent of GDP in 2011). The problem in Belgium is that state debt is the responsibility of the federal government, which has the authority over tax revenues, but not over sub-national expenditures. The federal financing of the Flemish, Walloon and Brussels regional governments and the French-, Dutch- and German-speaking communities is legally determined. Though regional governments aimed at balancing their own budget, they had no intention to make extra expenditure cuts in order to reduce the federal state debt. Flanders would well be capable of doing so, but had no incentive as a Flemish surplus would automatically be compensated by a Walloon deficit. Wallonia eternally had deficits. Moreover, the political parties in the federal government were not identical to the parties in regional governments, hindering compromises along that line, so federal government could do nothing but increase tax revenues. How the Belgian state debt will ever be resolved seems a mystery.

Source: Kickert (2012c)

however, we are not interested in political discussions about economics. Political decisions by governments to cut spending and raise taxes depend on more than economic considerations alone. Take, for example, the highly complex Belgian political system.

Financial authorities such as Finance Ministries and National Banks were well aware that the costly bank rescue packages and economic recovery programmes were resulting in excessively increasing budget deficits and state debts, that is, in a serious fiscal crisis, and incessantly warned governments that this would need to be compensated, by necessity, by serious public expenditure cutbacks and revenue increases, but politics were not yet ready to break the bad news. The next stage of the global crisis, the fiscal one, in almost all Western countries was addressed by governments only after the banking and economic crisis, for obvious political reasons. Announcing cutbacks and tax rises is not what makes politicians particularly popular, especially when general elections are approaching. The decision-making about the inevitably forthcoming but politically unpopular cutbacks was lifted over the elections by most incumbent governments.

In some countries, the reluctance of the incumbent government to make public budget cuts before general elections was due to political ideology. Social Democrats prefer to present themselves to the electorate as true advocates of

Reluctance to spending cuts in Britain

In Great Britain, Labour Prime Minister Brown refused to be clear about future spending cuts in view of the coming May 2010 general elections. The Conservatives accused the Labour government of the 'worst peacetime public finances ever known'. Brown replied in parliament that the choice was investment under Labour or massive cuts under a Conservative government. Brown's reluctance to be frank about public spending cuts became a major issue in the election campaign. The Treasury and the Bank of England warned of the high budget deficit. Several cabinet ministers tried to persuade Brown to be more open, candid and honest, and therefore more trustworthy, on deficit reduction, but Brown refused (Seldon and Lodge 2011). The government refrained from publishing a three-year Spending Review, which would have revealed the details of departmental spending. The December 2009 pre-budget report remained vague on spending cuts, and the March 2010 budget did not contain much information either.

After the May 2010 elections, the Conservative-Liberal Democrat Cameron-Clegg coalition cabinet, within a few days, announced severe deficit reduction measures.

Source: Kickert (2012b)

Reluctance to spending cuts in Germany

In Germany, the Christian Social Democrat grand coalition under Chancellor Merkel focused on economic recovery plans in view of the forthcoming September 2009 general elections. The Social Democrats wanted to prevent an economic crisis at all costs. In the election campaign, the SPD party leader Steinmeier wanted to make clear they were the true and only advocates of saving jobs and recovering the economy. Merkel was more or less forced to take over many Social Democrat proposals in order to politically 'neutralise' them, and reluctantly agreed upon a second additional economic recovery package.

The September 2009 elections resulted in a Christian/Liberal (CDU/CSU-FDP) coalition cabinet headed by Chancellor Merkel. The Liberal Party (FDP) had promised tax cuts during the election campaign, and both the Liberals and the Bavarian Christian Democrats (CSU) had advocated less and slower cutbacks. Finance Minister Schäuble (CDU), supported by Chancellor Merkel, during the coalition formation managed to push through a substantial cutback package, resulting in the July 2010 'Sparpaket'. The political position of the Liberals (FDP) was relatively weak, as early elections would probably wipe out the party, and regional elections had resulted in a sensitive loss of the Bavarian Christian Democrats (CSU). Both coalition parties were in a relatively powerless position.

Source: Kickert (2013b)

---

saving jobs and recovering the economy, and not as advocates of public sector cuts, as the following two country examples illustrate.

In 2008, the Spanish Socialist government under Zapatero had responded to the economic collapse of the building and construction sector and rising unemployment by a fiscal stimulus program of tax exemptions for households and companies and extra public investments for local governments, amounting to some 2 per cent of GDP (Beynet *et al.* 2011). The Spanish economy had fallen in recession, with rising unemployment (21 per cent in 2010) and soaring youth unemployment (43 per cent in 2010), so the Socialist government had good reason to further fiscally stimulate the economy. However, in early 2010, the Socialist government was externally forced to prepare for fiscal cutbacks. The Greek default made foreign investors question Spain's creditworthiness too, bond yields rose, and international credit ratings declined. Then, the Eurozone leaders, led by the German Chancellor Merkel, contacted Zapatero and urged him to take austerity measures if he wanted to keep counting on European support (this public secret was later confirmed by Zapatero in his memoirs).

Afterwards, in a May 2010 speech for parliament, Zapatero unexpectedly and suddenly announced a first round of cutbacks (in public employee salaries) and the withdrawal of fiscal stimulus measures. This lost him the support of his Socialist electorate, leading to defeats in regional and local elections in May 2011. Moreover, massive public protest and social unrest broke out. In July 2011, Zapatero resigned as party leader and called early elections, which his party lost. In December 2011, the newly formed right-wing People's Party government under Rajoy immediately announced further austerity steps, a labour reform, public sector cuts, and cutbacks in health and education (Kickert and Ysa 2014).

Likewise, the left-wing governments in Iceland and Ireland were more or less externally compelled to take drastic fiscal consolidation measures, that is, as a precondition for the bail-outs they received.

A counter-example of the usual political science assumption that right-wing governments tend to take harder and swifter consolidation and cutback decisions than left-wing governments is the French case. The right-wing (UMP) French government and President Sarkozy refrained from drastic cutback decisions. Although the right-wing Sarkozy was minister of Economics and Finances

Reluctance to spending cuts in the Netherlands

In the Netherlands, the coalition between Christian Democrats (CDA), Labour Party (PvdA) and the Christian Union (orthodox Protestants) under Prime Minister Balkenende lifted the political decision-making on budget retrenchment and cutbacks over the June 2010 general elections. The coalition decided, however, to have top officials already make policy preparations for the spending cuts. In autumn 2009, nineteen working groups were established to look at policy areas where there could be cuts (social security, health, housing, education, environment, etc.). The working groups comprised expert top officials chaired by a senior politician or official. These working groups had three scenarios: relatively minor cuts, more severe cuts, and drastic savings of about 20 per cent. The first scenario consisted of mere efficiency gains, the second cautiously introduced some stronger cuts, and the third consisted of what the policy sector experts knew to be fundamental cutback decisions. For insiders in central administration, it was clear that here, the fundamental priorities and retrenchments were spelled out. The working groups published their reports in April 2010, in time for the June 2010 elections. However, the reports received hardly any publicity and did not have much of a role in the election campaign, neither were they reflected in the October 2010 Christian-Liberal coalition agreement.

Source: Kickert (2012d)

before and had initiated reforms in public finances, and during his presidency strengthened his leadership and centralised his control over government, and therefore strict and severe fiscal policy was to be expected from this president, the French government hesitated between cutbacks and economic stimulus measures.

On the other hand, the landslide victory of the right-wing (FIDESZ) government in the 2010 Hungarian general elections, resulting in a grand parliamentary majority, enabled it to push through a severe cutback plan, thus confirming the aforementioned political assumption.

In other countries, the reluctance to implement spending cuts was not due to the political orientation of government (right/centre/left), but to the inherent difficulties of multi-party coalitions in consensual democracies to take resolute decisions. The following example illustrates how politicians in a multi-party coalition evaded their political responsibilities for setting priorities in spending cuts.

Among the countries we investigated, Denmark was a rare exception where the incumbent government, right before approaching general elections, took drastic cutback measures. The proposed measures were clear examples of fundamental political priority-setting, which was the more remarkable as the Liberal-Conservative coalition government only had a parliamentary minority. It lost the 2011 general elections.

Another example of a government not lifting the cutbacks over a general elections was Estonia. As we mentioned in the introductory chapter, the Estonian coalition government did not engage in economic recovery, but instead decided for immediate fiscal consolidation, right from the outset of the crisis

---

Cutbacks before elections in Denmark

The centre-right coalition between the Liberal Party (Venstre) and the Conservative People's Party, in power from 2001 until 2011, was a minority coalition supported in parliament by the right-wing populist Danish People's Party (DF). In May 2010, the government and the DF agreed to consolidate public finances, including the politically sensitive and unexpected measure to half the duration of the unemployment benefit period and double the qualification requirement for this benefit. In May 2011, right before the upcoming September 2011 general elections, the government announced another reform package, including the politically sensitive measure to finish the early retirement scheme. These measures constituted fundamental reforms in the Danish flexible labour market policy (Goul Andersen 2011), a combination of Liberal employment protection and generous unemployment support.

Source: Kickert (2013a)

in 2008. Moreover, the volume of fiscal consolidation was relatively very high. The Social Democrats opposed the drastic cuts and left the coalition in May 2009, turning it into a parliamentary minority. The minority government, however, did not call early elections, but managed to carry out significant cutbacks. Moreover, the same coalition won by an overwhelmingly grand majority the regular 2011 general elections, an exceptional case in many regards.

Does politics matter?

In this book, we are particularly interested in the politics of fiscal consolidation. How does politics affect the governmental fiscal decision-making about consolidation and cutbacks? Is the current worldwide crisis affected by political considerations, or is the global financial, economic and fiscal crisis primarily or only a matter of economic rationale?

Let us now draw an analogy with a debate in the political sciences from the 1980s about the post-war welfare state. In the seminal article by Castles and McKinlay (1979), the then overriding common opinion that the prime determinants of policy outputs were largely economic and social, rather than political, was contested. The conclusion from many policy studies used to be that the post-war creation and expansion of the modern welfare state was a matter of economic and social modernisation, and hardly affected by the political choice of voters and politicians. Politics had come to appear as irrelevant. Modern technology and an advanced economy were the overriding factors shaping societies, which largely converged into similar institutional patterns and social systems. Variety in political structures and ideas were relatively unimportant.

According to Castles and McKinlay (1979), one of the reasons for this misconception was that quantitative comparative techniques were mainly the expertise of economists and sociologists, and generally lacking in political science at the time. So they set up a quantitative comparative study, focusing on well-defined measures of welfare and examining their covariation with (economic and) political variables, such as political structure, leadership and political ideology. Although economic factors had some influence, the main findings were that political factors had a greater salience in determining public welfare outputs, especially whether a right-wing conservative party being in office mattered. The issue of whether 'politics does matter' has since gained wide attraction in political science (Castles 1981, 1982; Sharpe and Newton 1984). In retrospect, Castles and McKinlay (1997) emphasised the development of sophisticated quantitative methodology and the findings that politics matters in a variety of ways, more than only the right-wing/left-wing partisan control. The main focus of the comparative studies was on the post-war building of the welfare state, showing that in an age when ideologies were proclaimed to be dead, political choice remained significant. Castles and McKinlay (1997: 106) remarked that at the time, many argued that the post-war welfare state development was complete and even defunct, as states worldwide were rather cutting back welfare state arrangements. With the demise of the welfare state, domestic politics dissolved by a globalisation process, by international finance capitalism.

Although this political science debate was about developments of welfare states and did not refer to administrative reform trends, the Public Administration analogy would be that the worldwide convergent 'new public management' (NPM) reform trend would have occurred irrespective of different political orientations. International comparative studies of public management reform (e.g. Pollitt and Bouckaert 2000), however, clearly refuted that stance, and showed that politics mattered in these reforms.

As repeatedly mentioned before, the current worldwide financial, economic and fiscal crisis has extensively been investigated by scholars from an economic perspective. Economic recovery and restoring public finances allegedly are primarily a matter of economic rationale (OECD 2011). Politicians, parties and governments had better follow sound economic recommendations rather than political right-wing or left-wing ideology. Fiscal consolidation, after all, is chiefly about reducing budget deficit and state debt. Studies by political and administrative scholars are only beginning to appear. The impression might arise that political aspects are hardly relevant or interesting to study, and explain the crisis and consolidation.

In this book, we show that politics does matter in fiscal consolidation, and how so. Although we do not claim to use the sophisticated quantitative methodology referred to above, we do supplement the qualitative country case studies with quantitative comparative analysis in the chapters on causes and effects of fiscal consolidation.

Terminology

Before moving to the next chapter about the analytical framework used in this book, we first pay some attention to the rather affluent, and therefore now and then confusing, terminology about fiscal crisis and consolidation.

The titles of publications on cutback management in the 1970s and 1980s cited in the literature review by Raudla *et al.* (2013) reveal a wide variety of seemingly synonymous terms in use. The creativity with which English-language synonyms for cutbacks were invented is moving.

Likewise was the creative variety of synonyms for the term fiscal crisis.

More significant is the variety of terms indicating the main subject of investigation by the various political and administrative scientists. The seminal articles of Levine (1978, 1979) used the term 'cutback management', although

Synonyms for cutbacks

Austerity	Decrementalism	Savings
Cuts	Downsizing	Scarcity
Decline	Reductions	Shrinking
Decrease	Retrenchment	Termination

Synonyms for fiscal crisis

Fiscal distress	Fiscal pressure	Fiscal stress
Fiscal limitations	Fiscal strain	Fiscal squeeze

he later used the term 'managing fiscal stress' (Levine 1980). Titles such as 'managing the fiscal crisis' can also frequently come across in the literature (Raudla *et al.* 2013).

Besides the perhaps touching linguistic creativity of scholars in inventing appealing titles for their publications, the really significant point at stake here is that these terms are not synonyms. Cutbacks are only one of the measures to manage the fiscal crisis. At the national government level, a fiscal crisis is defined in terms of public finances, that is, the degree of public budget deficit and gross state debt. Restoring public finances, or the equivalent term 'fiscal consolidation' widely used by economists (IMF 2010; OECD 2011), is achieved by either expenditure cuts or revenue increases. A budget deficit being the difference between expenditures and revenues, deficit reduction measures can logically be distinguished into expenditure cuts or revenue rises. Cutbacks are not the only option. Increasing tax revenues was a measure that governments outside the United States, where that is widely considered a political taboo, especially in the Republican camp, were less hampered to adopt. The OECD (2011, 2012) review of fiscal consolidation measures of its member states confirmed that. Managing the fiscal crisis was not restricted to spending cutbacks.

Moreover, governments were not 'managing' the cutbacks, but were rather focused on the political decision-making leading up to the cutback and revenue measures. 'Managing' the fiscal crisis suggests that governments were involved in some sort of goal-oriented and rational control of the crisis, which they were not. A reduction of the public deficit can be the result of economic growth rather than cutback and revenue measures by government, and reversely, these measures may not lead to deficit restoration when the economy significantly deteriorates. Indeed, the fiscal crisis is by far not yet successfully resolved. 'Responding' to the fiscal crisis might be a more modest and accurate description of what many governments were desperately attempting to do (Kickert 2012a).

Therefore, neither of the words in the term 'cutback management' seems a proper description of what governments actually did in response to the fiscal crisis. The term 'cutback management' was often suitable at the lower organisational levels of ministerial departments or executive agencies or local government services. There, the option to increase own revenues is limited. Public organisations that obtain their entire revenues, or most of them, from the state generally undergo budget deficits as a consequence of cutbacks imposed by the state. At that organisational level of analysis, the term 'cutback management' is fully appropriate, as that is the only option departments, agencies or local public service organisations have: managing the externally imposed, determined and unalterable cutbacks. And these were the types of organisations mostly considered in the above-mentioned seminal publications of Levine (1978, 1979, 1980). In this book, however, the level of analysis is national government.

Economists tend to make a distinction between fiscal crisis and fiscal stress (while fiscal strain, fiscal pressure and fiscal squeeze are often used as synonyms or subcategories for fiscal stress). In general, 'fiscal stress' refers to a situation of chronic scarcity of budgetary resources (Schick 1980), in which the available revenues are not sufficient to cover the growth of expenditures, and as a result, budgetary decision-making is centred around constraining expenditure growth (Raudla *et al.* 2013). 'Fiscal crisis', in turn, refers to a situation of acute or total scarcity (Schick 1980), in which revenues are falling and the resulting gap between expenditures and revenues is perceived to be so large as to constitute a 'crisis' by the political decision-makers, causing for an adoption of austerity measures (Raudla *et al.* 2013). In the Eurozone, the degree of 'fiscal crisis' according to the Maastricht criteria depends on how much the budget deficit exceeds the 3 per cent GDP ceiling and how much the state debt exceeds the 60 per cent GDP ceiling.

While we recognise differences between fiscal crisis and fiscal stress, for the sake of terminological clarity we use the terms 'fiscal crisis' (excessive budget deficit and state debt) and 'fiscal consolidation' (reduction of budget deficit and debt accumulation, by expenditure cuts and revenue increase) (OECD 2012: 18) in this book.

Politics of fiscal consolidation

Our special interest in this book is in the political aspects of fiscal consolidation. That does not necessarily coincide with the economic volume of fiscal consolidation. Neither is it necessarily related to the economic outcomes such as restoration of the budget balance or economic recovery. How can we conceptualise and define the politics of fiscal consolidation as clearly as the economics of consolidation? We are looking for a political equivalent of the neat economic variable: the volume of fiscal consolidation (OECD 2011). This could be a sort of measure indicating how much political effort was involved in government's fiscal decision-making, a sort of 'volume' of political effort – the degree of political effort, the degree of endeavour, the pain and energy and time spent in reaching the decisions, or the political 'sweat'. The hyperbole 'sweat' indicates that political effort not only refers to concrete and specific consolidation measures, but also to framing, symbolism and ideational aspects of measures.

For the sake of conceptual clarity, we employ a plain context-action-effect scheme. The action concept is the political effort devoted by a government to fiscal decision-making. The political effort of a government to take hard and unpopular cutback decisions is dependent on the political context. In some political systems, it is more complicated for a government to reach a cutback decision than in others, and the political effort of a government to take a cutback decision is also related to the effects. The fiercer a government is expected to be politically opposed against its cutback decisions, the higher the effort to accomplish the decision. Here, we first have a look at the context and effects, and then return to the action concept of political effort.

Political context

The degree of political effort of a government to reach cutback decisions depends on the political context. For example, a one-party government in a majoritarian democracy allegedly is in a better position to take resolute decisions, even unpopular cutback ones. A multi-party coalition government in a consensual democracy is likely to be in a worse position to take resolute and unpopular decisions, more so when it only has a parliamentary minority. The government has to take account of both coalition and opposition parties, and in a corporatist democracy also of the multitude of interest groups and social organisations.

The degree of political effort is supposed to depend on the type of political system (majoritarian or consensus), on the type of government (one-party or multi-party coalition), on the degree of parliamentary majority (grand, simple or minority), and on the political orientation (right wing, centre or left wing) of governing parties. In Chapter 6 of this book, we investigate these relationships, both with qualitative country examples illustrating the alleged relationships, and with a quantitative statistical analysis of the correlations.

Political effects

The political effort of governments to take hard and unpopular cutback decisions also depends on the possible political effects. The classical definition of politics by Laswell (1936) in terms of 'who gets what when how' indicates that it is crucial who wins or loses, who gets the credit and who takes the blame. Not only who have to pay more taxes and are hurt by the spending cuts, but also the effects on voters, and therefore the electoral effects. A government that dares to take unpopular cutback decisions might be punished at the next elections. In Chapter 7 of this book, we investigate these electoral effects of fiscal consolidation both in a qualitative country example and a quantitative statistical correlation sense. The electoral effects appeared to be significant.

However, the adjective 'political' has a more encompassing meaning than only 'electoral'. Other 'political effect' variables can be conceived, such as party-political opposition in parliament, but also public opposition outside parliament, public protests and demonstrations, opposition by social interest and action groups, and resistance by civil servants. In countries that were so severely hit by the crisis that they had to be bailed out, social protest and unrest not only resulted in the ousting of the government in office, but, for example, in Hungary, Iceland and Ireland, also in structural reforms of the domestic political system. The political, public, social and administrative resistance, opposition and protest that a government's cutback decisions can bring about can have a variety of forms (see Table 2.2).

The political effort of a government in taking fiscal consolidation decisions is not only related to the electoral side effects and political party opposition in parliament, but also to these other forms of public, social and administrative opposition. Alternatively, to reframe it inversely and more optimistically, effort is related to political, public and social legitimacy.

TABLE 2.2 Forms of opposition

Political opposition in parliament	Sort and degree of opposition
	Walkout of parties
	Fall of coalition cabinet
Public opposition	Media coverage
	Protests and demonstrations
	Social unrest
Social opposition	Employees and trade unions
	Social interest groups
	Pressure and action groups
Administrative opposition	Resistance to austerity measures
	Saving one's own turf
	Strikes and protests

As public administration itself is an important target of austerity measures, civil servants can be seen as a specific internal 'interest group', which is not only the 'object' of cutbacks, but can influence the planning and implementation of consolidation measures through their expertise and role in policy-making. This leads to a broader discussion of the politico-administrative relations and the balance between political control that governments exercise over the administrative machinery and civil servants' involvement in the preparation and implementation of public policy (including consolidation measures). The question is also whether consolidation measures are mainly seen as a rational-technocratic exercise by allowing civil servants more latitude in managing cutbacks, or whether they are perceived as part of political priority-setting. Moreover, during the era of austerity, civil service can be seen more than ever as a political force in itself. In a situation where their own job security, pay and pensions are threatened, it can be hard for politicians to ask civil servants to plan and implement consolidation measures that run counter to their own 'social contract' (Kelman 2006), even if they are called upon to work as perfectly neutral professionals. Theories focusing on bureaucratic politics argue that if bureaucracies are assumed to act in a self-interested way (as assumed by public choice, for example), it can lead to officials trying to protect their turf and resisting operational expenditures, and, among operational expenditures, spending on salaries would be cut less than other operational expenditures (Downs and Rocke 1984; Hood *et al.* 1988). Civil servants can show their attitude towards consolidation through strikes and protests, and by inner-administration rivalry caused by a zero-sum game of cutbacks.

Notice the conceptual difference whether the opposition and protest took place during the decision-making process of government, therewith influencing the outcomes of the decision process, in which case it is an input indicator of 'political effort'. Alternatively, whether the public and social opposition and protest took place after the government had reached its political decision in parliament, in which case it is an output indicator of 'political effect'. The conceptual confusion between input and output further augments when the *ex post* protests against a severe cutback decision urge and persuade the government to take back its earlier decision and reach another one, which is not unusual in politics.

Although virtually each cutback measure affects some kind of vested interest, and therefore even small, across-the-board, cheese-slicing cuts can result in opposition and protest, the aforementioned indicators of public and social opposition rather point to the type of selective, targeted, political prioritised cutback decisions.

Political effort

Let us now return to the action concept of political effort of a government in fiscal consolidation. In this book, we interpret the 'political effort' of a government primarily in terms of the government's decision-making activities, and we further conceptualise that endeavour along the following lines.

First, we distinguish types of decision-making. Based on the basic distinction in the cutback management literature of the 1970s and 1980s between across-the-board (cheese-slicing, equal-proportional) cuts, on the one hand, and selective, targeted political priority-setting, on the other (Pollitt 2010; Raudla *et al.* 2013), we elaborate this classical rational-incremental dichotomy in decision-making and distinguish a number of characteristics of decision-making. The country studies revealed that in the few cases that the government decided to set selective political priorities, these were often implemented in cautious, slow, small and gradual steps, that is, in an incremental way. Apparently, one has to make a further distinction in phases of decision-making between agenda-setting, preparation and planning, taking the decisions, implementation and evaluation.

Second, we distinguish between stages of decision-making. Fiscal consolidation usually took place in a series of different stages. The initial stage typically consisted of politics denying the severity of the crisis, only taking temporary small measures, and postponing serious cuts. Only in later stages was the gravity and duration of the crisis recognised and first attempts at serious cutbacks were made. The longer the crisis took and the more severe it became, the higher the chance that, in the end, the government made selective targeted cuts based on political priority-setting.

Third, we take a closer look at the shifting power relations between political and administrative actors in crisis decision-making. Who gains more power while austerity measures are underway? We look both at the power relations between politicians and civil servants, and between the administrative units both at national and organisational level. Although the existing literature argues for both centralisation and decentralisation of cutback decision-making (Boin *et al.* 2008; Peters *et al.* 2011; Schick 2009), our study indicates a clear shift towards centralisation with particular empowerment of Ministries of Finance.

In the next chapter about the analytical framework, these challenges of decision-making are further explained and elaborated.

Chapter 3

Analytical framework

The analytical framework used in this book derives from the three questions that were addressed and presented in the first introductory chapter.

First, the informative and descriptive question: we describe and analyse how the European governments responded to the fiscal crisis. What fiscal consolidation measures were taken, and how did the decision-making take place? Thus covering both the economic aspects of the measures and the governments' political decision-making.

Second, the explanatory question: how to explain the similarities and differences in consolidation measures and decision-making in the various European countries from both an economic and a political perspective. And besides domestic factors, supra-national factors have also influenced the national governments' fiscal consolidation decisions.

Third, the evaluative and effectiveness question: What were the effects of the fiscal consolidation on the recovery of public finances and the economy, what were the political effects, and what were the effects on administration itself?

The analytical framework of both the 'economics' and 'politics' of fiscal consolidation therefore follows the conceptual 'cause-action-effect' scheme outlined in Figure 3.1. The constituent components of the analytical framework are outlined in the following sections.

The focus of this book is on the fiscal crisis and fiscal consolidation. To clarify the distinctive nature of the fiscal crisis, in Chapter 2 the previous two stages

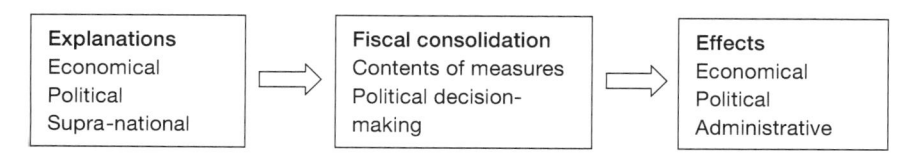

FIGURE 3.1 Outline of the analytical framework

of the global crisis were described, the initial first stage of the worldwide banking crisis and the subsequent second stage of the worldwide economic crisis. The banking and economic crises are only used as contextual information when necessary. Here, we investigate the national governments' measures to handle the domestic fiscal crisis. We therefore neither separately investigate the joint multi-national decision-making at the European level, as this is too different from, and hardly comparable with, the national level. The European Union's fiscal rules and regulations, and the Eurozone crisis, undoubtedly had a major impact on the economic and fiscal crisis in the Eurozone countries and their consequent domestic fiscal consolidation measures. In this book, we interpret this as a supra-national factor influencing the national governments' fiscal decisions, that is, as an additional set of explanatory factors.

3.1 FISCAL CONSOLIDATION

The fiscal consolidation measures taken by European governments to address their domestic fiscal crises were described and analysed in the country studies for the COCOPS seventh work package These were described both from an economic perspective (the contents of the consolidation measures) and from a political one (the political decision-making). Let us now outline and explain these two key concepts.

Fiscal consolidation: contents of measures

From an economic perspective, the central approach to 'fiscal consolidation' is the contents of the measures taken by governments to restore their public finances in order to reduce the budget deficit and state debt (IMF 2010; OECD 2011; World Bank 2008). The usual economic classification of consolidation measures are:

- expenditure cuts; and
- revenue increases.

Expenditure cuts are further subdivided according to the following categories (see OECD 2011, 2012):

- Operational measures (cutting operational costs or running costs of the administration).
- Programme measures in policy sectors (transfers and grants).
- Cuts in capital expenditures (investments).

Tax revenue measures are further divided into a number of subcategories, such as consumption tax, income tax and corporation tax.

The economic classification of consolidation measures is presented and illustrated with some examples in Table 3.1.

In this book, we pay particular attention to the expenditure cutbacks targeted at Public Administration, that is, operational cuts. This analytical framework is built on the basis of many cutback studies from the 1970s and 1980s, which have been summarised in a thorough literature review by Raudla *et al.* (2013).

Reductions in operational expenditures are commonly categorised by the object of the expenditure, and by distinguishing between personnel expenditure and non-personnel expenditure (Wolman and Davis 1980: 232). For example, the measures for cutting personnel costs usually include reducing the number of workers, working time or remuneration, and the list of tools involve a number of options, ranging from reducing overtime to dismissal. The literature of the 1970s and 1980s addresses the following measures used in cutting personnel costs: reduced (over)time; furloughs; salary cuts; salary freeze or reduction in the rate of salary increase; slowdown of promotion; filling positions with less-credentialed, lower-paid staff; reducing pay grades of vacated job lots; early retirement; reshuffling of staff; and hiring freeze and lay-offs (e.g. Cayer 1986; Dunsire and Hood 1989; Greenhalgh and McKersie 1980; Hood and

TABLE 3.1 Classification of consolidation measures

Expenditure measures	Revenue measures	Other measures
Operational expenditures Hiring or pay freeze Wage reduction Staff reductions Reorganisations Efficiency cuts	*Consumption tax* e.g. VAT, excise taxes on alcohol, tobacco, energy	Addressing tax evasion and social security fraud Financial sector
Programme expenditures in policy sectors Social security Health Education Housing Welfare Other sectors	*Income tax* e.g. top incomes *Corporation tax* e.g. bank bonuses *Non-fiscal revenues*	Energy sector e.g. sustainable economy
Capital expenditures Cuts in or postponement of investments		

Source: OECD (2011)

Wright 1981; Levine 1978, 1985; Marando 1990; Rubin 1980; Wolman and Davis 1980; Wright 1981). The experience of that era shows that within the 'menu' of cutback options, the hiring freeze was the most popular measure for cutting personnel expenditure, often applied as the first response during crisis to achieve cutbacks (Dunsire and Hood 1989; Levine *et al.* 1981, 1985; Schick 1988; Wolman 1983; Wolman and Davis 1980). Non-personnel cutbacks of operational expenditure included restrictions or bans on spending on utilities, supplies, equipment, travel and communication (Lewis and Logalbo 1980; Wolman and Davis 1980).

Several studies show that politicians generally prefer cuts to operational expenditures over programme cuts; administrative cost cutting is less visible to the public and likely to cause less opposition from other political parties and voters (Banner 1985; Glennerster 1981; Downs and Rocke 1984; Lewis and Logalbo 1980; MacManus *et al.* 1989). Programme cuts are seen as decreases in transfers to the citizens (e.g. entitlements), but so are changes in expenditures that lead to reduced levels of public services (Dunsire and Hood 1989; Lewis and Logalbo 1980; Kogan 1981). Dunsire and Hood (1989) pointed out that different streamlining and quality-reducing activities were aimed either at smoothing out the inputs or levelling down the outputs of public services. The former involved activities such as formalising access by clients, standardising forms and treatments, establishing quotas, raising prices, etc. The latter predominantly comprised reducing the variety of available service tasks, reducing the frequency of service provision (e.g. of waste collection), reducing service hours, and/or reducing the number of service outlets (e.g. libraries) (Dunsire and Hood 1989; Lewis and Logalbo 1980: 187). In addition, the main means of achieving cutbacks in public services was to change the nature of service providers (by using part-time, third-party or volunteer counterparts) (Dunsire and Hood 1989).

Among the cutback instruments that deal with transfers, common options involved straightforward cutbacks in the coverage or size of entitlement payments, but also shifting part of the entitlement costs elsewhere (e.g. on to the private sector, to citizens or just further away from the central government budget). For example, making employers pay part of sickness fund payments, increasing waiting times, delaying payments, establishing item charges and user fees for services (Dunsire and Hood 1989; Hood and Wright 1981: 188, 211).

Finally, capital expenditures can take different forms, such as elimination of capital spending from the budget, but can also include softer measures, such as postponing capital projects, spending freezes on new projects and cutting maintenance costs (Lewis and Logalbo 1980). In the literature, several authors warn against these approaches, as the related future costs might be far in excess of present savings and may lead to more costly capital acquisition in the long term (Lewis and Logalbo 1980; McTighe 1979; Tarschys 1981).

In Table 3.2, we summarise the main cutback measures of the 1970s and 1980s (Raudla *et al.* 2013) according to the three categories.

TABLE 3.2 Main cutback measures

Category	Measures
Operational expenditures	
Personnel costs	Reduced overtime or working time
	Slowing down of promotion
	Early retirement
	Wage freeze
	Reduction in the rate of salary increase
	Filling positions with less-credentialed, lower-paid staff
	Reducing pay grades of vacated job lots
	Salary cuts
	Reshuffling of staff
	Furlough
	Hiring freeze
	Lay-off
Non-personnel costs	Spending limits and bans on utilities, supplies, equipment, travel, communications, etc.
Programme expenditures	
	Cut service provision
	Shorten the reception time, limit service hours
	Reduce the frequency of service provision, reduce the number of service outlets
	Reduce the quality requirements for service provision
	Programme termination
	Engage voluntary, part-time and third-party counterparts in service provision
	Reduce transfers
	Shift part of the entitlement costs to the private sector or citizens
Investments/capital expenditures	
	Capital spending freezes on new/non-essential capital projects
	Transfer of cost to private capital
	Postponing procurement
	Deferral of maintenance
	Book-keeping expenditure cuts on capital account

Source: Raudla *et al.* (2013)

Fiscal consolidation: political decision-making

Besides analysing the contents of the consolidation measures, we are particularly interested in the political efforts of governments in taking fiscal consolidation measures. At the end of Chapter 2, we explored the concept of political effort and concluded by focusing on political decision-making. Although it was clear that the political aspects of fiscal consolidation can be considered in many different ways, in this chapter we operationalise the concept of political decision-making by distinguishing three key aspects:

1 between different types, or characteristics, of decision-making;
2 between different stages of decision-making; and
3 the shifting of power relations, particularly the centralisation and politicisation of decision-making.

The characteristics of decision-making

The most often used distinction in cutback management is the one between across-the-board cuts, on the one hand, and targeted cuts, on the other (Pollitt 2010; Raudla *et al.* 2013). Across-the-board measures refers to cuts in equal amounts or percentages for all institutions and/or policy fields, while targeted cuts means that some institutions and sectors face a larger cut than others (Raudla *et al.* 2013). This dichotomy has been labelled in various ways. The across-the-board tactics have variously been dubbed 'cheese-slicing' (Pollitt 2010; Tarschys 1985), 'decrementalism' (Bartle 1996; Levine 1985; Levine *et al.* 1981), and 'equal misery' approach (Hood and Wright 1981).

Targeted cuts involve an array of possible tactics, such as 'strategic prioritisation' and 'managerial' cuts (Bartle 1996; Behn 1980; Hendrick 1989; Levine 1978, 1979). A strategic response to fiscal stress would involve decisions on the department's mission and core services and corresponding prioritising in resource allocations (Levine 1985: 692). Such a response could mean that in making reductions to programmes, low-priority programmes would be cut more than high-priority programmes (Levine *et al.* 1981: 15). In the managerial approach, the cuts are also selective, but instead of using rational analysis for making the cuts, the officials use programmatic criteria related to mandatory and non-mandatory expenditures to determine requests and appropriations (Raudla *et al.* 2013).

Most analysts of the 1980s called for rational approaches (e.g. Levine 1985; McTighe 1979) by suggesting political decision-making on the basis of fundamental core-task analysis, strategic prioritisation and long-term decision-making. Other authors argue pragmatically that rational approaches may not be the most feasible option in the middle of a fiscal crisis, and suggest decremental approaches based on compromise and shorter timescales are used in practice (e.g. Hood and Wright 1981). The literature review by Raudla *et al.* (2013) reveals the following characteristics of across-the-board versus targeted cuts.

Proponents of across-the board cuts argue that they reduce decision-making costs as they do not require comprehensive analysis and comparison of various institutions and policy programmes, which implies that cutbacks can be decided upon rather swiftly without going through long negotiations and analysis (Banner 1985; Hood and Wright 1981; Schick 1988). They also argue that decremental cuts diminish the likelihood of conflicts between both political and administrative institutions as they avoid distinguishing between cutback winners and losers (Hood and Wright 1981; Schick 1983; Tarschys 1985). Furthermore, equal cuts are presented as being more equitable, fair and legitimate than targeted cuts, which is why they have also been called 'the equal misery approach' (Hood and Wright 1981) and 'sharing the pain' (Biller 1980).

Proponents of targeted cuts argue that they represent a more rational and strategic approach towards cutbacks as they take into account differences in the importance and urgency of tasks in different policy sectors and specific public services (Banner 1985; Levine 1985). They distinguish between different public organisations and their specific circumstances (Levine 1979), and avoid situations where equal cuts could accumulate and lead to declining service quality (Behn 1980; Levine 1985). It is notable that the basic distinction in the cutback management literature between across-the-board and targeted cuts resembles the classical dichotomy in decision-making between rational-comprehensive and incremental (Lindblom 1959; see Table 3.3).

Peters *et al.* (2011) have further elaborated this classical dichotomy and sub-divided decision-making dilemmas into a number of strategic characteristics, such as:

- fundamental priorities versus incrementalism;
- swift and drastic versus slow and small decisions;

TABLE 3.3 Rational-incremental dichotomy in decision-making

Rational-comprehensive	Incremental-compromise
Political priority-setting	No political priorities, no rational analysis
Fundamental rational core-task analysis	Across-the-board, cheese-slicing, equal cuts
Strategic long-term decision-making	Pragmatic short-term compromise decisions

Source: Lindblom (1959)

TABLE 3.4 Characteristics of decision-making

Fundamental political priority-setting	*Incremental pragmatic compromises*
Swift, large and drastic decision-making	Slow, small and gradual steps
Centralised decision-making	Decentralised decision-making
Coherent and systematic decision-making	Incoherent patchwork
Long-term sustainable solutions	Short-term quick fixes

Source: Peters *et al.* (2011)

- centralised versus decentralised decisions;
- coherent systematic versus incoherent patchwork; and
- long-term sustainable solutions versus short-term quick fixes (see Table 3.4).

Stages of decision-making

Types and characteristics of decision-making may differ in various stages of crisis. When faced for the first time with fiscal crisis necessitating spending cuts, governments can be tempted to deny or delay the cuts, instead of deciding and implementing actual cuts. This reaction pattern resembles the social-psychological 'coping cycle' (Carnall 2003) about 'resistance to change': people first deny the need for change, then defend the advantages of the current situation, but afterwards recognise and comply with the need for change, and in the end agree to take action to change.

The literature on change management (for surveys, see Burnes 2009; Carnall 2003) is based on the empirically confirmed observation that initiatives to transform organisations often fail, and is about the actions and steps that have to be followed in order to successfully implement a 'planned change'. Theories on 'planned change' are based on the seminal work of the social psychologist Lewin (1951), who developed the famous three-phase model of change:

- *Unfreeze.* Create the need for change, due to dissatisfaction with the status quo.
- *Move.* Identify and mobilise the resources required to effect the change.
- *Refreeze.* Embed the new ways of working in the roots of the organisation.

Organisational members have to be convinced of the need for change, have a sense of urgency, otherwise nobody is willing to move. And a new situation after the change has to be institutionalised, the members of the organisation have to embed new behavioural patterns, new working methods, new values and norms, otherwise people will soon return to their old habits from prior to the change.

Following the original three-phase model of Lewin, many different multi-phase models of managing change have been developed (e.g. Burnes 2009; Carnall 2003; Fernandez and Rainey 2006; Kanter 1983; Kotter 1996; Senior 1997). Despite the justified criticism of such relatively simple models of change management (e.g. Kickert 2014), we take a further look at the approach by Carnall (2003: 210), who developed a five-stage 'coping cycle' consisting of the following steps:

- ◼ *Denial.* The first reaction of people and groups is to deny there is a need for change.
- ◼ *Defence.* People will defend their past practices and behaviours and deny that the new ones are better suited.
- ◼ *Discarding.* When change is inevitable, people start to recognise that past behaviour is no longer suitable for the current situation.
- ◼ *Adaptation.* People must adapt to the new ways, but the new ways must also adapt to the people.
- ◼ *Internalisation.* People reach the stage where they see the changes no longer as new, but as normal, the way things should be.

Other phase models emphasise the components: 'need to change, capacity to change, best interest to change, all behind the change, change is right' (Armenakis and Bedeian 1999).

The theories of change management teach us that resistance to change is not a strange aberration, but a normal human reaction pattern. People have to be convinced of the need for change, feel a sense of urgency, recognise that the status quo is inappropriate, otherwise nobody is willing to change. Unsurprisingly, politicians in governments do look like ordinary people, as the same 'resistance to change' pattern could be recognised in cutback decision-making by governments.

The experience with cutback management during the fiscal crisis of the 1980s has taught us that cutbacks took place in a series of stages (Raudla *et al.* 2013). After the initial stages of denial and defence were overcome, a first round of small cutbacks usually came about. Because politicians were not yet fully convinced of the gravity and duration of the crisis, the measures were moderate and temporary, cutbacks were postponed, and expenditure cutbacks were shifted to the capital investment account, thus disguising the cuts and sparing the service delivery to citizens. Only in the later stages of cutbacks did governments come to realise that the crisis was more severe and persistent than expected, and the cutbacks became more serious and severe. Wages were frozen, as was hiring, but wage cuts and dismissals were still avoided, as were

TABLE 3.5 Stages of cutback decision-making

Stages of cutback decision-making	Types of cutback measures
Denial. Defend advantages of present situation. Unconvinced of gravity and duration of crisis	Temporary small measures. Moderate adjustment to status quo. Cuts postponed
Compliance with the need for cutbacks	First attempt at serious cutbacks
Internalised need for cutbacks. Action. Resolute cutback decisions	First across-the-board and efficiency cuts. Later targeted downsizing and cuts of public tasks. Ultimately fundamental political priority-setting

cuts in public service delivery. It was only several rounds of cutbacks later that governments had to concede that cuts in salaries and employment were inevitable and that political priorities had to be set for targeted downsizing and cutting of public services. Table 3.5 provides an overview of these different stages of cutback decision-making.

The existing literature shows that the longer lasting and the more severe fiscal stress was, the more likely it was that the authorities started imposing targeted cuts rather than implementing across-the-board cuts (Hood and Wright 1981; Levine 1979, 1985; Levine et al. 1981; Raudla et al. 2013). Levine (1979: 182) argued that at the beginning of the austerity, across-the-board cuts were more likely because the 'sharing the pain' option was likely to be perceived as more equitable and hence to generate less conflict and resistance, but if these measures were not sufficient, more targeted cuts on the basis of prioritisation would be adopted (Hood and Wright 1981; Pollitt 2010). Therefore, across-the-board cuts may be appropriate for dealing with small cuts, whereas achieving deeper cuts necessitates targeted cutbacks (Levine 1984; Schick 1983: 21).

As is shown later in the empirical analysis, countries have not all gone through these stages in the same order. In particular, countries that were hit so hard by the crisis that they were incapable of domestically solving their fiscal crisis and had to be rescued externally by a 'bail-out', received these large loans on the explicit precondition that drastic consolidation measures were immediately to be carried out. In these countries, the severity of the crisis was overriding. They did not have the opportunity to deny or delay the cuts, but had to get involved in radical cutback decisions.

Shifts in power relations

Finally, we take a look at shifts in consolidation decision-making processes compared to 'normal' times. The governments' response to the fiscal crisis is likely to change the conventional patterns of decision-making, and the established roles and functions of politicians, civil servants, external experts and other stake-holders. The existing research shows that one of the central issues of cutback decision-making is related to the centralisation-decentralisation dilemma (Boin *et al.* 2008; Kickert 2012a; Peters *et al.* 2011; Schick 2009). Has the crisis brought about a shift towards more centralised or decentralised modes of decision-making? Centralisation has been considered inherent in any sort of crisis management and decision-making (Boin *et al.* 2008). When faced with crisis, governments tend to centralise decision-making, primarily, because it enables quick legitimisation of decisions (Peters 2011). It is widely accepted that finan-cial decline triggers movement towards mechanistic structures and hierarchy-based procedures in organisations, first and foremost because budgeting, naturally assumed to be in the domain of the chief executive, becomes a central issue of governing (Bozeman 2010; Peters 2011; Stern and Sundelius 1997). As several authors (Behn 1980; Levine 1985; Schick 1983) have argued, central-isation of decision-making during retrenchment is necessary because the organisational subunits would be very unlikely to volunteer the making of cuts. As any prioritisation assumes a certain degree of centralisation (Wildavsky 2001), a government's decision to carry out cuts based on strategic prioritisations automatically leads to centralised decision-making. Moving towards centralisa-tion can be achieved either through standardisation of procedures, empowering the central budgetary departments, setting limits and ceilings to organisational spending, borrowing and activities, or by general priority-setting by the govern-ment (Peters 2011; Pollitt 2010). The need to cut back budgets reinforces top-down and rule-based budgetary procedures and increases the power of budgetary institutions (Schick 2009: 10).

In addition, we explore whether the crisis has increased the autonomy of civil servants or if there have been attempts to politicise the decision-making. Has the power of politicians increased in the decision-making process? Several authors (Kickert 2012a; Peters 2011; Peters *et al.* 2011) point out that a typical feature related to governments managing the fiscal crisis is the centralisation of the decision-making process around the political elite and distancing 'the career civil service' from the key actors. Even technocratic and operational decisions commonly in the responsibility of officials might move into the political arena during cutback management (Peters 2011); public service can be cast aside because it is treated as part of the problem resistant to changes, but not part of the solution (Peters and Pierre 2004). That is why even technocratic and operational decisions commonly in the responsibility of officials might move to the political arena during cutback management (Peters 2011), and tasks involv-ing greater share of responsibility, accountability and blame are expected to be carried out by political leaders (Boin *et al.* 2008: 150). On the other hand, it has been argued that in times of crisis, the intense engagement of competent public officials becomes especially critical due to the intensified role of high-quality policy analysis (Kickert 2012a; Pollitt 2010). Also, relying on the administrative apparatus or other sources of expert advice can serve the aim of obscuring or shifting blame (Boin *et al.* 2008; Peters *et al.* 2011). Posner and Blöndal (2012: 29) call the delegation of hard choices to agencies the 'time-honoured strategy' of scattering political responsibility.

All in all, we assume, based on the existing literature, that governmental cutback strategies and measures, as well as types of decision-making, differ in various stages of crisis, because decision-making and the selection of particular consolidation measures is highly dependent on the phase and acuteness of the crisis. Next, we will look at the possible explanations for a better understanding of fiscal consolidation.

3.2 EXPLANATIONS OF FISCAL CONSOLIDATION

We distinguish between three types of explanatory factors in analysing consolidation measures and decision-making during the fiscal crisis: financial-economic factors, political-administrative factors and supra-national influences.

Economic factors

As the primary aim of fiscal consolidation is to restore public finances (OECD 2011, 2012), that is, to reduce the budget deficit and state debt, it is evident that the size of fiscal consolidation plans of European governments are dependent on the 'financial size' of the fiscal crisis. In Eurozone countries, the latter is explicitly expressed in terms of the 3 per cent deficit ceiling and 60 per cent debt ceiling. As a rule of thumb, the volume of fiscal consolidation in EU member states is related to the size of budget deficit to be resolved over a certain period.

For governments, restoring public finances is not a goal in itself, but rather a means to restore the economic growth and employment. Consequently, factors such as GDP, GDP growth and unemployment also affect the size of the governments' fiscal consolidation plans. The size (and to some degree also the contents) of national fiscal consolidation plans in most Western countries is based on sophisticated mathematical simulation models forecasting the economic indicators such as GDP and unemployment rate, operated by either national Budget or Finance Ministries, National Banks or by independent economic forecasting institutions (such as the British 'Office of Budget Responsibility', the Danish 'Economic Council' or the Dutch 'Central Planning Bureau'). The Budget Directorate of the European Commission also employs an economic forecasting model to check the correctness and effectiveness of the fiscal consolidation plans of its member states.

As administrative scholars not versed in economics, we take a modest stance in the economic explanation of the fiscal consolidation. The fiscal consolidation plans of the investigated European countries are only correlated to explanatory factors such as GDP growth, gross debt and budget deficits (Eurostat) over the period 2008–2012.

Although it is self-evident that the size of fiscal consolidation is related to the size of the budget deficit, its correlation with gross state debt is less clear. As long as the public budget runs a deficit, the state debt rises in any case. As we will see finally, some countries had a very high state debt though a modest budget deficit. The correlation between fiscal consolidation and economic (GDP) growth is ambivalent. Fiscal consolidation measures were, in the economic sense, the reverse of the economic recovery measures taken previously at the time of the economic crisis: spending cuts and tax rises instead of extra spending and tax cuts. Many economists and politicians argued that fiscal consolidation therefore logically leads to economic deterioration, and large spending cuts should hence be avoided – more or less the viewpoint of the present French (Socialist) President Hollande.

Political factors

Economic factors are undoubtedly important and necessary, but not sufficient, in explaining cross-country variation. Here, we also use political-administrative factors. Political-administrative factors gain even more importance since the analysis not only addresses the contents of cutback measures, but also the decision-making processes leading to these measures. For example, according to Pollitt (2010: 21–2), cuts based on political priorities or effectiveness evaluations (e.g. programme cuts) tend to be political decisions, whereas across-the-board cuts rather reflect administrative decisions. Political factors are especially useful for explaining the types of political decision-making by governments, that is, across-the-board versus targeted decisions, or slow and small versus swift and drastic ones.

In our comparative study of political factors, we will employ some of the variables that are commonly utilised in comparative politics and government (Hague *et al.* 1993). The following box presents a brief overview of the usual categories in comparative politics and government, that is, politics and society, state and government, and administration and policy. Our interest in this book is on the political aspects of governments' fiscal decision-making, so our comparison is restricted to the categories of politics and government only.

Characteristics of political and government systems are considered, including general state structure (e.g. unitary, decentralised or federal state); type of political system (majoritarian or consensus); type of government in power (single-party or multi-party coalition; minority, simple majority or grand majority government); political orientation of the governing parties (right/centre/left); electoral cycle; and the role of various actors in political decision-making.

Comparative politics and government

In most comparative politics and government studies (e.g. Blondel 1990; Hague *et al.* 1993; Hancock *et al.* 1993; Page 1992; Ziller 1993), the following categories are utilised:

Politics and society. Political scientists discuss the types of parliaments (number of chambers, committees), election systems (majority systems where the winner takes all seats, versus proportional systems where seats are obtained by quota), political parties (two-party system versus multi-party systems), types of governments (majoritarian single party cabinet or multi-party coalitions, which can be grand coalitions, minimal winning coalitions or even multi-party minority coalitions), types of political executives (prime ministers or presidents) and more. Society is taken into account by paying attention to culture in general and to civic culture in particular (collectivism versus individualism, post-materialism in affluent societies), to social movements (environmental, feminist, etc.), to interest groups and interest mediation by the state (pluralism versus neo-corporatism). Sometimes, special attention is paid to socio-political cleavages (labour class, unions), church and religion (Protestant versus Catholic).

State and government. Studying government structures usually starts with the constitution. Is the constitution codified or unwritten? The constitutional framework determines whether the state is unitary, decentralised unitary or federal. The degree of decentralisation can vary (e.g. the degree of functional and regional autonomy, or the central-regional-local share of public budget and public employment). The constitution also determines the judiciary (independence and recruitment: direct election, elected by parliament or appointment by government) and whether the administration is subject to a separate judiciary.

Administration. The national type of bureaucracy is usually rated in the former category 'government', but sometimes administration is studied separately. The usual starting point is the classical Weberian bureaucracy. Distinctions can be made between career bureaucrats and political appointees. What is the mode of political control over bureaucracy? What are the relationships between politicians and bureaucrats? How are bureaucracies organised? How are bureaucrats recruited? Is there a typical administrative culture?

Public policy scholars like to also add separate chapters on policy, sometimes divided into policy sectors. Sometimes, the military and police are treated separately.

In our comparison, we make particular use of the political science findings about majoritarian single-party governments and consensual multi-party coalition governments. At the end of the 1960s, Lijphart (1968, 1969) invented the political science theory of 'consociational democracy'. Lijphart had extensively studied the Dutch pillarisation and pacification democracy. He perceived similar social, political and cultural fragmentations in Belgium, Switzerland, Austria and Scandinavia. In all those states, some form of consociational democracy existed in which the political elites of fragmented political subcultures cooperated in coalitions. This led Lijphart (1977) to the following four characteristics of consociational democracy:

- grand coalition (more than minimal winning coalition);
- mutual veto for minorities;
- proportional election system; and
- segmental autonomy and federalism.

In his later empirical comparative book about democracies in twenty-one countries, Lijphart (1984) rejected the term 'consociationalism' as too vague and broad and hardly empirically measurable, and introduced the 'consensus' model of democracy versus the majoritarian Westminster model of democracy (see Table 3.6).

In his review of twenty-one governments, Lijphart (1984) distinguished multi-party coalition executives into minimal winning cabinets, oversized cabinets and minority cabinets. That original distinction later evolved into the categories of parliamentary minority coalition (less than half of parliament),

TABLE 3.6 The Westminster and consensus model of democracy

Westminster model	Consensus model
1 Concentration of power in one-party majoritarian cabinets	1 Power sharing in grand coalitions
2 Fusion of power, cabinet dominance	2 Separation of powers
3 Asymmetric bicameralism	3 Balanced bicameralism and minority representation
4 Two-party system	4 Multi-party system
5 One-dimensional party system	5 Multidimensional party system
6 Pluralistic election system	6 Proportional election system
7 Unitary centralised government	7 Federalism and decentralisation
8 Unwritten constitution	8 Written constitution with minority veto
9 Exclusively representative democracy	

Source: Lijphart (1984)

Consensus democracy in various countries

The seminal work of Lijphart induced several political scientists at the time to investigate consensus democracies in various countries (Daalder 1971, 1987), albeit under various titles. Lehmbruch (1967) published on the so-called 'Proporzdemokratie' in Switzerland and Austria – in German, the term 'Konkordanz' is used as well. Steiner (1974) named the system in Switzerland 'amicable agreement'. Elder *et al.* (1982) used the term 'consensual democracies' for the Scandinavian states, and Huyse (1970, 1986) used Lijphart's Dutch term 'Verzuiling' (pillarisation) to typify the Belgian situation.

simple majority (just more than half) and grand majority (more than two-thirds) (Müller and Strom 2003).

Let us now return to the political science findings on majoritarian and consensus governments and apply them to our subject of interest: types of decision-making.

The common political science assumption is that unitary states are better able to take drastic and uniform decisions than decentralised or federal states (Lijphart 1984: 169). It does indeed seem evident that unitary states are better capable of taking centralised and uniform measures, but it is less evident whether they are also better capable at taking swift and drastic measures.

The political science assumption normally used to be that majoritarian one-party governments were more stable and more effective (Lijphart 1984: 107), and thus better capable to take swift and drastic actions than multi-party coalitions in consensus democracies, where the consultation and deliberation between different parties in search of consensus generally results in patchwork compromises of an incremental nature (slow, small and gradual steps). Moreover, within the category of multi-party coalitions, another distinction can be made as to the margin of parliamentary majority. In cases where the coalition has a grand majority in parliament (more than two-thirds, in most parliaments sufficient for constitutional reform), it seems to have the power to take swift and drastic decisions without being hindered by political opposition. In cases where the coalition only has a parliamentary minority (less than half, not unusual in the Danish and Norwegian political traditions), it will have to form ad hoc coalitions with opposition parties for each major decision to be reached. Danish governments traditionally used to negotiate and cooperate with opposition parties. The Dutch government (where minority coalitions are a rare exception) is presently learning that lesson. The usual assertions that minority coalitions are associated with crises, conflicts and polarisation, and that they are unstable, unviable and ineffective, have been disputed by Strom (1990).

Another assumption is that the political orientation of government affects its fiscal decision-making. When the political party orientation (right/centre/left) is defined with respect to economic policy, as in the World Bank Database of Political Institutions (World Bank 2012), it seems plausible to assume that right-wing parties (Conservative, Christian Democratic, etc.) in government tend to take more drastic and swifter fiscal consolidation and cutback decisions than left-wing parties (Communist, Socialist, Social Democratic, etc.). At least that is how they normally present themselves in election campaigns, which does not necessarily imply that, once in government, they also entirely succeed in realising their political ideas.

A political science assumption is that the electoral cycle affects governments' decision-making. Governments supposedly are not keen on taking hard cutback measures right before upcoming general elections, as these are widely unpopular and so inevitably cost votes for the parties in office. As we mentioned in Chapter 2, the fiscal crisis was addressed after the banking and economic crisis. Although financial authorities were aware that deficits and debts were alarmingly increasing and fiscal consolidation was strongly required, politicians were not ready to take unpopular cutback measures, especially with general elections approaching. With only a few exceptions (e.g. Denmark and Estonia), in most investigated countries governments lifted politically unpopular cutback decisions over the general elections.

In the political decision-making about fiscal consolidation, the top officials of the Budget and Finance Ministries play an important role. In times of fiscal crisis and spending cuts, the power of the ministry of Finance over the spending departments usually increases, as does the power of the budget offices within ministerial departments. These trends were confirmed in the COCOPS public executives' survey (Hammerschmidt *et al.* 2013).

In some countries, independent financial institutions play an important role in budgetary decision-making. In the Netherlands, the independent and expert 'Central Planning Bureau' (CPB) plays a crucial role in the macro-economic forecasting underlying the Budget preparation. Denmark has an 'Economic Council' consisting of 'wise men', that is, professors of economics and public finances who publish independent and authoritative economic forecasts. In Britain, the (Conservative) Chancellor of the Exchequer, Osborne, right after the general elections in 2010, established an independent 'Office of Budget Responsibility' (OBR), chaired by an independent expert, and later also staffed by independent specialists.

Apparently, the crisis in some countries led to stricter budget procedures and budget discipline. For example, the German Finance Minister, Schäuble, in 2008, introduced a constitutional brake on state debts (Schuldenbremse). The annual increase in the structural federal state debt was to be limited to 0.35 per cent (as of 2016). The regional governments (Landesregierungen) were prohibited any debt increase (as of 2020). Furthermore, in 2010, the German minister of Finance introduced a 'top-down budget procedure' in which the ministry of Finance annually starts by determining a fixed financial framework, and ministries subsequently draw up their estimates and budgets within this predetermined frame.

Supra-national influences

The way governments decided to manage the fiscal crisis not only depended on the domestic financial-economic and political-administrative situation, but to a large extent also on worldwide financial-economic circumstances. The worldwide banking crisis in 2008 triggered a collapse of the interbank loan system and a break-down of the international financial system, forcing national governments to rescue domestic banks. The national banking crises were internationally caused. Without the worldwide financial crisis, in many Western countries national banks might have remained sound and safe. Likewise, the ensuing domestic economic crisis was chiefly caused by the worldwide economic crisis. The domestic fiscal crises also depended on worldwide financial-economic circumstances. The worse the economy, the less the tax revenues (particularly corporation taxes), and the higher the public expenditures (particularly social security), hence the higher budget deficit. In small and internationally open economies, domestic economic recovery is mostly more dependent on world-wide economic developments than on national governments' economic recovery measures (which was the reason why the Belgian Prime Minister wanted to refrain from costly national economic recovery measures). The Belgian, Danish and Dutch economies are strongly connected to the German economy (components suppliers for German industrial products), which recovered quickly and well from the economic crisis thanks to the increase in industrial exports to Asia. The economic recovery in these three neighbouring countries was partly due to the German success.

Another supra-national factor strongly influencing the domestic governments' fiscal consolidation decisions, especially in the Eurozone, was the EU Stability and Growth Pack requirement of a 3 per cent ceiling for budget deficit and a 60 per cent ceiling for state debt. Although in many countries the strict necessity of the EU ceiling on budget deficit was politically debated and disputed, and further nourished the mounting political aversion against the allegedly excessive Brussels regulatory influences on domestic policies, it is undeniable that the EU ceilings had a foremost influence on the domestic decisions, in some countries more openly admitted than in others. In its strong desire to join the Eurozone, the Estonian government took radical cutback measures to display its resoluteness in strictly obeying the Maastricht criteria.

Furthermore, the Eurozone crisis of Southern European sovereign state bonds led to major European bail-out measures, which further increased state debts and deficits in EU member countries requiring further rounds of domestic cutback measures. Although in Germany the picture was the opposite: due to the Eurozone crisis, Germany became a safe haven for foreign investors, and the run on German bonds reduced the interest rates and hence the state's borrowing costs. Germany was therefore able to soften its initial spending cuts (the 2010 'Sparpaket'). In the countries that were bailed out, the supra-national influence was imperative. There, the fiscal consolidation measures were externally prescribed and imposed. When the hugely oversized Icelandic banking sector collapsed in 2008 and Iceland was bailed out by the IMF, the loan was received on strict conditions for financial restructuring and fiscal consolidation. When Greece, Portugal and Ireland were bailed out by the EU, ECB and IMF Troika, in return for the financial rescue packages they had to comply with strict conditions for fiscal consolidation and cutbacks, sometimes accompanied by requirements for major administrative and policy reforms. When the ECB massively bought up endangered Italian and Spanish state bonds to prevent further interest rate rises, and the ECB provided a multibillion-Euro loan to Spain for rescuing and restructuring its failing banking sector, the ECB sent a letter to the Italian and Spanish governments containing several 'recommendations' for financial and fiscal measures. The Italian Berlusconi government furiously reacted upon this 'intrusion in domestic affairs' and refused. As mentioned before, the Spanish (Socialist) government under Prime Minister Zapatero prepared an austerity plan that cost him the support of his party's

TABLE 3.7 Explanatory factors

Financial-economic	Political-administrative	Supra-national influences
Socio-economic and financial indicators prior to and during the crisis	State system: unitary or federal	Worldwide economic developments
GDP per capita	Political system: majoritarian of consensus	EU regulations (ceilings on budget deficits and debt, conditions for joinig the Eurozone)
GDP growth	Ideology of governing parties	Eurozone crisis
Gross debt	Electoral cycle	IMF, EU and ECB conditions for loans
Government deficit	Political-administrative relationships	
Unemployment rate		

backbenchers and rank and file, leading to him stepping down and calling early elections, which his party lost. In the end, the refusal of Berlusconi to carry out drastic cutbacks indirectly also led to his downfall. His fiscal unreliability made Italy so untrustworthy and vulnerable that he was forced to resign and be replaced by the financially trustworthy 'technocrat' Monti.

Table 3.7 (above) summarises the three types of explanatory factors.

3.3 EFFECTS OF FISCAL CONSOLIDATION

Effect measurement and evaluation

However interesting an international comparative analysis and explanation of national fiscal consolidation decisions may be from a scientific point of view, practitioners, politicians and policy-makers always ask the inevitable questions: Did fiscal consolidation work? Was it successful? Which country did better, and why? What were the success and failure factors? As already mentioned in the introductory chapter, direct evaluation of success and failure is impossible.

First, it is far too early to assess the successfulness of fiscal consolidation. The fiscal crisis is not yet over by some long way. In many countries, new cutback packages are repeatedly being made. Although early signs of economic recovery are surfacing nowadays, definite economic recapture still seems far away. Neither is the Eurozone crisis yet over by some long way, with its detrimental effects on national budget deficits. The previous worldwide economic and fiscal crisis of the late 1970s and 1980s lasted for more than a decade – more than a decade of round after round of cutbacks in policy sectors such as social security, health, education, welfare and administration itself. Without wanting to make a pessimistic impression, there is little chance that this time the torment and suffering will be over any sooner. The fiscal crisis is still continuing, and so are the fiscal consolidation and cutbacks. Even though the economic figures show signs of restoring economic growth, the influence of fiscal crisis on Public Administration and management is likely to continue for several years to come (Pollitt 2010). Moreover, Posner and Blöndal (2012: 11) argue: 'In contrast to previous recessions, the return of strong growth will not end the fiscal gaps facing these nations but will serve as the prelude for even more difficult and wrenching choices.' The fiscal crisis is still continuing, and so are the fiscal consolidation and cutbacks.

This raises a major methodological question, that is, the normative one of evaluation. What are the criteria for success or failure of fiscal consolidation measures? It seems reasonable to measure the success of fiscal consolidation in terms of decrease of public budget deficit and debt. But the ultimate criteria for success are the recovery of economic growth and especially employment. The citizens of a country hit by the global economic crisis are not interested in all kinds of high-brow economic and fiscal indicators, but in their own private economic situation, that is, chiefly work and income. However, the recovery of a domestic economy is dependent on many more factors than the domestic government's fiscal consolidation measures alone. Moreover, it is questionable whether success is only to be measured in fiscal and economic terms. Are the political and social aspects of success and failure not just as important? Cutbacks in social security such as increasing pension age and reductions in unemployment benefits were socially, publicly and politically highly contested.

In order to avoid the practical and methodological pitfalls of evaluating success, we have restrained ourselves to the less normative and more neutral measurement of effects. What were the effects of the fiscal consolidation measures taken by the European governments? In this book, we concentrate on three types of effects. Evidently, the first category of effect is the fiscal and economic one. After all, fiscal consolidation was primarily aimed at deficit reduction and economic recovery. The second category is the political effects of consolidation, in line with the twofold perspective on economics and politics throughout the book. And the third is the administrative effects, reflecting the undeniable fact of both authors being administrative scholars.

Economic effects

From an economic perspective, the intended effects of fiscal consolidation are, first, the reduction of budget deficit – resulting in a reduction of state debt increase – and, second, a recovery of the economy – economic growth. As mentioned before, the recovery of domestic public finances and economic growth depends on many more variables than the government's fiscal consolidation efforts alone. Moreover, our country studies finished mid-2013 and our survey data in 2014, while fiscal consolidation in many countries only started in 2010, leaving too little time for the measurement of the effects of domestic consolidation plans on the recovery of budget deficit and the economy. Notwithstanding the limitations, the comparative effect-measurement statistics are conducted. As expected, the statistical correlation between fiscal consolidation and budget deficit reduction appears to be only vague, and there is no clear correlation between fiscal consolidation and economic recovery.

Political effects

The political effects of national governments' fiscal consolidation efforts first of all recount the electoral effects of governments taking unpopular cutback measures. Politicians were well aware that the electorate would most probably punish them for taking cutback measures. All countries but Denmark and Estonia postponed these electorally suicidal actions until after the next general elections. And all but Baltic governments decided to spread the hard, and hence unpopular, cutbacks over a longer time period, starting with relatively small, and thus less harmful, cuts and only increasing the pain, with the largest cuts emerging at the end of the plan period after general elections for new governments to come. Nevertheless, postponement and spreading of the painful measures did not save the investigated European governments from electoral punishments.

The data from the COCOPS country case studies, which we analyse finally, show that all but one (Estonia) of the general elections in the investigated countries were lost by the incumbent government. The study also reveals that more than half of these elections were early elections called by incumbent governments, and that all but one (Belgium) of these calls for early elections were due to the fiscal cutback plans of governments.

Furthermore, many of the multi-party coalition governments were confronted with coalition partners leaving the cabinet transforming it into a parliamentary minority coalition. In all but one (Belgium) countries, this was due to the parties refusing to support the cutback plans of governments. In most countries, once the coalition was deprived of its parliamentary majority, it had to call early elections, which it lost.

Apparently, the electoral effects of the consolidation efforts for governments were quite devastating. Besides the quantitative analysis of the electoral effects, more in-depth explanations can be found in the specificity of the country cases. The electoral and governmental course of events in the countries is described in relation to the governments' consolidation efforts. This offers the opportunity to consider more than electoral-political effects, as mentioned at the end of Chapter 2 about 'political effects', where we distinguished between different forms of opposition. The subsequent cross-country study seeks answers to the following questions.

What forms did party-political opposition in parliament have? Were there walkouts of parties? How did the fall of coalition cabinets take place?

What about public opposition? Was there social unrest, and was it widespread? How about public protests and demonstrations? How did these affect the decision-making by governments?

How did trade unions and employer organisations react upon the fiscal cutback measures, especially the cuts in social security? How did other interest groups react? What about pressure and action groups?

Effects on Public Administration and management

In this book, particular attention is also paid to the effects of the fiscal crisis on Public Administration itself, not only in terms of the spending cuts on administration itself, the so-called operational expenditures mentioned in section 3.1.1, such as hiring and pay freeze, staff lay-offs, salary cuts, efficiency cuts and reorganisations, but also the effects on reforms in Public Administration and management. We aim to explore if the fiscal crisis has triggered administrative reforms and identify particular reform trends and shifts in public management patterns during the fiscal crisis.

The current global crisis resembles the previous worldwide economic and fiscal crisis of the 1980s. Roughly speaking, the oil crisis of the 1970s unleashed an international economic crisis, which, at the end of the 1970s and the beginning of the 1980s, resulted in such state debts and deficits that Western welfare states were forced to take drastic cutback decisions. Substantive cutbacks in social security, health, education and other sectors became inevitable. Moreover, the crisis led to a major reform trend in Western administrations, called new public management (NPM). Governments were forced to increase their cost-effectiveness and cost efficiency, leading to the widespread introduction of models and techniques from the private business sector. Cutback management in the 1970s and 1980s clearly emphasised the rhetoric, which was later translated into the main slogans of NPM, such as 'cost-consciousness', striving for 'efficiency', 'result orientation', calls for 'flexibility' in personnel regulations and financial management, and 'performance measurement' as a basis for decision-making. The question arises whether the current crisis once again leads to a major administrative reform trend. Has the contemporary crisis caused only temporary short-term changes? Alternatively, can we expect more fundamental administrative reforms and shifts in public management?

The popular saying is not to waste 'a good crisis', but to use it for carrying out long-awaited changes and even structural reforms. Political and administrative leaders, as well as management consultants, have tried to take a positive stance on crisis by emphasising the window of opportunity that the fiscal stress creates, and by using downturn as a catalyst for reforms. Also, the existing academic literature indicates that the fiscal crisis and its immediate aftermath are likely to lead to (structural) reforms in Public Administration (e.g. Green 2012; Peters *et al.* 2011; Pollitt 2010; Rodrik 1996; Tompson 2010; Vis *et al.* 2011). Bouvard *et al.* (2009: 3) argue: 'Reform is now a necessity, not a choice. As governments assume a broader, more significant role in response to the crisis, it becomes ever more important that they should be efficient and effective – otherwise, they would compound the severity of the problems. This crisis is the public sector's ultimate test.'

It has been noted that crises can create significant reform opportunities, both by demonstrating the unsustainability of the status quo and by disrupting the interest coalitions that have previously resisted reforms (Tompson 2010). Institutionalists claim that crisis may create a critical juncture at which it is possible to divert from the original path of incremental development and initiate structural reforms (e.g. Drazen and Grilli 1993; Thelen 1999; Vis *et al.* 2011). As crisis causes uncertainty and urgency, it is likely to foster the acceptance of previously unacceptable ideas to transform Public Administration radically and rapidly (Béland and Cox 2011). Economists and business management scholars, in their turn, tend to rely upon an incentive-based view by arguing that a crisis in finances or resource flows forces change, as only when faced with problems do people seek new approaches (Kelman 2006). In addition, several studies have concluded that the occurrence of the global financial crisis was, among other factors, caused by the systemic failures in governance and Public Administration, including, for example, problems of vertical and horizontal coordination in government, inadequate regulation of financial institutions, shortcomings in principal-agent relationships, and fragmented steering and control mechanisms (Green 2012; Khademian 2012; Lodge and Hood 2012; Peters *et al.* 2011; Pollitt 2010; Potter 2012). This is likely to lead to structural reform proposals to address these deficiencies in order to improve the existing system, to avoid the occurrence of similar crises in the future and to help achieve longer-term fiscal sustainability (Cepiku and Savignon 2012).

However, the assumption that crisis encourages reforms is controversial. Several authors (e.g. Behn 1985; Cayer 1986; Kelman 2006; Levine 1979; Peters *et al.* 2011; Pollitt 2010; Schick 1988) offer the antithetical approach by arguing that crisis inhibits change. As claimed by Peters *et al.* (2011: 16): 'Restructuring within the public sector is itself disruptive, and attempting to implement institutional change in the midst of the crisis may appear to be a recipe for confusion and failure.' Schick (1988: 532) noted that because of the time pressure involved in curbing budget deficits, policy-makers' attention has been diverted from comprehensive and time-consuming preparation and implementation of structural reforms. In a crisis context, people face time and workload pressures that reduce their ability to explore new approaches and change (Amabile and Conti 1999).

Fiscal crisis sets limits to both financial and human resources necessary for planning and implementing structural reforms (Levine 1979; Pollitt 2010). Organisations that are forced to cut their operational or programme costs are not likely to accumulate funds for preparing, piloting and carrying out reforms (Cayer 1986; Pollitt 2010). The difficulty with structural reforms is that the costs tend to be incurred upfront, while the benefits take longer to materialise. In addition, Levine (1979: 180) argued already in the 1970s that when public organisations need the analytical capacity the most, they may not be able to afford it. Preparation of reforms requires high-level expert advice at the time when the best experts are overburdened and/or demotivated. Furthermore, the cutback situation puts civil servants under pressure, as they need to fulfil extra tasks related to cutbacks and crisis more generally (see Lodge and Hood 2012), as well as to fill in the gaps left by lay-offs or hiring freeze. In fact, the entire organisational climate during the cutbacks may not be supportive of reforms and public-sector innovation (Kelman 2006; Pollitt 2010).

Because of the time pressures that usually accompany cutback management, the focus of the governments is likely to be on short-term measures rather than on structural reforms, although it is in fact structural reforms that could help the governments to achieve longer-term fiscal sustainability (Cepiku and Savignon 2012). Whether the current crisis triggers larger Public Administration reforms or not, it is likely to cause changes in public management practices because of the need to adapt to changes both in the internal and the external environment. How scarce resources are perceived and reacted to by Public Administrators is shaped by both the 'objective' characteristics of the cutbacks and various contextual conditions both inside and outside the organisations (Jick and Murray 1982: 159). For instance, the objective characteristics of cutbacks involve the severity of the cuts, the time pressure involved and whether the cuts could be anticipated or not (Jick and Murray 1982: 160). Contextual factors, such as the individual characteristics of key decision-makers and differences in organisation design, are also likely to play a role.

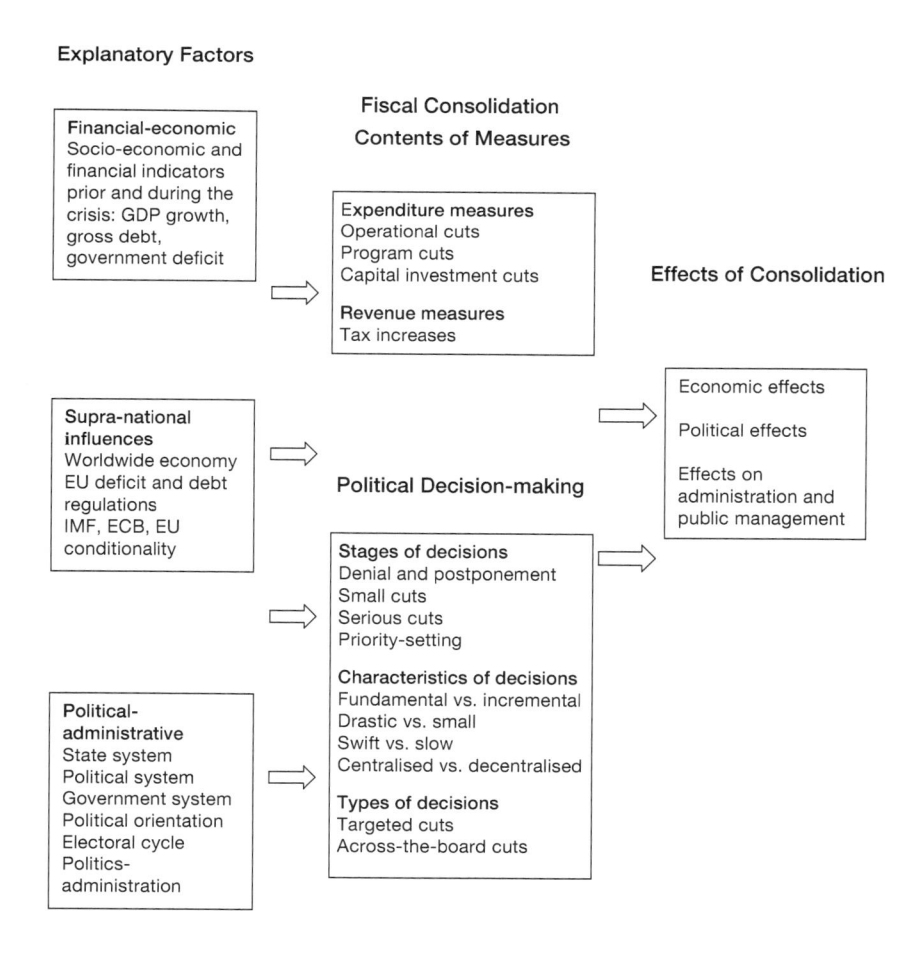

FIGURE 3.2 Analytical framework

All in all, there is a certain contradiction between the 'windows of opportunity' for reform that crises can present, and the ability and willingness of the politicians to seize that opportunity. The argumentation pro and contra the reforms during the era of fiscal crisis presents a puzzle that the current book aims to address. Although designing and carrying out substantial changes during the cutbacks can prove very difficult, the cutback environment may contribute to 'setting the scene' for the changes and reforms in the future when the immediate crisis with cutbacks is over, and there is more time, funds, focused attention and motivation of politicians, public managers and civil servants to prepare and implement changes.

The aforementioned ingredients altogether constitute the following analytical framework presented in Figure 3.2 (above).

Part two

Fiscal consolidation

Chapter 4

Fiscal consolidation contents of measures

In this chapter, the contents of the fiscal consolidation measures undertaken by European governments are considered. Our methodological approach to information gathering here is threefold.

First, a general overview is provided of the contents of the consolidation measures taken in the thirteen countries – with Norway being left out since it was only very slightly affected by the fiscal crisis. Following the analytical framework that was introduced in the previous chapter, we distinguish between expenditure and revenue measures, and further subdivide these into subcategories and briefly review them. This first general overview is based on country studies, and on the highly informative OECD (2012) cross-country report on fiscal consolidation.

Second, we pay particular attention to the expenditure cutbacks targeted at Public Administration, that is, operational spending cuts. In virtually all countries studied, reducing the costs of administration has been a prime government objective. What were the measures taken by European governments to curtail the costs of administration itself? Besides presenting an overview of the measures in the countries studied, we provide in-depth country examples of the specific measures taken to freeze and cut public-sector payment and employment. Herewith, we complement the general overview with specific information per country. The possible longer-term effect of the cuts on the functioning and reform of Public Administration is a subject addressed later in Chapter 7 about the effects of consolidation.

Third, in addition to the general country overview and specific country examples, we present the quantitative results of the COCOPS survey of public sector executives (Hammerschmidt *et al.* 2013). What were the public executives' perceptions of the main operational cutback measures, such as hiring and pay freeze, staff lay-offs and pay cuts? Were existing policy programmes cut and/or new programmes cancelled or postponed? The executives indicated to what extent each of these cutback measures were used in their organisation.

4.1 CONSOLIDATION MEASURES

Despite the rich abundance of economic studies and publications about the global financial and economic crisis, and despite the multiple availability of comparative data about economic growth, budget deficits and state debts in the Eurostat, EU, IMF and World Bank databases (though they mutually differ), it is very hard to obtain comparative data about fiscal consolidation measures in different countries. Currently, the only available international comparative source of information about the size of national consolidation measures is the OECD (2011, 2012) report on fiscal consolidation measures taken in the OECD member countries.

In our country studies, data were collected on the size and contents of fiscal consolidation measures. We followed the normal economic classification of consolidation measures into expenditure and revenue measures, subdividing the first into hiring and pay freeze, staff and wage reduction, reorganisations and efficiency cuts, and looked further at the so-called programme measures in specific policy areas such as social security, health and education.

Table 4.1 reviews the expenditure and revenue measures comprising the fiscal consolidation. The overview is based on the information presented in the short country reports and country case studies, and the OECD (2012) cross-country report on how governments restored their public finances. In the next section, both sources of information are utilised, the OECD (2012) report with specific references, and our country studies, unreferenced.

Most countries relied on expenditure measures rather than revenue increases in their fiscal consolidation (see also OECD 2012: 40). The countries that almost exclusively took expenditure reduction measures were the ones with smaller consolidation plans (e.g. the Netherlands). Still, many countries with large consolidation plans also focused on expenditure reduction (e.g. Britain, Iceland, Ireland, Germany and Spain). In the following analysis, we take a closer look at both expenditure and revenue measures (partly based on Kickert *et al.* 2013).

Expenditure measures

Following the categorisation provided in Chapter 3, expenditure measures are subdivided into programme measures, operational measures and capital investments.

Programme measures

In terms of the volume of cutbacks, the largest expenditure reductions involved programme measures. As social protection, including social welfare, is the largest category of government spending and steadily increasing, and public health expenditures the second largest, followed by education (OECD 2012:

TABLE 4.1 Overview of expenditure and revenue measures

	BEL	ESP	EST	FRA	GBR	GER	HUN	IRL	ISL	ITA	LTU	NLD	SLO
Expenditure measures													
Operational measures													
Hiring freeze	+	+	+	+	n/a	+	+	+	+	+	+	+	+
Wage reduction	–	+	+	–	n/a	–	+	+	+	n/a	+	–	+
Pay freeze	–	+	+	+	+	–	+	+	+	+	+	+	+
Staff reductions	+	+	+	+	+	+	+	+	n/a	+	+	+	+
Reorganisations	–	+	+	+	+	+	+	+	+	n/a	+	+	+
Efficiency cuts	+	n/a	n/a	+	+	+	n/a	+	n/a	n/a	+	+	+
Programme measures													
Health	+	+	+	+	+	–	+	+	+	+	+	+	+
Education	n/a	+	–	+	+	–	+	+	n/a	n/a	+	+	+
Pensions	+	+	+	–	+	+	+	+	n/a	+	+	+	+
Unemployment	–	+	+	–	+	+	n/a	+	+	n/a	+	+	+
Other social security/welfare	+	+	+	+	+	+	+	+	+	+	+	+	+
Infrastructure	+	+	n/a	+	n/a	–	n/a	+	+	n/a	n/a	n/a	+
Investment reductions	+	–	n/a	n/a	–	n/a	+	n/a	n/a	n/a	+	+	n/a
Revenue measures													
VAT	–	+	+	+	+	–	n/a	+	+	+	+	n/a	+
Consumption tax (e.g. alcohol, tobacco, energy)	+	+	+	+	+	n/a	+	+	n/a	+	+	+	+
Income tax	+	+	+	+	+	–	n/a	+	+	n/a	Re.	+	+
Corporation tax (bank bonuses)	–	–	n/a	n/a	+	n/a	–	+	n/a	+	+	Re.	n/a
Non-fiscal revenues	+	+	n/a	n/a	n/a	n/a	+	n/a	n/a	+	n/a	n/a	n/a

+ indicates that in this country, the specific measure has been reported.
– indicates that in this country, the specific measure has not been reported.
n/a indicates that information on the specific measure is not available.
Re. indicates that tax rates were lowered.

Source: Composed by Riin Savi (Kickert *et al.* 2013)

42), it was not surprising that cuts were targeted there. Education, however, has relatively been spared. During the retrenchment period, the most frequently targeted areas for savings were thus health care, pensions, welfare and infrastructure (OECD 2012: 52). In the following, we focus on the cutback trends in the social security sector and, in particular, politically sensitive areas of pension systems, unemployment systems, social security benefits and the health sector.

Pension-related cutbacks were applied in numerous countries, but the character of the cutbacks varied to a great extent. Suspending, freezing and decreasing the rise in pension payments or restructuring of the pension schemes (e.g. increasing the employee contribution rates) were applied in several cases (Estonia, Slovenia, Spain, the United Kingdom). To cut back the government expenditure in the long run, the (early) retirement age was increased in several countries during the crisis (Belgium, Estonia, the Netherlands, the United Kingdom). In addition, savings were sought by levelling down the differences between public- and private-sector pension regimes by raising civil servants' pension contribution to the private-sector level (Belgium and France). In Hungary and Italy, the crisis impelled a structural revision of the pension system with the aim to produce significant cuts to the government expenditure in the long-term perspective (OECD 2012: 66).

The crisis brought along severe cuts in other *social security benefits* (besides pensions) in most of the countries. In general, the overall public social expenditure was reduced by cutting unemployment and welfare benefits, increasing social security contributions, etc. For example, in Ireland, the unemployment and welfare benefits were cut by approximately 10 per cent in 2009–2010, and in Hungary, Ireland and Slovenia, parental benefits were curbed.

Nearly half of the studied countries reported *cuts in the health sector* during the crisis. The cuts varied to a great extent in terms of both size and contents of the cutbacks between the countries. In Ireland, the total volume of cuts in health services outweighed all other spending cuts, and in Belgium and Spain it made up a remarkable share of the expenditure savings (OECD 2012: 53).

In some countries, rather *exceptional cuts in specific policy fields* could be observed. In Lithuania, the national defence sector was the main loser in austerity measures (the expenditure dropped by 27 per cent from 2007 to 2011). In Ireland, the largest proportion of cuts affected cultural and arts policies, which were cut by 65 per cent. In Spain, cutback measures strongly affected both college and non-university education, materialising in more teaching hours and more students per teacher, as well as a reduction or cancellation of free school transport and school lunches. In Slovenia and the United Kingdom, grants for pupils and students were reduced.

Operational measures

Although the reduction of programme expenditures in most countries took the largest share of the consolidation, savings in operational expenditures were also widely undertaken (OECD 2012: 47), especially in bail-out countries (e.g. Ireland) and countries with alarming debt sizes and bond yields (e.g. Hungary, Slovenia and Spain). Wage cuts and staff reductions were frequently applied in the countries, especially in the aforementioned troubled countries. Hungary, Ireland, Slovenia and Spain undertook serious wage cuts, and a number of countries were reported to have reduced their public employment, most of them by freezing replacement and hiring (OECD 2012: 51).

In the analytical framework as presented in the previous chapter, cutbacks in operational expenditures were categorised into hiring and pay freeze, staff and wage reduction, and reorganisations and efficiency cuts. Here, we briefly review these categories. In the next section, more in-depth information is provided about what these measures involved in various countries based on the qualitative country studies.

When looking at the expenditure reductions of governments' running costs, it can be observed that *hiring and pay freeze* were very popular measures applied to combat the fiscal crisis in numerous countries. In some countries, the period of pay or hiring freeze was explicitly fixed (e.g. in the United Kingdom, a two-year pay freeze was foreseen in 2011); in others, their duration was treated more flexibly.

Wage reduction was a cutback measure that followed the more modest and less contested pay freeze in those countries where the budgetary problem and pressure were considerably higher. However, some governments, such as those of Estonia and Lithuania, volunteered unpopular decisions of wage cuts immediately after the outset of crisis. Meanwhile, other countries that had received financial assistance from the IMF and the EU, such as Iceland, Ireland, Italy and Spain, were requested to carry out these politically more sensitive forms of cutbacks. Germany, on the other hand, has a special legal civil service system that prohibits wage reductions and even pay freeze.

Reduction of staff was applied as a cutback measure in at least half of the countries studied. Interestingly, however, very different tactics were applied to achieve this goal. At one end of the extreme, in Estonia and in Lithuania, lay-offs were applied at the beginning of the retrenchment (in Lithuania, the executive and its institutions experienced a decrease of 11 per cent in the filled positions). In France, the non-replacement of one out of two retiring civil servants was put in place, while in Spain a 10 per cent replacement rate for all staff in the public sector was implemented.

Several governments also opted for *reorganisations* to reduce the expenditure side of the budget. Lithuania stands out in this respect as all ministries and many agencies were restructured when the government initiated broad organisational reforms affecting all types of public-sector institutions. In the United Kingdom, a 'Public Bodies Reform' plan was initiated in 2010, with the aim to reorganise about 500 arm's-length bodies either by abolishing, merging or substantially reforming the agencies. In Spain, the restructuring of government included the abolition of duplicated bodies at the regional and central levels.

Efficiency savings seem to have been the least popular measure. Here, the United Kingdom serves as a pioneer by having introduced the 'Operational Efficiency Program' for all departments targeted at savings in back-office operation, equipment, ICT reforms and collaborative procurement, as well as increased cost saving in the public-sector estates. Seeking efficiency gains was on the agenda in Lithuania as well, where the efficiency assessment of staff functions was carried out at the central governmental level and also centralisation of procurement functions and standardised state property management were applied.

Capital investments

In numerous countries, either real cuts (Ireland, Spain) or cuts planned in the future (Slovenia and Spain) were targeted at public infrastructure investment projects. In Ireland, nearly 40 per cent of the adjustments to the state budget were achieved by the cancellation of planned capital and infrastructure projects. In Iceland, the reduction of road maintenance costs contributed strongly to fiscal balance (OECD 2012: 154). On the contrary, in countries receiving EU structural support (Estonia and Lithuania), the lion's share of the (EU co-financed) infrastructure projects were not cut.

Revenue measures

In Table 4.1, taxes were divided into income taxes, consumption taxes and corporation taxes. Other categories include taxes on goods and services, property taxes and social security contributions (OECD 2012: 57). Various tax revenue measures were applied in most of the countries. As a rule, governments relied more on increasing the rates of existing taxes rather than introducing new ones, with the exception of France, where twenty-three new taxes were established during the period 2007–2012 (Kickert *et al.* 2013).

Most countries announced increase in *consumption taxes* – most frequently excise duties on tobacco and alcohol, followed by VAT and environmental taxes (OECD 2012: 60). In many countries, the excise taxes were increased repeatedly – in Slovenia, excise taxes on fuels were increased for six times in a row during 2010. Also, the rate of *value added tax* (VAT) was increased in numerous countries (OECD 2012: 61), and in Estonia and Lithuania several VAT exemptions were abolished. In France, so-called 'social VAT'-related cuts meant the reduction of pensions for retired people aiming at general cutbacks in tax shelters. By contrast, in Slovenia, the VAT rate was reduced, and in Belgium the VAT rate in the catering sector was lowered. Some countries also reported new consumption taxes such as levies on telecom services and lotteries (Estonia, Hungary) and motor-vehicle tax (Slovenia). In addition, new taxes were often introduced in the area of sustainable energy and ecology

– such as new environmental and carbon taxes (Iceland), taxes on nuclear energy production (Germany) and eco-taxes on airline tickets (Germany, the Netherlands).

Also, *income tax measures* were applied by a number of countries (OECD 2012: 62). Though in general the share of income tax measures in the total revenue increase was smaller than the share of consumption taxes (OECD 2012: 59), in Ireland the increased income tax could be considered as the most important measure on the revenue side as it widened the base that had narrowed down during the pre-crisis period. In Spain, the changes introduced to income taxation were rather encompassing – the government first increased the tax burden on the highest incomes and later on almost all tax rates. Similarly, higher tax rates for the top incomes were introduced by the Labour government in the United Kingdom and by the Socialist president in France. Exceptionally, in Lithuania, personal income taxes were lowered from 24 to 21 per cent.

4.2 CUTBACKS IN ADMINISTRATION

In all countries but Norway, the public expenditure cutbacks were, to a considerable degree, targeted at governments' operational costs, that is, the costs of Public Administration itself (OECD 2012: 47). In this section, more detailed in-depth and country-specific information is provided about the cutbacks concerning the salaries of public-sector employees and the size of public-sector employment. In the following sequence of country examples – in alphabetical order of country name – the varying scope and form of the spending cuts in administration is illustrated. The country examples draw from the country studies.

Belgium

Regarding operational measures, the Belgium government relied upon staff reductions and efficiency cuts. The government took an opportunity offered by an ageing civil service by not replacing every retiring civil servant (i.e. used hiring replacement freeze accompanied by limited hiring). The government also reduced staff through the non-prolongation of contracts of definite duration. These measures led to a 5.5 per cent reduction in the civil service workforce in 2008–2012, corresponding to a 1.1 per cent decrease in remuneration expenses in 2011–2014. The civil service legislation did not allow the use of either pay freeze or pay cuts. The Belgian government also forced individual departments and agencies to take up efficiency measures by streamlining the previous underutilisation of operational budgets.

Source: Troupin *et al.* (2013)

Estonia

All three supplementary cutback budgets that the government adopted during 2008–2009 contained extensive cuts in the operational expenditures of the central government, predominantly achieved by curtailing personnel expenditures. Concurrently, dismissals, salary cuts, decreased work time and lay-offs were applied during the cutback period. In 2008, the central government abolished about 3,000 positions and laid off about 1,000 civil servants. For example, the State Chancellery and ministry of Finance laid off 16 and 11 per cent of their respective workforce (Kattel and Raudla 2013; Peters *et al.* 2011; Raudla 2013). During the retrenchment period, civil service salaries were sliced back in several stages; in total, salaries were cut by 10–20 per cent. Besides the pay cuts, civil servants faced a cut in their benefits when additional pay funds, training funds and one-time support schemes (e.g. compensation for health-related activities, financial support for festive occasions) were abolished.

Source: Savi and Randma-Liiv (2013)

France

Within the General Public Policy Review aimed at cutting costs and increasing productivity, initiatives were undertaken to restrict state expenditure. The 2008 Budget Bill set the operational expenditure increase at no more than projected inflation, which was in effect until 2012. Rather than laying off staff or delaying promotions, a civil service recruitment freeze was implemented through the replacement of only one in two retiring state employees. This resulted in the elimination of 150,000 public service jobs in 2008–2012, leading to annual savings of €800 million a year. One significant measure was taken for the civil service wage bill, with a freeze on the point value of civil service pay in 2010. The French government also introduced efficiency measures by addressing the optimisation of procurement, examinations and training, the use of IT systems, and management of the automobile fleet.

Source: Bezes and LeLidec (2013)

Germany

Due to the specific legal status of civil servants (Beamten), staff lay-offs were not possible. Likewise, pay cuts of civil servants were legally prohibited except in the case of special allowances (e.g. holiday, Christmas) and bonuses, or in the case of externally contracted staff. Due to the legal basis for periodic seniority-based pay rises, salary freeze was not a viable option either. The common approach to realising savings was to freeze hiring and replacement.

Source: Osterheld *et al.* (2013)

Hungary

In 2002, for electoral reasons, public-sector wages were increased by 50 per cent, and a thirteenth-month salary was added. In response to the fiscal crisis in 2009, the government took the measure to freeze public-sector wages (at the previously increased level) and eliminate the thirteenth-month allowance.

Source: Hajnal (2013)

Iceland

The Icelandic government was bound by the IMF agreement (2008–2013) to aim at fiscal consolidation, as the restoration of the banking system cost the tax-payers enormous amounts of money. As Iceland is not a member of the Eurozone, it devalued its own Króna, which automatically affected real income and purchasing power, even without nominal wage cuts. In addition to devaluation, expenditure cuts were, in most cases, achieved through a combination of cuts in civil service wages and wage-related benefits, as well as through postponement of investments and infrastructure expenditures.

Source: Kristinsson (2013)

Ireland

In Ireland, following the onset of the crisis in late 2008, public-sector pay increases scheduled for payment in 2009 were not paid, a 'pension levy' was introduced for all existing public servants, and in 2010 public-sector pay was cut again on a tiered basis. Adjustments to future but not current pension provisions were introduced. As a result of these measures, the gross rates of public service pay were reduced by about 14 per cent cumulatively over 2009 and 2010 (cf. EU-IMF progress report of March 2012).

In December 2009, the government concluded an agreement with the labour unions (Croke Park Agreement), which guaranteed that public-sector employees would not suffer any further direct cuts to their pay. An immediate implication of the agreement was that expenditure savings in the public sector would be enforced through control over the numbers employed rather than through pay rates. The government was committed to securing shrinkage in numbers through further voluntary retirement schemes, in addition to early-retirement and career-break incentives introduced earlier in the crisis.

Changes to the terms of pension entitlements encouraged some 9,000 public servants to depart by the end of February 2012, with the government indicating that it would recruit about 3,000 replacement personnel to the service. An overall reduction of about 25,000 people (albeit on pre-crisis 2008 figures) by 2014 was agreed with the EU-ECB-IMF in November 2010 as part of Ireland's bail-out deal.

Source: MacCarthaigh and Hardiman (2013)

Italy

The austerity plans launched in 2010 consisted of a freeze of temporary contracts, a vacancy replacement rate of 20 per cent for 2010–2013, a freeze of public-sector wages for 2010–2013, and a cut in salaries that exceeded €90,000 The budget for temporary contracts was halved.

The reduction in the number and costs of public employees went further back. The first attempts in the late 1990s to reduce the permanent workforce were undone by an increase of temporary positions, leading to a marginal decrease of public employment. The brief period of the centre-left Prodi government (2006–2008) also led to only a slight reduction. In 2008, the centre-right Berlusconi government launched another reform, downsizing the workforce mainly by tightening the replacement rates (at 10 per cent in 2009 and 20 per cent in 2010–2013), and by halving the budget for fixed-term contracts. Managerial positions were to be reduced by 20 and 15 per cent. A marked reduction of public employment was the result, which continued during the Monti government period (2011–2012). Dismissals were announced but not implemented.

Source: Ongaro *et al.* (2013)

Lithuania

In view of the forthcoming 2008 general elections, expansions in public-sector costs had taken place, such as an increase in public-sector wages and the introduction of automatic indexation. The successive rounds of cutbacks in 2008–2011 led to a reduction of staff expenditures (the so-called remuneration fund) from 13 to 11 per cent of total government expenditures. The remuneration fund diminished by an overall 17 per cent in the period 2008–2010, varying between different ministries. Civil service salaries were cut in a progressive way, resulting in top officials experiencing the deepest cuts. In the period 2008–2010, the lay-offs at the state and municipal levels amounted to an average of about 10 per cent, varying between branches and levels of government.

Source: Nakrosis *et al.* (2013)

The Netherlands

In October 2010, the new cabinet announced a cutback package of up to €18 billion in 2015. The largest cuts (about €1.5 billion) were to be realised in national administration. Salaries of civil servants were frozen, as was hiring of new personnel. A reduction in the number of civil servants was proposed, although lay-offs were not planned. Some ministries were merged, and departmental reshuffles took place. Cutbacks of 1.1 billion were imposed on the provincial and municipal funds. Provinces were to restrict themselves to their core tasks. Mergers of provinces in the 'Randstad' (the Amsterdam-Utrecht-Rotterdam-The Hague area) were proposed. In total, the cutbacks in Public Administration amounted to €6.1 billion in 2015 (on a total of €18 billion).

In April 2012, another €14 billion of cutbacks were announced, including an additional freeze of civil servant salaries and another round of cutbacks for provinces and municipalities. In October 2012, the new coalition cabinet endorsed the €14 billion of cutbacks. The coalition agreement contained far-reaching announcements about territorial reform. The existing thirteen provinces were to merge into five regions, one specific interprovincial merger was proclaimed, and other mergers were invited. Municipalities were to increase their size to 100,000 inhabitants. Central administration was cut by an additional €1.1 billion, to be realised by managerial efficiency measures in ministries and agencies.

Source: Kickert (2013c)

Slovenia

During 2008–2011, the cutback measures of the Slovenian government were aimed at reducing the operational costs of government, either by reducing the salaries and other work-related benefits of public servants and governmental officials, or by reducing the material costs of government and the public sector as a whole. More specific measures to decrease the labour costs of government included the withholding of the wage increases due to the new law on salaries of public servants (adopted in 2008), the reduction of the number of total employees in state administration by 2 per cent, with consolidation of selected activities and organisational units, the reduction of basic salaries of governmental officials by 4 per cent until the end of March 2010, and the reduction of governance-related fees and other payments. In January 2010, the rationalisation of the public sector was combined with the reform of the pension and health-care system, which should ensure fiscal sustainability in the long run. Furthermore, the wage freezes for governmental officials were prolonged until 2010. The plans of the newly elected government in 2012 foresaw for the salaries of public servants to be reduced by 8 per cent (combined with the elimination of all discrepancies still not being realised from the 2008 system); the work-related benefits and awards were reduced; the wage increase due to additional work was limited to 20 per cent; job promotion was enabled only after June 2013, and related wage increases only to follow in 2014; and additional employment was allowed only upon a special permit.

Source: Pevcin (2013)

Spain

Public-sector wages were cut by 5 per cent in 2010 and frozen in 2011. Hiring was frozen, and the vacancy replacement rate was set at 10 per cent for all public-sector jobs, which were to be cut by 7 per cent in 2013. New temporary jobs were forbidden. The austere fiscal crisis measures led to a massive loss of public support, which forced Prime Minister Zapatero (Socialist Party) to call new general elections in 2011, resulting in the People's Party's success. However, the new Rajoy government could only embrace the harsh fiscal measures. In 2012, neither fixed nor temporary staff was to be hired. Weekly working hours of civil servants were brought up from 35 to 37.5 hours. For arm's-length bodies such as agencies, the vacancy replacement rate was also set at 5 per cent. The streamlining of the public sector by restructuring central administration, merging and closing agencies, and by reaching agreements with the autonomous communities and municipalities to stabilise public expenditures, which was started by the Zapatero government, was continued by the Rajoy government, which imposed fiscal retrenchment plans upon the autonomous communities.

Source: Clifton and Alonso (2013)

> ## United Kingdom
>
> In 2010, the new Cameron-Clegg government announced a drastic spending-cuts programme amounting to savings of £83 billion in all policy areas by 2014–2015. Public spending was to be reduced by 25 per cent and some 490,000 public-sector jobs were to be cut. The 2010 budget announced large-scale job cuts (downsized to 330,000) in the public sector, as well as a two-year freeze on public-sector pay rises and public-sector pension reforms. Plans were made for a 33 per cent cut in administrative costs of government departments. The government announced a 'Public Bodies Reform' to reduce the number of arm's-length bodies. In sixteen departments, 904 public bodies were reviewed, of which a total of 496 were suggested to be dissolved, merged with others or reformed.
>
> *Source:* James and Nakamura (2013)

Table 4.2 provides an overview of the cutbacks in Public Administration in different government periods in all thirteen countries studied (until 2013). The government periods refer to either newly elected governments or government changes without elections (e.g. Estonia), which also is the reason why periods differ country by country.

The overview in Table 4.2 confirms the general picture emanating from the country examples. Virtually all countries studied had to resort to measures of freezing payment and hiring (usually by freezing replacement) to reduce the costs of their public services. Politically more sensitive measures to actually cut salaries and lay off staff were not widely undertaken, but only in those countries where the fiscal crisis was most severe, or where such measures were prescribed and imposed by the Troika.

After this presentation of the results from the qualitative country studies, we now move to an additional quantitative source of information, that is, the COCOPS questionnaire of public-sector executives.

4.3 PUBLIC-SECTOR EXECUTIVES' PERCEPTIONS OF CUTBACK MEASURES

In the COCOPS senior executives survey (Hammerschmidt *et al.* 2013), the perceptions of public-sector executives were asked with regard to cutback measures applied during the crisis. More specifically, the occurrence of personnel cuts (hiring freeze, staff lay-offs, pay freeze, pay cuts) and programme cuts (postponing or cancelling new programmes and cuts to existing programmes) were addressed. Each executive indicated to what extent the specific cutback

TABLE 4.2 Cutbacks in administration

	Belgium		Estonia			France	Germany	
	(–2011)	(2011–)	(2007–2009)	(2009–2011)	(2011–)	(2007–2012)	(–2009)	(2009–)
Hiring freeze	Yes	Yes	Yes	Yes	Yes	Yes	No	Yes
Pay freeze	No	No	Yes	Yes	Yes	Yes	No	No
Public-sector wage cuts	No	No	Yes	Yes	No	No	No	No
Public-sector job cuts	Yes	Yes	Yes	Yes	No	No	Yes	Yes
Reorganisation	No	No	No	No	No	Yes	No	Yes

	Hungary		Iceland	Ireland	Italy			Lithuania
	(2008–2010)	(2010–)	(2009–)	(2011–)	(–2008)	(2008–2011)	(2011–2012)	(2008–2012)
Hiring freeze	No	Yes	Yes	Yes	Yes	Yes	Yes	No
Pay freeze	No	Yes	Yes	Yes	Yes	Yes	Yes	Yes
Public-sector wage cuts	No	Yes	Yes	Yes	No	No	No	Yes
Public-sector job cuts	No	No	Yes	Yes	No	No	Yes	Yes
Reorganisation	Yes	Yes	Yes	Yes	No	No	Yes	Yes

	Netherlands		Slovenia		Spain		United Kingdom	
	(2012–2012)	(2012–)	(2008–2011)	(2011–2013)	(2004–2011)	(2011–)	(–2010)	(2010–)
Hiring freeze	Yes	Yes	Yes	Yes	Yes	Yes	No	Yes
Pay freeze	Yes	Yes	Yes	Yes	Yes	Yes	No	Yes
Public-sector wage cuts	No	No	No	Yes	Yes	Yes	No	Yes
Public-sector job cuts	Yes	Yes	No	Yes	Yes	Yes	No	Yes
Reorganisation	Yes	Yes	No	Yes	Yes	Yes	No	Yes

instrument was used in his or her organisation. The results are analysed in a seven-point Likert scale.

What strikes the eye immediately in the results of the survey is the clearly deviant position of Norway. In Norway, 54 per cent of the respondents claimed that no cutback measures were applied, thus confirming the general understanding that due to its wealthy gas and oil revenues, Norway was only slightly affected by the global financial and economic crisis. Norway did not endure a fiscal crisis, and Norwegian administration remained unaffected.

The COCOPS survey shows that among personnel cuts, hiring freeze was the most widely applied cutback measure in Europe. Pay freeze was clearly the second most used personnel cut, followed by pay cuts and the reduction of staff through lay-offs (Figure 4.1).

According to the responses of the public executives, *hiring freeze* was the most popular measure taken in response to the crisis. In particular, extensive use of hiring freeze was reported by executives from Ireland and Spain, but also from Hungary, the United Kingdom, Austria, Italy and France (Figure 4.2). In Norway, the respondents estimated that hiring freeze was rarely applied; similarly, in Germany, hiring freeze was reported as a measure of rather low importance. This is interesting because hiring freeze was paradoxically the only personnel cut supported by the German civil service legislation – indicating that German public-sector personnel cuts were altogether very limited compared to other European countries.

Pay freeze was also applied extensively during the retrenchment in the European countries, especially so in the United Kingdom, Spain, Ireland and Estonia (Figure 4.3). Exceptionally, pay freeze was not so common in Norway as there was no need for substantive personnel cuts. Also, in Germany and Hungary, the officials asserted pay freeze was not common. Whereas the German civil service legislation did not support pay freeze, in Hungary the government opted for more radical personnel cuts through applying lay-offs more than any other European country.

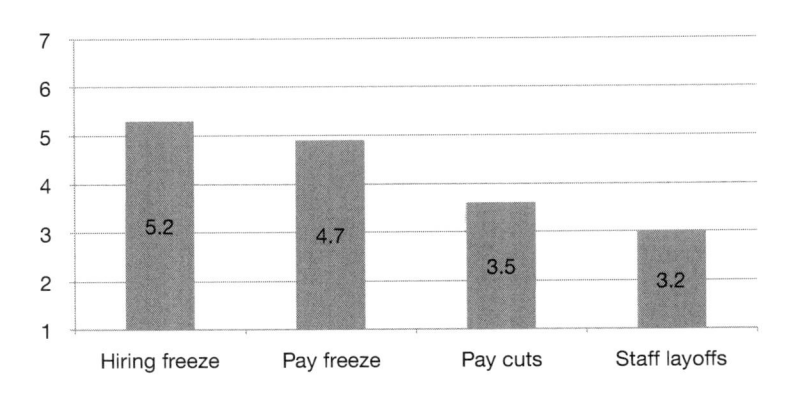

FIGURE 4.1 Perceived personnel cuts (1 = not at all; 7 = to a large extent)

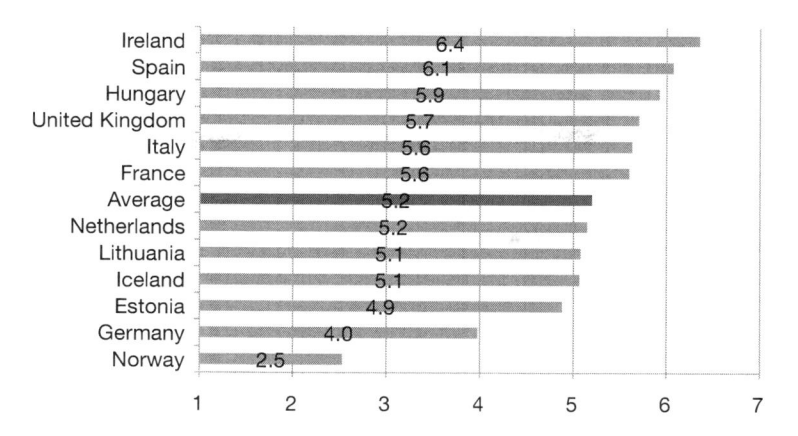

FIGURE 4.2 Perceived cutback measures: hiring freeze (1 = not at all; 7 = to a large extent)

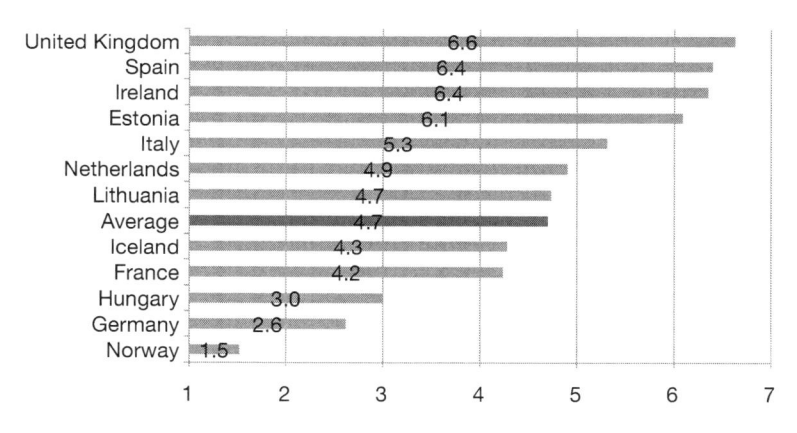

FIGURE 4.3 Perceived cutback measures: pay freeze (1 = not at all; 7 = to a large extent)

Pay cuts and lay-offs are more radical personnel cutback measures compared to hiring or pay freeze. *Pay cuts* were widely used cutback instruments in the countries most severely hit by the crisis (Figure 4.4). Wage reduction was a cutback measure that usually followed the more modest and less contested pay freeze in those countries where the budgetary problem and pressure were considerably higher. They appeared to be a very widely used cutback instruments in Ireland and Spain. Also, public executives from Lithuania and Estonia reported extensive pay cuts. Strikingly different results were reported by top officials from Norway and France, where pay cuts occurred in exceptional cases. Also, in Germany and the Netherlands, pay cuts remained marginal when fighting the crisis.

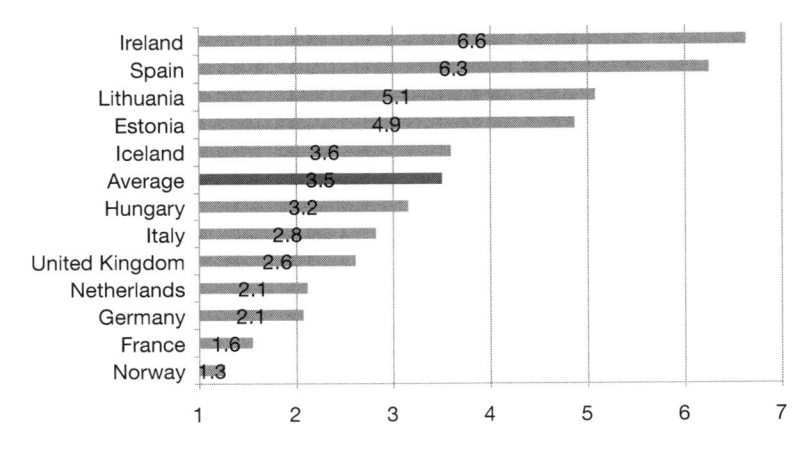

FIGURE 4.4 Perceived cutback measures: pay cuts (1 = not at all; 7 = to a large extent)

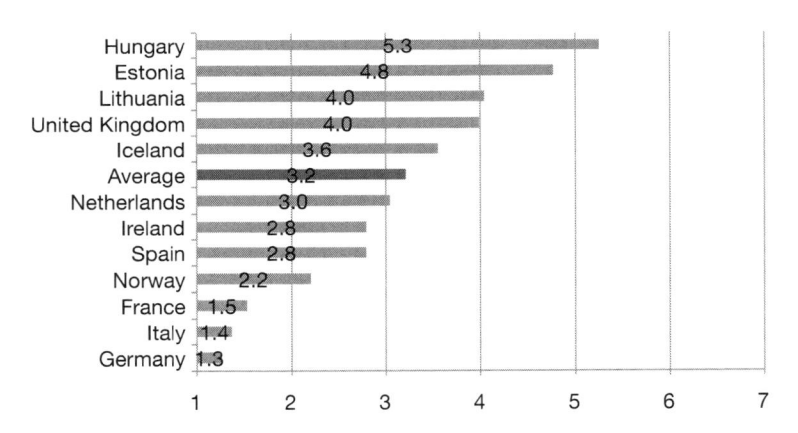

FIGURE 4.5 Perceived cutback measures: staff lay-offs (1 = not at all; 7 = to a large extent)

Staff lay-offs were rather extensively applied in response to the crisis according to the executives in Hungary and Estonia (Figure 4.5). Lay-offs were also rather common in Lithuania and the United Kingdom. The Eastern European countries have very limited civil service tenure allowing the governments to undertake such radical cutback measures. The responses of top officials from Germany, Italy and France point in an opposite direction, where staff lay-offs were used only in exceptional cases. It is also interesting to note that very hardly hit countries such as Ireland or Spain were able to manage the crisis without having to lay off a considerable number of civil servants.

In addition to public-sector personnel cuts, a great majority of European governments had to *cancel or postpone new policy programmes* and cut expenditure on the existing programmes. According to the survey, postponing or cancelling new programmes to alleviate the crisis was a relevant measure in most of the countries studied (Figure 4.6). Cancelling or abandoning new programmes was substantial in hardly hit Spain and Iceland, followed by Ireland and the United Kingdom. Only in Norway did top officials claim new programmes were rarely postponed or cancelled.

With regard to *cutting expenditure on already existing policy programmes*, in Spain, Iceland, Ireland and the United Kingdom, executives claimed that cuts to existing programmes were extensive and commonly used throughout the public sector (Figure 4.7). On the contrary, Norway stands out as an exception where programmes were not cut extensively. As a rule, policy programmes were most strongly curtailed by cutbacks in countries utmost hit by the crisis.

There are some similarities but also certain differences between countries included in the COCOPS survey. For example, it can be observed that the positive budgetary and fiscal situation in Norway, which made it rather unnecessary to reduce the public-sector wage bill, is reflected by the answers of the Norwegian respondents who rated highest in denying pay cuts, pay freeze and hiring freeze. Rather surprisingly, Norway did not rate the highest in denying staff lay-offs.

The survey results indicate that the selection of particular cutback measures was not only affected by the depth of the crisis in each country, but so are the national civil service systems and respective legislation. In Germany, the special legal regime for civil servants (Beamten) prohibits lay-offs and wage cuts, and even pay freeze, therefore freezing hiring (and replacement) was the only way

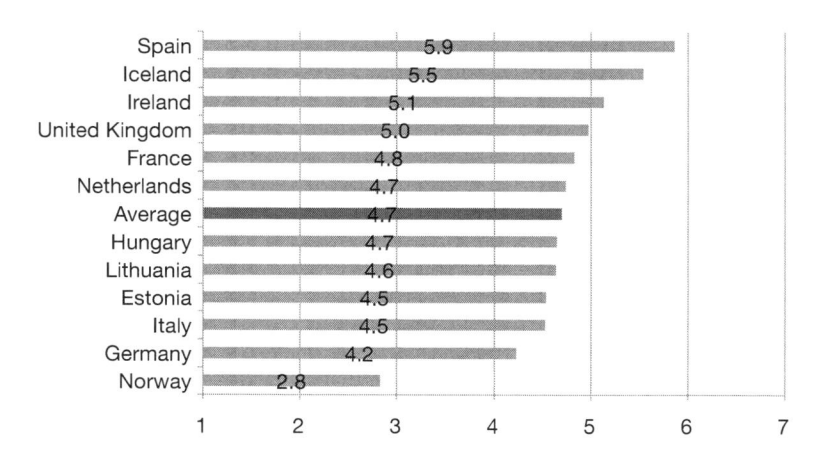

FIGURE 4.6 Perceived cutback measures: postponing/cancelling new programmes (1 = not at all; 7 = to a large extent)

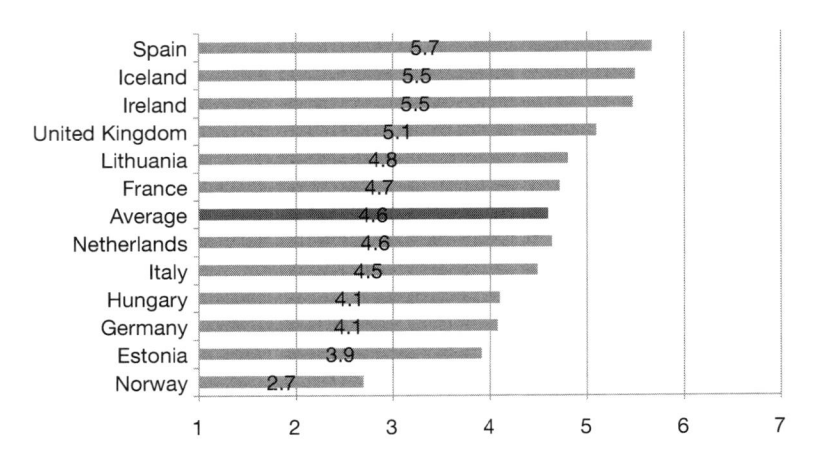

FIGURE 4.7 Perceived cutback measures: cuts in existing policy programmes (1 = not at all; 7 = to a large extent)

to realise savings in Germany, which was still rather modestly applied compared to other European countries. On the other hand, radical personnel cuts (e.g. lay-offs) were more usual in Eastern European countries that do not have civil service tenure and where the legislation allows for cutting both personnel and pay. Finally, in countries where the fiscal crisis was too excessive and aided by the IMF or the Troika of IMF-ECB-EU, such as Iceland, Ireland and Spain, the fiscal consolidation measures were the most radical and large-scale. Countries such as Germany and neighbouring Belgium and the Netherlands were economically better off and suffered a more modest fiscal crisis, which was reflected in their relatively negligible consolidation measures.

There are a few differences between qualitative country studies and survey results. One of the possible explanations for such differences is the fact that country studies explicitly addressed the measures taken by the national government as a whole, while the survey asked questions about measures taken within the respondent's organisation. Cutback management within specific public organisations does not necessarily always and completely coincide with general central government policy.

All in all, the survey confirms the general picture from the country studies that hiring and pay freeze were widely applied, but that real pay cuts and staff lay-offs were rather an exception. Also, the survey confirms the finding of the OECD (2012: 40) that, in most countries, the largest expenditure reductions involved programme measures. The great majority of European governments had to both cancel new programmes and cut expenditure on existing policy programmes.

Chapter 5

Fiscal consolidation decision-making

This chapter offers an overview of the political decision-making processes by governments leading up to the fiscal consolidation measures reviewed in the previous chapter. As explained in the analytical framework in Chapter 3, in our analysis of the political aspects of consolidation we concentrate on characteristics of decision-making, changes in decision-making patterns triggered by the crisis, and stages of decision-making. At the end of Chapter 2, we reflected upon the concept of political effort of a government's fiscal consolidation, a kind of political equivalent of economic volume of a government's fiscal consolidation, as so clearly measured by the OECD (2012). Though the concept of 'political effort' can be interpreted in many various ways, as discussed in Chapter 2, the choice was made to describe and analyse it in terms of political decision-making – first, by distinguishing different characteristics of decision-making; second, by looking at the degree of centralisation in decision-making; and third, by distinguishing different stages of decision-making.

In this chapter, these aspects of political decision-making are described and analysed. The core parts of this chapter therefore are, first, the extensive and thick description of the political aspects of the governmental decision-making in various European countries. Second, we use the results of the COCOPS survey in order to shed light on the shifting decision-making patterns during fiscal consolidation, with particular attention paid to the degree of centralisation. Third, we look into thick descriptions of the stages of cutback decision-making in a number of countries. In the following chapters, a quantitative statistical analysis of the economics and politics of consolidation is carried out. In this chapter, the primary focus is on qualitative exploration by means of in-depth country case studies.

In line with the methodological pluralism and variety advocated by the authors, we occasionally alternate the qualitative country examples with quantitative results from the COCOPS questionnaire. Some characteristics of decision-making are described and analysed by means of country examples, and other characteristics primarily in terms of the survey's response results.

5.1 CHARACTERISTICS OF DECISION-MAKING

Decision-making in preceding phases of crisis

This book focuses on the decision-making about fiscal consolidation, which was distinct from the different sorts of decision-making in the preceding phases of crisis. As mentioned before, the fiscal crisis was preceded by the banking crisis of 2008 and the economic crisis of 2009, in which different types of decision-making occurred (Kickert 2012a). Let us now briefly review the different decision-making practices.

During the 2008 banking crisis, the severity, magnitude and urgency of the crisis forced governments into very rapid and highly centralised crisis management. Only a few actors – usually the Prime Minister, Finance Minister and President of the National Bank, assisted by a handful of top officials – had to take decisions under enormous time pressure. In virtually all countries affected by the banking crisis, the decision-making was very quick and drastic, and highly centralised and targeted at saving specific banks.

During the 2009 economic crisis, several European governments devised economic recovery plans. However, this time the crisis was not as urgent and severe, and decision-making followed the usual political and parliamentary path, often including extensive consultations with employers' and employees' organisations. Moreover, the crisis in some countries was not considered severe enough to justify large extra expenditures. Decision-making during the economic crisis was neither drastic, nor swift, nor centralised in most European countries.

The Eurozone crisis that erupted in 2010 provides a totally different type of decision-making pattern, this time not restricted to domestic government decisions, but a highly complex and multi-layered cooperative decision-making by all Eurozone states together. As the primary focus of this book is on domestic decision-making by national governments, and joint multi-national Eurozone decision-making is incomparable to domestic decision-making, we did not try to encompass this much more complex multi-level type of decision-making into our analytical framework, and so the Eurozone crisis is only treated as contextual information.

In 2010, most European governments arrived at the phase where budget deficits – often far exceeding the EU ceiling of 3 per cent of GDP – required fiscal consolidation measures. At the outset of the fiscal crisis, political and social actors in several European countries were far from being convinced of the need for expenditure cutbacks and, for example, debated the strictness of the European deficit limit, thus slowing down the decision-making process. As the need for more radical cutbacks grew, governments faced a need for more severe cutbacks often requiring centralisation of their decision-making processes. Here, we now have a closer look at the characteristics of governments' decision-making in the phase of fiscal crisis and consolidation.

Decision-making on fiscal consolidation

In this section, we follow the distinctions between types or characteristics of decision-making presented in the analytical framework. Starting from the basic distinction in the cutback management literature (Raudla *et al.* 2013) between across-the-board (cheese-slicing, proportional) cutbacks, on the one hand, and targeted (selective, priority-setting) cuts on the other, the classical dichotomy between incremental and rational-comprehensive decision-making was elaborated into the following characteristics (based on dichotomies provided in Peters *et al.* 2011).

Were governments able to swiftly reach drastic and targeted decisions? Alternatively, were the decisions slow, small and of the across-the-board type?

In Table 5.2, the characteristics of the government's decision-making, as described in the country case studies, are summarised per country for different government periods (until 2013). The entries in this table characterise the size and speed of the cutback decisions, whether the decisions were across-the-board or targeted, and how centralised the decision-making was. They refer to cutback decisions at the national government level. The different government periods refer to either newly elected governments, or government changes without elections (e.g. Estonia in 2009).

In Table 5.3, the characteristics of cutback decision-making from Table 5.2 are summarised in frequency counts.

Table 5.3 clearly confirms that fiscal consolidation and cutback decisions were taken centrally. As is shown in the section below on 'centralisation of decision-making', the relative power of the Ministries of Finance over the spending departments increased during the fiscal crisis. Table 5.3 also refutes that swift,

TABLE 5.1 Characteristics of decision-making (repeated from Chapter 3)

Fundamental political priority-setting	Incremental pragmatic compromises
Swift, large and drastic decision-making	Slow, small and gradual steps
Centralised decision-making	Decentralised decision-making
Coherent and systematic decision-making	Incoherent patchwork
Long-term sustainable solutions	Short-term quick fixes

TABLE 5.2 Characteristics of cutback decision-making by central government

	Belgium		Estonia			France	Germany	
	(–2011)	(2011–)	(2007–2009)	(2009–2011)	(2011–)	(2007–2012)	(–2009)	(2009–)
Small/moderate/large cuts	Small	Moderate	Large	Large	Small	Moderate	Small	Moderate
Swift/slow	Slow	Slow	Swift	Swift	Slow	Slow	Slow	Swift
Targeted/across-the-board	Across	Across	Across	Across	Targeted	Across	Across	Targeted
Centralised/decentralised	Central	Central	Central	Central	Central	Central	Central	Central

	Hungary	Italy			Iceland	Ireland		Lithuania
	(2010–)	(2006–2008)	(2008–2011)	(2011–2012)	(2009–)	(2008–2010)	(2010–2012)	(2008–2012)
Small/moderate/large cuts	Large	Moderate	Moderate	Large	Large	Moderate	Large	Large
Swift/slow	Swift	Slow	Slow	Swift	Swift	Slow	Swift	Swift
Targeted/across-the-board	Targeted	Across	Across	Targeted	Across	Across	Targeted	Across
Centralised/decentralised	Central	Central	Central	Central	Central	Central	Central	Central

	Netherlands		Slovenia		Spain		United Kingdom	
	(2010–2012)	(2012–)	(2008–2011)	(2012–2013)	(2004–2011)	(2011–2013)	(–2010)	(2010–)
Small/moderate/large cuts	Moderate	Large	Small	Moderate	Large	Large	Small	Large
Swift/slow	Slow	Swift	Slow	Swift	Slow	Swift	Slow	Swift
Targeted/across-the-board	Across	Targeted	Targeted	Across	Targeted	Targeted	Across	Targeted
Centralised/decentralised	Central	Central	Central	Central	Central	Central	Central	Central

TABLE 5.3 Frequency counts of characteristics of cutback decisions

Size of cutback decisions		Speed of cutback decisions		Across-the-board versus targeted cuts		Centralisation of cutback decisions	
Small	5	Slow	12	Across-the-board	14	Decentralised	0
Moderate	8	Swift	12	Targeted	10	Centralised	24
Large	11						

drastic and targeted cutback decisions were less frequently used than slow and moderate across-the-board cuts. Large cutbacks occurred more frequently than moderate and small ones, swift cutback decisions as often as slow ones, and targeted cuts based on political priority-setting almost as often as proportional, across-the-board, cheese-slicing cuts.

Another finding of the country summaries in Table 5.2 is that the distinction between successive government periods enables us to draw the conclusion that the fiscal crisis and consolidation indeed consisted of different stages and that, with the only exception of Estonia, the size of the consolidation and cutbacks increased in subsequent stages. In Estonia, the exception can be explained by the fact that the country was the earliest cutter in Europe and cutbacks were basically finished by 2011. In a following section on 'stages of decision-making', that subject is addressed in more detail.

The data in Table 5.2 merit some empirical-methodological comments. The entries in this table are based on the country reports and case studies carried out by the COCOPS partners in these countries (see Chapter 1), and were checked by the partners before the publication of this table in the COCOPS seventh work package's trend report in September 2013 (Kickert *et al.* 2013). The entries hence represent subjective judgements by highly qualified experts from different countries. However, the empirical-methodological limitations of such data are obvious.

In Table 5.4, we counted the coincidence of the variable 'size of cutback decisions' with the variable 'targeted or across-the-board cuts', and with the variable 'speed of cutback decisions'. From a statistical perspective, the three variables, as measured in Table 5.2, are absolutely not independent, but almost one-to-one correlated.

It is therefore not entirely irrelevant that in the next section, a number of country examples are presented that provide additional in-depth information about the cutback decision-making, thus placing the entries in Table 5.2 in a clarifying context.

TABLE 5.4 Correlation between variables in Table 5.2

Coincidence large cuts and targeted cuts	22 out of 24
Coincidence moderate cuts and across-the-board cuts	5 out of 5
Coincidence small cuts and across-the-board cuts	1 out of 2
Coincidence large cuts and swift decisions	23 out of 24
Coincidence moderate cuts and slow decisions	4 out of 5
Coincidence small cuts and slow decisions	2 out of 2

Before turning to the extensive and thick descriptions of the specific country examples of political cutback decision-making, we first present the result of the COCOPS public executives questionnaire about across-the-board versus targeted decision-making.

Targeted versus across-the-board cuts

The COCOPS survey (Hammerschmidt *et al.* 2013) asked how public sector executives perceived the cutback decision-making. In the survey, the dichotomy 'targeted versus across-the-board cuts' was expanded to the following three partitions: targeted cuts according to priority-setting, proportional across-the-board cuts, and productivity measures (efficiency gains) (Figure 5.1).

Figure 5.1 indicates the perceptions of European public-sector executives on cutback strategies in their respective countries. Norway hardly experienced an economic and fiscal crisis, so it is not surprising that the survey yielded the highest outcome of 'no cutbacks' regarding this question, as 53 per cent of respondents reported no cuts were taken at all. Targeted cuts were perceived as a prevailing strategy of cutbacks in Spain, where an outstanding 64 per cent of the respondents assured that targeted cuts were undertaken during consolidation. Targeted cuts to budgets were also stated as prevalent in the United Kingdom, Hungary, Germany, France and the Netherlands. Proportional across-the-board cuts were reported as the main strategy for curbing the budget of public executives in Italy and Iceland by 62 and 61 per cent, respectively, and, to a lesser extent, were also perceived as an important approach during retrenchment in Estonia and Ireland. In Italy, however, the new Monti government introduced more targeted cutbacks in 2012 – the year when the survey was carried out – which might be the reason why this is not adequately reflected

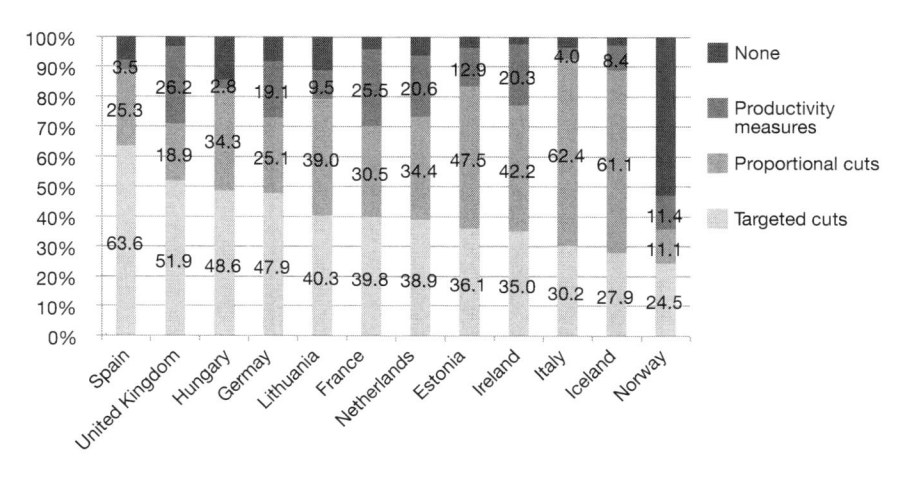

FIGURE 5.1 Perceived types of cutback decisions by public-sector executives

in the survey results. Interestingly, productivity measures made up the smallest portion among different strategies in most European countries, most often made use of in the United Kingdom, France, the Netherlands and Ireland. For example, the British government introduced the Operational Efficiency Program for all departments targeted at saving in back-office operation, equipment, IT reforms and collaborative procurement, as well as increased cost saving in the public-sector estates.

The findings clearly show that European governments applied a mix of different types of cutback strategies during the crisis. The drastic and fundamental cutbacks taking place in Spain and the United Kingdom are reflected by the high proportion of 'targeted cuts' in the survey. The survey is thus partly in line with the previous findings that the extent to which the cutback decisions were targeted or across-the-board was related to the size of the fiscal crisis. The bigger the necessary cuts, the higher the chance that across-the-board measures will not be sufficient, and targeted cuts become inevitable. Large-scale cuts in hardly hit Iceland and Estonia were carried out by using across-the-board cuts as prevailing cutback strategies.

In other countries such as France, Germany and the Netherlands, the relatively high perception of 'targeted cuts' in the survey somewhat differs from the information provided by country studies. This may result from the fact that often it is not possible to draw a clear-cut line between targeted and across-the-board cuts, as governments tend to use a combination of the two. In addition, while the country studies explicitly addressed the measures taken by the national government as a whole, the survey asked questions about measures taken within the respondent's organisation. Cutback management within individual public organisations does not necessarily always and completely coincide with general central government policy. This is especially the case of the national-level across-the-board cuts, where the responsibility for deciding upon particular operational cuts is often left for political and administrative leadership in individual departments and agencies, leading to a situation where the cutback practices across the public sector may vary to a great degree (Savi and Cepilovs, forthcoming). Most often, governments tend to use a combination of the targeted and across-the-board cuts, leading to a wide variety in the perceptions of public-sector executives.

Country examples of political decision-making

This section illustrates the specific characteristics of the political decision-making in European countries with examples drawn from the country studies. Qualitative in-depth case studies improve our comprehension of the specificity of governments' political decision-making. In this section, we pay particular attention to the same characteristics of decision-making as presented in the analytical framework above, that is:

- the size and speed of the decision-making; and
- across-the-board versus targeted decisions.

We begin with a presentation of the most prominent and well-known example of swift and drastic cutback decisions, the United Kingdom, and show how the newly formed coalition between the Conservatives and Liberal Democrats managed to very quickly announce and work out an unprecedented volume of cutbacks. We also show what efforts the Cameron-Clegg coalition government took to stimulate fundamental priority-setting of spending cuts.

Second, we present the example of a country with a unitary state, a single-party government and a strong president, who was a proponent of strict budgetary policy, that is, a country in which swift and drastic cutback decision-making was most probably to be expected, but yet did not take place: France. We present some insights into the political decision-making by President Sarkozy in order to understand the paradox.

Third, we present the example of a lesser-known country that is unique in many respects: Estonia. The Estonian government was among the first European countries to opt for immediate and large cutbacks right at the outset of the crisis, despite the fact that the budget deficit remained modest and state debt minimal. When one party left the coalition and the government was reduced into a parliamentary minority, the government did not call early elections, remained in power, still managed to urgently push cutbacks through parliament, and won the next general elections with a grand majority.

Subsequently, we turn to the 'normal' example of a multi-party coalition government having to deliberate, negotiate, make compromises and find consensus on fiscal consolidation and cutbacks, that is, Germany, an example of relatively slow and small decision-making.

We then turn to the example of a country where the decision-making about fiscal consolidation was extremely politicised, as it coincided with the formation of a new multi-party coalition after the general elections, that is, the Netherlands. As would be expected, the cutback decision-making was slow, small and gradual, and resulted in a patchwork of political compromises.

Finally, we present an example of a country that took eighteen months to form a new coalition cabinet after the general elections, that is, Belgium. Though confronted with a serious deficit and a very excessive state debt, and lacking a parliamentary-approved annual budget, under extreme pressure of the EU to get the budget in order, and with falling credit rating of Standard & Poor's, the lengthy formation of the coalition was more concerned with Flemish-Walloon political language-group conflicts and the reform of the Finance Act than with fiscal consolidation.

United Kingdom: swift and drastic cutbacks

The swift and drastic cutbacks were not taken by a single-party government, but by a coalition cabinet. Despite the fact that the 2010 Cameron-Clegg coalition was reached between two ideologically opposing parties, in which case one would normally expect long and tedious negotiations, the massive cutback decisions were taken more or less overnight. The following box illustrates how swift the coalition's political decision-making was, and the second box illustrates the attempt at fundamental priority-setting of the spending cuts.

Not only was the new government's cutback decision-making in the United Kingdom relatively very swift, but the government also devised a special decision-making instrument to especially stimulate fundamental political priority-setting in the departmental spending cuts, the so-called 'Star Chamber'.

Moreover, the government conceived an instrument to enhance the commitment of public-sector workers and the general public in the spending cuts, the so-called 'Spending Challenge'.

Political decision-making in the United Kingdom

The general elections of May 2010 produced a hung parliament for the first time in twenty-six years, with no party having an absolute majority. The day after the elections, the Conservative leader Cameron made a 'big, open and comprehensive' offer of a coalition with the Liberal Democrats, and the negotiations soon resulted in a Conservative-Liberal Democrat coalition government with Cameron (Conservative) as Prime Minister and Clegg (Liberal Democrat) as deputy Prime Minister, and with Osborne (Conservative) as Chancellor of the Exchequer and Alexander (Liberal Democrat) as Chief Secretary to the Treasury.

During the election campaign, budget cutbacks played an important role, but the fear of a double-dip recession of the economy rather dominated the campaign. During the election campaign, the Conservatives said that they would cut faster and deeper than Labour. The Liberal Democrats before the elections rather supported a more cautious approach, somewhat similar to Labour. Right after the elections, the new Cameron-Clegg cabinet decided on a hard cutback package, going much farther than the Liberal Democrats had promised they would do in the election campaign. The Liberal Democrats had changed their position on the economy almost 180 degrees from a broadly Keynesian one to a much more fiscally conservative one. It was the price they paid for concessions by the Conservatives on constitutional reform of the general elections system, which the Liberals craved.

The announcement the new Cabinet made days after the election to drastically cut the budget deficit and state debt was worked out in the Emergency Budget delivered by Chancellor Osborne in the June 2010 Emergency Budget and in the Spending Review four months later. This was remarkably fast because there was no 2009 Spending Review, so there were no fixed budgets for departments. The alarming financial economic situation was used by the new government to justify the need to urgently make a clear fiscal plan in order to restore confidence in the markets and with the public. The Treasury and other departments had made preparations from the time the election was called. The Treasury knew well in advance that, sooner or later, a detailed plan for spending budgets of departments would be required (Treasury Committee 2010).

In preparing the Budget and Spending Review, regular meetings also took place between the Prime Minister (Cameron) and the deputy Prime Minister (Clegg), and Chancellor (Osborne) and Chief Secretary (Alexander) in order to involve and commit the coalition partners. Normally, the Prime Minister and the Chancellor would decide on fiscal and taxation measures, but both Cameron and Osborne were Conservatives. The Liberal Democrats needed to be constantly involved in the decision-making on the Budget and Spending Review. The quadrilateral meetings served that purpose.

Source: Kickert (2012b)

Star Chamber

After the Treasury published its Spending Review framework, a new form of cabinet decision-making was announced by the Chancellor in June 2010. The Public Expenditures Committee (PEX) was revitalised and called a 'Star Chamber' after a Canadian example in the 1990s. In the 'Star Chamber', all of Whitehall's spending would be scrutinised. The initial PEX consisted of the Chancellor of the Exchequer as chair, the Chief Secretary to the Treasury as deputy chair, the Minister for the Cabinet Office and Paymaster General. Other Cabinet ministers could only become members of the 'Star Chamber' once they had settled their departmental allocation with the Treasury. The idea was to build collective Cabinet commitment and to stimulate fundamental reconsiderations of departmental budgets. The wheeling and dealing in bilateral negotiations between departments and the Treasury was settled before. Cabinet ministers thus had an incentive to deliver their spending cuts early and then pressure their colleagues in the Star Chamber. The commitment for fiscal consolidation in the coalition Cabinet was high.

Source: Treasury Committee (2010)

> ## Spending Challenge
>
> In preparation for the Spending Review in June, public-sector workers and the general public were invited to suggest money saving through the 'Spending Challenge' website, again after a Canadian example. Although the Treasury was positive about the useful contributions made by public-sector workers and the public, it was also criticised as being half-hearted and not genuinely involving the public.
>
> *Source*: Treasury Committee (2010)

France: only moderate consolidation

France is a unitary state, has a single-party government, and since 2007 had a strong-minded and right-wing president, Sarkozy, who was an outspoken proponent of strict budgetary policy. One would therefore be tempted to presume that once the fiscal crisis broke out, France was in an outstanding position to enable swift and drastic decisions. However, quite the contrary happened. The super-energetic and reform-minded French President Sarkozy, for electoral reasons, refrained from hard and unpopular cutback measures. France once again reconfirmed its image of hard-to-reform welfare state.

President Sarkozy believed that he would be punished by the electorate if he undertook drastic retrenchments. Despite the pressure from Eurozone partners, especially Germany, to adopt a more resolute policy of reform and retrenchment, especially after the sovereign debt crisis threatened to spread to Italy and Spain as well, the French president instead chose for moderate consolidation. Sarkozy lost the May 2012 presidential elections to the Socialist Hollande.

The new French President Hollande was an even more explicit opponent of fiscal austerity and proponent of economic stimulus measures. Although Hollande in his election campaign had promised to redress some fiscal cutback measures of his predecessor, he had no choice but to adopt the same budgetary consolidation measures.

> ## Political decision-making in France
>
> In June 2007, the right-wing (UMP) President Sarkozy was elected for five years, meaning that the crisis was tackled entirely within his mandate together with his Prime Minister Fillon (UMP). The election campaign's main theme was a break with the old welfare state towards a more Liberal and business-friendly policy, along with tax reductions. Cutting public expenditures was a primary

political objective. Sarkozy was minister of Economy, Finance and Industry earlier and strongly advocated reforms in public finances. President Sarkozy strengthened his leadership and centralised his control of the government by frequently chairing interministerial council meetings and by tightening the control over ministries through a small number of close top officials.

In July 2007, he launched a General Public Policy Review (RGPP) aimed at 'rethinking the state' in view of the fiscal crisis. The RGPP aimed at swift, wide and drastic reforms to reduce the administration's costs and inefficiencies. Ministries were to plan spending cuts, to reform and to restructure their public service delivery. Spending Reviews and cutbacks were conceived before the global crisis erupted in 2008. The 2008 budget contained a spending freeze for the entire period until 2012 (next elections). A hiring freeze was installed, and a multi-annual budget based on the RGPP was introduced. On the other hand, the tax reduction package of July 2007 (TEPA) ran counter to the austerity policy. Business taxes were relieved, as were the tax burdens for top incomes (the UMP electorate), and the accumulated total of income, property and wealth taxes for individuals was maximised at 50 per cent (tax shield).

Once the crisis broke out in 2008, for a considerable period of time the government hesitated between cutback and economic stimulus measures. The policy was framed in the neologism 'ri-lance', a combination of the two words 'rigueur' (rigour) and 'relance' (stimulus). The result was a combination of, first, a economic recovery plan for 2009–2010 with extra spending of €26 billion, associated with several cutback measures that were not directly linked to the crisis, and second, the launching of a number of cutback measures beginning in 2010.

In 2009, a pension reform was announced to the advantage of ageing and retired people, who had voted massively in favour of Sarkozy. French pensions already were among the highest in OECD countries.

As of 2010, President Sarkozy moved to the end phase of the electoral cycle (2012) and refrained from sensitive and unpopular cutback measures. A freeze on public expenditures was announced in the 2011 budget, and particularly a pay freeze for civil servants. Spending cuts were extended to other public bodies such as agencies. A sudden cut in the central government's financial transfers to local authorities was rejected by the President in favour of a more gradual freeze. The planned reductions were postponed until after the 2012 presidential elections. Right before the May 2012 presidential elections, a number of politically well-timed tax measures were announced: an 'exceptional tax on very high earnings', an increase in top income tax, and increases in capital gains and dividends taxes. The stigma of Sarkozy as 'president of the rich' was to be redressed. An increase in VAT was politically sensitive, and was postponed until after the presidential elections (May 2012).

Source: Bezes and LeLidec (2013)

Estonia: immediate and drastic cutbacks

Estonia is a unique case because instead of denying and postponing cuts, it was among the first European countries that implemented immediate and drastic cutbacks right at the outset of the crisis, as early as 2008. The following box also illustrates other unique aspects of the Estonian government's decision-making. It pushed through three successive rounds of cutbacks in parliament, even after the coalition was brought down to a minority government. It did not call early elections, stayed in power until the next elections, and yet won them.

The initial volume of fiscal consolidation in 2009 (9.2 per cent of GDP) in Estonia far surpassed the British accumulated consolidation volume. The speed with which the cutback decisions were taken also outdid the British example. The cutbacks were front-loaded and immediate. In fact, the relatively unknown and small country Estonia is the most prominent example of immediate and drastic consolidation and cutbacks.

Estonia was withdrawing from the cutback measures, and thus reducing the cumulative impact of consolidation, by 2012 (OECD 2012: 36).

Political decision-making in Estonia

Prior to the crisis, Estonia enjoyed one of the highest economic growth rates among OECD countries, and had fiscal surpluses since the early 2000s. The 2008 worldwide financial crisis hit the small and open economy hard, with the economy sharply declining and unemployment suddenly rising. Estonia did not face a banking crisis and was not forced to save banks because the Estonian banking sector was almost completely dominated and operated by Nordic banks. Neither did Estonia engage in costly economic recovery packages. It decided for immediate fiscal consolidation, mainly because of the government's priority to join the Eurozone. So, the Maastricht treaty ceilings on deficit and debt were imperative (Kattel and Raudla 2013; Raudla 2013). The budget deficit remained modest and the state debt minimal.

The Estonian government took consolidation measures in three negative supplementary budgets, first in June 2008 and two more in February and June 2009. The size of the fiscal consolidation measures was exceptionally high (9.2 per cent of GDP in 2009) and front-loaded.

The government decided to make a negative supplementary budget in spring 2008, and installed a so-called 'Crocodile Commission' consisting of members of parliament and ministers from the three coalition parties to work out the cutbacks and revenue measures. One month later, the commission was dismissed as it was unable to propose solutions. The government then decided to opt for a top-down mode of decision-making to determine the cutback targets and revenue increases in the June 2008 supplementary budget. As all ministers defended their own interests in the cabinet, the cabinet opted for across-the-board cutbacks in the first supplementary budget.

In order to speed up consensus finding and to break the ministerial boundaries in making a second supplementary budget, the government installed another informal budgetary working group, comprising one Member of Parliament and one minister from each of the three coalition parties. Moreover, an expert committee was established of three economics professors and the deputy Governor of the Bank of Estonia, who presented their proposals in a cabinet session in February 2009. After the government concluded its second supplementary budget in February 2009, it was very quickly pushed through parliament, bypassing the normal lengthy processing of budget bills, and placing the opposition parties off-side.

The sharp political conflict and tension in parliament reached its peak during the preparation of the third negative supplementary budget. Unable to agree on further cutbacks, the Social Democrats left the coalition in May 2009, resulting in a two-party coalition with parliamentary minority (50 out of 101 seats). This time, the parliamentary approval of the third supplementary budget took much longer. It was ultimately approved due to a bargain with the Green Party – in exchange for its support, the minority government increased environmental fees and taxes. The third supplementary budget was strongly disapproved by societal actors from trade and industry and opinion leaders – the VAT rate was increased overnight.

It is remarkable that a minority government was able to urgently push through the cutback measures, contradicting the usual political science assumption. A number of reasons can be brought up. First, the lack of systematic resistance to cutbacks by civil servants. Despite wage cuts, lay-offs and increased workload, most civil servants displayed loyalty and commitment to the government's decisions. Second, the absence of strong opposition by trade unions, societal actors or corporatist institutions. Civil society in the new democracy of Estonia has not yet developed to the full extent. Third, the public opinion was predominantly anti-statist and in favour of fiscal consolidation and cutbacks. The neo-Liberalism embodied in the two coalition parties was widely shared by the population. Fiscal discipline and, above all, joining the Eurozone was strongly supported by the citizens.

The minority government did not call early elections, but remained in power until the regular general elections in 2011, which it won with a grand majority (74 per cent).

Source: Savi and Randma-Liiv (2013)

Germany: normal case of coalition politics

Germany seems a 'normal' example of consensual democracy with multi-party coalition governments. Deliberations, negotiations and compromises usually result in slow and small decision-making. Moreover, Germany is not a unitary state, but a federal republic. The central government's decisions are influenced by the regional (Länder) governments, represented in the 'Bundesrat' (senate). The 'Bundesrat' has become more important the last decade, especially in fiscal affairs (right of budget approval). Furthermore, the German Chancellor is not a 'primus inter pares', as is the usual case in many consensus democracies. The Chancellor has more central authorities (Richtlinienkompetenz), but German ministers do have certain autonomy in their policy area (Ressortprinzip).

Political decision-making in Germany

Politically unpopular decision-making on public budget cutbacks was postponed until the September 2009 elections, which, in October 2009, resulted in a Christian-Liberal (CDU/CSU-FDP) coalition cabinet headed by Chancellor Merkel (CDU), with Schäuble (CDU) as minister of Finance, and Westerwelle (FDP) as Foreign Minister and Vice Chancellor.

The Liberal Party (FDP) had promised tax reductions during the election campaign, and both the FDP leader Westerwelle and the CSU leader Seehofer wanted fewer and slower cuts in spending. The FDP blamed the previous government for the huge state debt and budget deficit, and was reluctant to share responsibility for severe cutbacks. Finance Minister Schäuble (CDU), supported by Chancellor Merkel, during the coalition negotiations managed to push through a substantial cutback package to balance the books sooner, resulting in the July 2010 'Sparpaket'. The FDP did not give up its intentions to reduce taxes, and repeatedly announced proposals. The political position of the FDP was, however, relatively weak as early elections would probably wipe out the party. Regional elections had resulted in a sensitive loss of the Bavarian Christian Democrat party CSU. Both coalition parties were in a relatively powerless position.

The political debate on the savings package ran along the usual party lines. The Social Democrats accused the government of disproportionally hitting the poor, elderly, unemployed and families. However, the Social Democrats, during the 2005–2009 'grand coalition' with the Christian Democrats, had supported curbing the state debt and deficit. Actually, there seemed to be a broad political consensus, at least among the political leaders, that fiscal consolidation was absolutely necessary.

The July 2010 'Sparpaket' was devised by Chancellor Merkel in close cooperation with Finance Minister Schäuble, seconded by Merkel's economic top advisor in the chancellery, Weidman (who became President of the Bundesbank in 2011) and by Schäuble's finance 'Staatssekretär' Asmussen (who became a board member of the European Central Bank in 2011) and budget 'Staatssekretär' Gatzer. They were the key players in the strategic decision-making on the 'Sparpaket'. At a second level, the coalition partners Westerwelle (FDP) and Seehofer (CSU) were informed and consulted. And at a third level, the parliamentary fractions in the Bundestag were informed and persuaded of the measures. CDU faction leader Kauder had to 'sell' Merkel's measures to parliament. Moreover, the 'Koalitionsausschuss' – the coalition committee consisting of government representatives, parliamentary faction leaders and party leaders – played an important role in coordinating the cooperation between the coalition partners in government and parliament.

Source: Kickert (2013b)

Historical legacy of financial chaos

After the First World War, Germany had experienced a chaotic financial situation. The warfare costs had led to huge state debt, and moreover Germany was forced to pay huge retributions to the Allied victors. It reacted by printing extra money, leading to price inflation. The hyperinflation reached its peak in 1923 when the German 'Deutschmark' lost virtually all value. Banknotes had become worthless. The crisis further culminated when the French and Belgians occupied the Ruhr area. This chaotic situation formed the fertile breeding ground for the rise of the National Socialist party of Hitler. This historical legacy explains why long-term financial and economic stability and a sound fiscal state household are such highly valued goods in German public opinion.

Euro crisis and Greek bail-out

Chancellor Merkel had long resisted aid for Greece, and only gave in to a combined IMF and EU rescue plan for Greece in April 2010. At later stages of the Euro crisis, when Ireland and Portugal also required bail-outs, Chancellor Merkel long refused to let Germany pay the checks for failing Euro members. Other much bigger economies of Italy and Spain were expected to follow, and, as we know in hindsight, the Greek financial crisis was not solved by the 2010 rescue plan, but continued and required additional rescue measures from the healthy EU members. The economically largest EU member, Germany always pays the highest price, which German tax-payers do not appreciate at all. In several regional elections in 2010 and 2011, the German electorate made that absolutely clear. Germans want a thrifty government.

Source: Kickert (2013b)

The centralisation of decision-making power in the hands of the Chancellor (together with her Finance Minister) that had started during the banking crisis, seemed to have persisted and although parliament complained it was in no position to resist Merkel on the issue of the 'Sparpaket'. German public opinion was more concerned about long-term economic stability and safeguarding pensions than about short-term advantages of tax reductions. The 2009 general elections had resulted in a loss of the Social Democrats who had profiled themselves as advocates of extra economic stimulus measures. German tax-payers preferred a thrifty government that maintained a sound household.

An important contextual factor influencing the decisions on the German fiscal crisis was the European sovereign debt crisis, especially the Greek bail-out measures. Most Germans believed that Greece was in trouble because of its own overspending and that German tax-payers should not pay the price. Chancellor Merkel was aware of a voter backlash if she risked German tax-payers' money, which actually happened at the regional elections in North Rhine-Westphalia in May 2010 that resulted in a defeat of the regional centre-right government.

The Netherlands: politicised decision-making

The cutback decision-making was highly politicised as it coincided with the formation of a new multi-party coalition after the general elections. In the Netherlands, that generally is a hectic process of political deliberation, negotiation, compromises and consensus, in which fundamental political priority-setting is impossible. The cutback decisions were a patchwork of political compromises. Let us now give an impression of the political aspects of the coalition formation in 2010.

Political decision-making in the Netherlands

The decision-making about spending cuts coincided with the cabinet formation process. The cutback measures were part of the negotiations involved in the coalition formation, which was a sequence of alternating political party com-binations. During the coalition formation, 'cabinet informers' negotiated with the party leaders and their adjutants, while every deal was extensively discussed in the party factions, and also publicly debated when leaked to the press. The 'cabinet informers' were assisted by a secretariat made up of officials seconded from the Ministry of General Affairs. The cabinet informers' questions about policy issues were answered by officials in these ministerial departments. Departments had long before prepared answers to every possibly conceivable question to make sure that the cabinet informers were immediately served when a request arrived. Furthermore, hundreds of different interest groups tried to make their views count. No wonder that in such a hectic circus, fundamental priority-setting could hardly take place. Moreover, cutbacks were not the only political hot issue discussed. The final coalition agreement had a financial attachment, which specified the cutback measures.

During the formation of the coalition, the 'main negotiation table' was composed of the party leaders, Rutte of the (conservative) Liberal Party (VVD), Verhagen of the Christian Democrats (CDA) (former Prime Minister Balkenende retreated as party leader after losing the elections), and Wilders of the right-populist party PVV. Besides the 'main table', there was a financial 'sub-table' where the financial specialists of the negotiating parties convened. The CDA representative De Jager was Minister of Finance of the outgoing cabinet (he became the new minister of Finance), and played a highly influential role in the financial and economic parts of the coalition agreement (as did the officials of his ministry).

Source: Kickert (2012d)

Fundamental priority-setting of spending cuts

The decision-making about the fiscal crisis was politically sensitive as cutback measures are unpopular. By the time the Christian-Social Democrat coalition cabinet Balkenende announced its economic recovery plans in March 2009, it was already clear that, somehow, this had to be compensated by major retrenchments. The cabinet, however, had no intention of taking unpopular cutback actions in its last government year before the 2010 general elections. Instead, in autumn 2009, the cabinet installed nineteen 'reconsideration working groups' on all relevant policy areas. The working groups were staffed with expert top officials and chaired by a senior politician or top official. These working groups worked out three scenarios: one with relatively minor cutbacks, a second with more severe cuts and a third with drastic savings of about 20 per cent. The third scenario proposals of the working groups comprised the fundamental cutback decisions the sector experts knew to be possible and feasible. For insiders in administrative The Hague, it was clear that here, the realistic and achievable fundamental priorities for spending cuts were spelled out.

The working groups published their reports in time for the June 2010 general elections. The reports received hardly any publicity, hardly played a role during the election campaign, and hardly influenced the October 2010 cutback plans of the new cabinet.

Source: Kickert (2012d)

The fiscal consolidation package contained in the coalition agreement was a patchwork of political compromises consisting of a variety of small and gradual across-the-board steps. Fundamental political priority-setting is not likely to happen in a consensual political process of multi-party negotiations and compromise finding between ideologically different parties. That is not to say that no attempts were made at priority-setting of spending cuts. In the Netherlands, that politically unpopular task was handed over to top officials. In Chapter 2, we showed how the Dutch government evaded its political responsibility for setting priorities in spending cuts. It installed nineteen reconsideration working groups. Here, we briefly summarise that.

In the first round of fiscal consolidation measures in 2010, the fundamental priorities for spending cuts were not endorsed by the coalition partners. As is shown later in the section on stages of decision-making, in the later rounds of consolidation measures in 2012, some of the ideas about fundamental cutbacks conceived by the 'reconsideration working groups' emerged and materialised.

Belgium: cutback decisions behind the scenes

From an outsider's perspective, it might seem that the Belgian government did not take any significant measures during the eighteen months between the June 2009 general elections and the November 2011 coalition agreement. The caretaker government 'under resignation' was not allowed to make a new budget or a drastic cutback plan – it was only allowed to handle 'current affairs'. Whereas most Western governments took measures in 2010 to consolidate their public finances, the Belgian federal government might appear not to have acted until November 2011. For sixteen months, the bumpy coalition formation concentrated on state reform, and only during the last two months of the lengthy formation were budget and fiscal measures debated. However, the caretaker government actually took several fiscal consolidation measures, starting in October 2009 with the 2010–2011 budget. After the May 2010 elections, the government 'under resignation' stretched the concept of 'current affairs' up to its extreme. Seemingly small pragmatic decisions such as freezing health care expenditures, and freezing and delaying departmental expenditures, in fact added up to substantial retrenchments. The March 2011 budget agreement contained billions of structural reductions. The impression that the Belgian government did virtually nothing to consolidate its household until November 2011 is absolutely wrong.

The Belgian political system is not only highly complex, but also full of countervailing forces, blocks and vetoes. At best, Belgium's political system is capable of small adjustments in existing arrangements – decision-making is pragmatic and incremental. Low-profile decisions, seemingly of a mere technocratic nature, avoiding political publicity, realised by informal political deliberations behind the scenes.

Political decision-making in Belgium

Although at first sight one might get the impression that the Belgian caretaker government did not take any fiscal consolidation measures until the November 2011 coalition agreement, in actual fact several consolidation measures were taken before.

After the (early) general elections of June 2010, the 'government under resignation', headed by Prime Minister Leterme, was only allowed to handle 'current affairs'. Although significant decisions cannot be taken by a government under resignation, it received parliamentary backing for some quite significant and politically sensitive decisions, such as participation in the war in Libya. Actually, the government under resignation handled much more than merely 'current affairs', which is hard to avert when remaining in function for one and a half years. The constitutional provision to handle 'current affairs' was meant to last no longer than a couple of formation months. Apparently, the broad common-law-like definition of 'current affairs' was flexible enough to be stretched up to the extreme.

In September 2010, the Leterme government decided to temporarily freeze the legally fixed 4.5 per cent annual rise in health care insurances, indirectly resulting in a substantial (€2 billion) cutback.

The Leterme government under resignation was not permitted to pass a new budget in parliament, neither was it allowed to propose a budget retrenchment plan to parliament. In December 2010, the IMF sounded the alarm over Belgium and the international rating agency Standard & Poor's lowered its credit rating for Belgium, leading to dramatic bond interest rates on its very high state debt, all pressures urging the government to finally make a budget. The government proposed the Di Rupo formation team to make a new budget for 2011 and proposed extra fiscal consolidations, with no result. In the absence of a new budget being approved by parliament, the government under resignation was legally allowed to acquire and spend monthly revenues and expenditures to the amount of the Budget approved in the year before the general elections (so-called 'preliminary twelfths'). Indirectly, this represented a substantial budget reduction as the normal annual rise in expenditures was frozen. The Leterme government also decided to establish a monthly monitoring of departmental expenditures and revenues. Departmental dossiers over €45,000 henceforth had to be submitted to the cabinet, thus leading to a substantial delay in departmental expenditures. The government under resignation took various other measures, which at first sight might seem minor, but together amounted to substantial cutbacks.

At the end of 2010, the bi-annual negotiations between social partners in the Central Council of Trade and Industry on wage increases again came to a standstill. When the social partners do not reach an agreement, the government can legally impose a wage norm, which it did at 0.3 per cent.

After this wage increase agreement, the Leterme government again insisted on reaching a new budget agreement. The international pressure on Belgium had further increased. In March 2011, an agreement on the 2011 budget was accepted. The Budget consisted of substantial expenditure cuts at federal and regional levels. Federal expenditures were to be structurally reduced by €2.29 billion in 2011.

The mounting Euro-crisis, the very high state debt and alarmingly rising bond yields put an enormous pressure on the government to show Belgium's credibility in managing its public finances. The European Union was putting an ultimatum for Belgium to finalise a budget. In August 2011, the Prime Minister under resignation offered the Di Rupo formation team to prepare the annual budget for 2012. Legally, the Budget had to be submitted to parliament before 31 October. That deadline was not met. In October, the government under resignation proposed a €10 billion consolidation package, herewith further increasing the pressure on the coalition team. Then, Prime Minister Leterme announced he would leave Belgian politics (he had accepted a job at OECD), which put an additional pressure on the coalition negotiators. Before reaching an agreement in November 2011, Di Rupo once again offered his resignation to the King. The by then tremendous pressure to finally deliver Belgium a government meant that the Budget negotiations were rounded off in one last weekend with an agreement on cuts worth €11.3 billion.

Source: Kickert (2012c)

The previous country examples have illustrated the characteristics of decision-making that were summarised in Table 5.2:

- size and speed of decision-making; and
- across-the-board versus targeted decisions.

First, we presented a well-known example of swift and large cutback decision-making; second, a counterintuitive example where swift and large cuts were to be expected but yet did not occur; third, an almost completely unknown and unique example of swift and large cutback decisions; and finally, three examples of consensual multi-party governments where swift and large cutback decisions are hardly possible, in ascending order of political complexity.

Implicitly, some first attempts were made at indicating what possible explanations might be given for the specificity of the country cases (e.g. in terms of the political system, type of government and political orientation). Explanatory factors for fiscal consolidation are explicitly and extensively considered in the following Chapter 6.

5.2 CENTRALISATION OF DECISION-MAKING

In the previous section, particular attention was paid to the first set of characteristics derived in the analytical framework, that is, targeted versus across-the-board, swift versus slow, and large versus small decisions. Let us now pay attention to the next set of characteristics, the degree of centralisation of decision-making during the fiscal crisis, first by presenting the relevant results from the COCOPS survey, and second by illustrating it with specific country examples. The methodological variety alternates between quantitative survey results and qualitative country examples, as announced before.

Survey results

The survey results show that responding to the fiscal crisis brought along several changes and power shifts in the conventional decision-making patterns in European governments (Figure 5.2). Namely, extensive increase in the power of Ministries of Finance and, to a slightly lesser extent, in the power of organisational budget-planning units were reported, alongside the general increase in centralisation of organisational decision-making. According to the respondents, politicians gained more power during cutback decision-making when compared to the pre-crisis period.

The survey results portray that in all of the countries studied, the *power of the ministry of Finance* increased during the fiscal crisis (Figure 5.3). A substantial increase was reported by the public executives of Ireland. It is interesting to

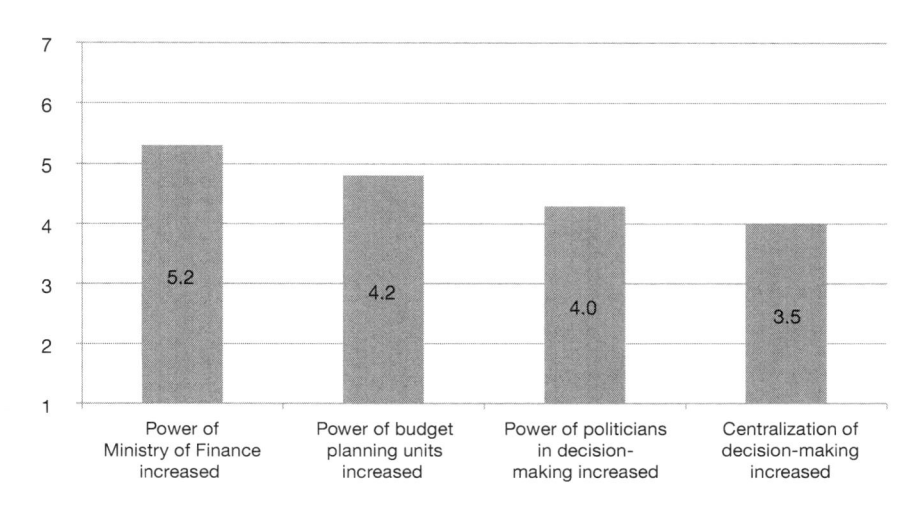

FIGURE 5.2 Perceived changes in decision-making during fiscal consolidation (1 = not at all; 7 = to a large extent)

notice that even a country not severely hit by the crisis – Norway – encountered a remarkable increase in the power of the Ministry of Finance vis-à-vis the line ministries. This trend is a function of more centralised arrangements in fiscal governance to achieve cutbacks, often including the adoption of a more top-down approach to budgeting by setting limits and bans on spending. Consequently, both control and coordination functions of the Ministry of Finance tended to intensify during the period of fiscal consolidation.

Similarly, *centralisation of decision-making within public organisations* occurred in all of the countries studied (Figure 5.4). The answers of the top officials show that, during retrenchment, the decision-making in respondents' organisations was estimated as more centralised. Similarly to the increase of the power of the Ministry of Finance, it is interesting to remark that the country responses of twelve European countries vary only slightly. Although the evidence from Norway, but also to a lesser degree from Iceland and Germany, shows somewhat less centralisation, the overall trend is still followed. Centralisation of decision-making occurs during retrenchment because the organisational subunits are unlikely to volunteer for cuts and tend to believe they have exceptional characteristics not suitable for cuts. Therefore, top-down processes are at times indispensable for the achievement of systematic spending cuts.

Public-sector executives perceived that *the role of budgetary units* in public-sector organisations increased as a consequence of crisis. The biggest rise in the power of budgetary units was reported in Ireland, Italy, France and Spain. The public executives of the other countries claimed rather similar shifts in the power of budgetary units. The increased power of budgetary units in relation to their horizontal counterparts reflects the fact that, during cutbacks, the organisational units become to be seen as 'budget holders', and planning and implementing cuts receive most of the management's attention.

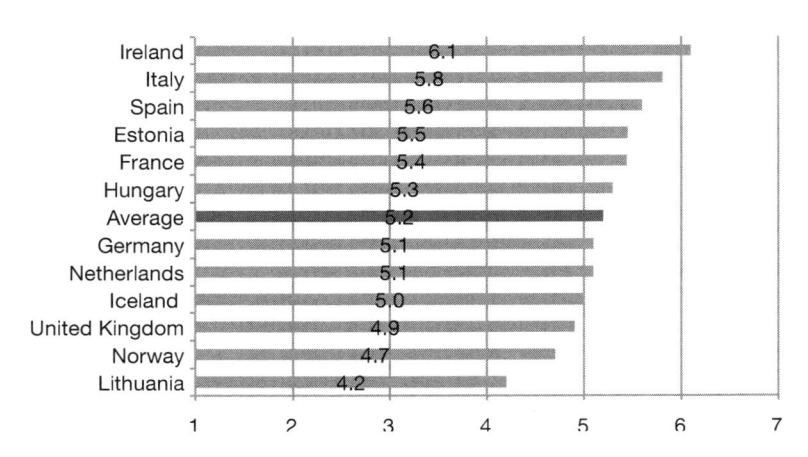

FIGURE 5.3 Increase in the power of Ministry of Finance (1 = not at all; 7 = to a large extent)

Finally, the increase in *the power of politicians* was also perceived by the public-sector executives during the crisis decision-making. Clearly, the largest increase in the influence of politicians in the decision-making process was reported in Spain, followed by Estonia, Ireland and Italy – all countries hit very hard by the crisis. In Norway, the increase in the power of politicians was seen as the lowest, but still confirmed the general trend towards the growing role of politicians in decision-making. Taking into account that budgeting is inherently political, and decisions on cutbacks determine the losers and winners, the bigger role of politicians could be expected.

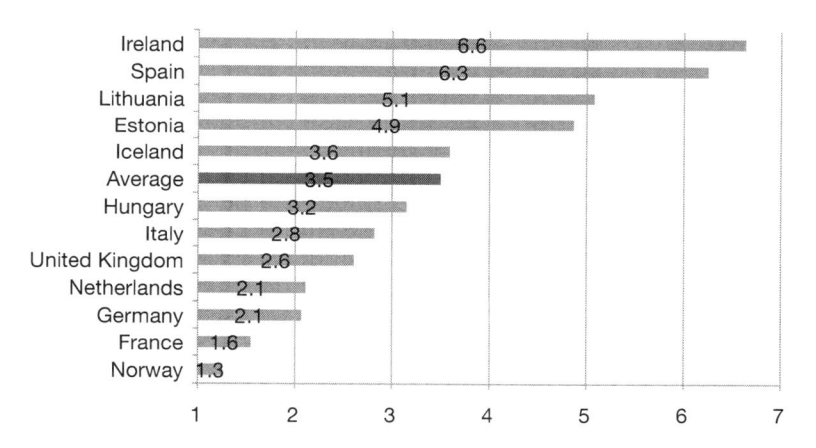

FIGURE 5.4 Perceived centralisation of decision-making in organisation (1 = not at all; 7 = to a large extent)

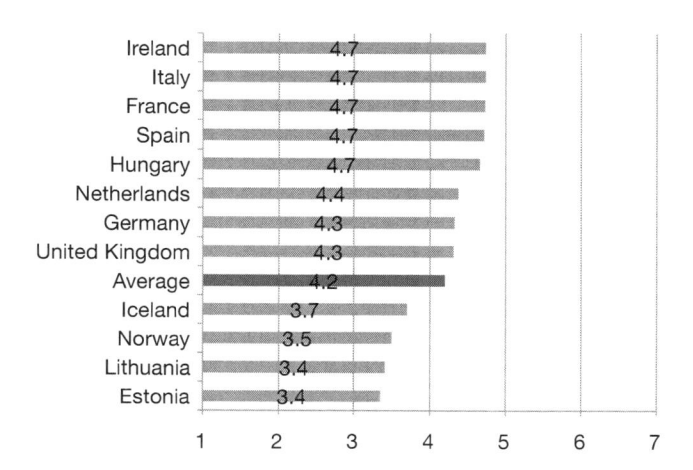

FIGURE 5.5 Perceived increase in the power of budget-planning units (1 = not at all; 7 = to a large extent)

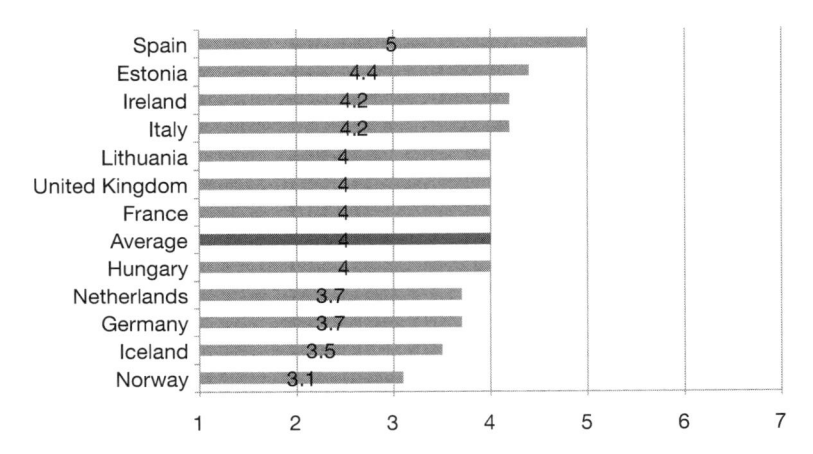

FIGURE 5.6 Increase in the power of politicians in decision-making (1 = not at all; 7 = to a large extent)

The survey results are illustrated by more specific country examples in the next section.

Country examples

The following country examples provide some additional in-depth insights into how the centralisation of the decision-making process in the hands of the Ministries of Finance took place in some countries.

Centralisation of budgetary decision-making in Estonia

During the preparation of the supplementary budgets, the Ministry of Finance became the central key player between the government and the line ministries. At first, the Ministry of Finance mainly provided the cabinet, but also the ad hoc working groups, with financial-economic information that remained technical and numerical in form. Then, the ministry of Finance began orchestrating the cutback decision-making processes in the line ministries, by setting duties and deadlines. Subsequently, the cabinet further increased the central fiscal control of the Ministry of Finance by appointing representatives of that ministry to the boards of state foundations and state-owned enterprises. The primary aim was to achieve control over the borrowing authority of these entities, and the local governments' borrowing procedures were restricted by central government by granting the Ministry of Finance the right of permission.

Source: Savi and Randma-Liiv (2013)

In the previous section, we presented the Dutch country case as an example of highly politicised cutback decision-making. As it coincided with the formation of a new multi-party coalition cabinet, the fiscal consolidation package contained in the new coalition agreement was a patchwork of political compromises. However, in the Netherlands, besides this 'political world', a second financial-economic 'world' existed in which the financial framework for the cutbacks was predetermined and maintained, and where budget discipline was predominant. One is tempted to conclude that the financial frames and the cutback volumes were determined in the one 'world', and that the political 'world' was about policy-making substance within these predetermined financial constraints. The experts of the Ministry of Finance and the Central Planning Bureau determined the financial figures, the politicians the policy contents.

In Great Britain, the budgetary procedure was massaged by Prime Minister Brown. Allegedly, even the economic facts and figures were manipulated by Labour in view of the upcoming general elections. In many countries, financial-economic experts enviously look at the Dutch independent, authoritative and expert Central Planning Bureau.

Budget discipline in the Netherlands

Before general elections, a regular procedure is that a 'study group on budget-room' produces a financial and economic advisory report. The study group consists of top officials from various ministries and from the Central Planning Bureau and the National Bank, and is headed by the Treasury General of the ministry of Finance. The study group works without interference from politics, and cabinet forwards the study group's advice to parliament without adding any commentary. The advice is a major financial-economic expert input for the coalition deliberations after the elections. The study group's April 2010 report contained major retrenchment proposals.

Another regular procedure before elections is that the Central Planning Bureau (CPB) publishes its economic forecast. The forecast in 2010 was that the budget deficit could rise to €29 billion. All political parties (except the left-Socialist and the right-populist parties) in their party programmes used this long-term figure, which therefore became leading in the political debate on cutbacks. Party programmes before elections are economically checked by the Central Planning Bureau. Another influential role of the Central Planning Bureau is that they economically check the financial outcomes of the final coalition agreement, that is, the financial attachment (which was probably more or less written by the Ministry of Finance).

Source: Kickert (2012d)

Office for Budget Responsibility in Great Britain

Alleged political massaging of economic forecasts by Labour led the new Conservative Chancellor Osborne to establish an independent Office for Budget Responsibility immediately after the 2010 elections. The OBR is chaired by an independent committee. Its staff, which, in the first months of its existence, were seconded from the Treasury, became employed by OBR itself. The reliability and credibility of its independent forecasts have become good.

Source: Kickert (2012b)

Also, in Germany, the fiscal crisis has led to a tightening of the budget procedure and an increase in the power of the Ministry of Finance.

Budget discipline in Germany

In order to ensure that the hard cutback measures for consolidating the fiscal crisis (Sparpaket) would not be jeopardised by subsequent political wheeling and dealing, Finance Minister Schäuble decided to tighten the German budget preparation procedure. The prior federal budget procedure was that politics had the first say, then external independent experts were consulted, then the Ministry of Economic Affairs would present an economic forecast. Next, the Finance Ministry had to work that out in budget proposals, which were debated in parliamentary special committees for budget and finance, and finally decided upon in parliament. The new 'top-down' procedure, which was announced in 2010, was to be that the Finance Ministry would annually start by presenting a fixed financial framework, and that the other ministries would subsequently make their estimates and plan their budgets within that predetermined framework. The Finance Ministry gained more central power to curb excessive spending of ministries.

The German Finance Minister at the time of the economic recovery packages had introduced a constitutional brake on state debts (Schuldenbremse) that enacted structurally balanced budgets for both the federal and regional 'Länder' governments as of 2016 and 2020, respectively.

Third, in 2010, a 'Stability Council' was established consisting of the federal Ministers of Finance and of Economic Affairs and the Finance Ministers of the 'Länder'. The council regularly was to monitor the budgets of the federal and regional governments based on a set of indicators.

Source: Kickert (2013b)

> ## Central Council of Trade and Industry
>
> In this council, employer organisations and trade unions deliberate about wage developments. Together with the National Labour Council, it publishes reports on the development of wages and employment. Annually, it reports the maximal margin of wage development in Belgium, thus setting the margins for the bi-annual negotiations between social partners. In late 2008, the social partners could not reach a compromise on wage increase because of the economic crisis, which was a main reason why the government made up a economic recovery plan in the first place. In late 2010, the bi-annual negotiations again failed. This time, the Prime Minister took over and imposed a wage norm by decree.
>
> *Source*: Kickert (2012c)

In Belgium, the budgetary procedure is explicitly politicised. Even the economic forecasts and figures are the outcome of political compromises between the government, employer organisations and trade unions. Belgium has a legal procedure of bi-annual negotiations between social partners about wage development.

In Belgium, budget discipline was only accomplished under external pressure from the IMF, EU and ECB. During the lengthy coalition formation, Belgium did not even have an approved annual budget, which did not go unnoticed by Standard & Poor's.

Our analysis shows that centralisation has been a common pattern in all fourteen European countries during fiscal consolidation. Centralisation can take different forms, but in most cases it has been related to the increase in the power of Ministries of Finance in the decision-making process, and also the other central decision-making bodies have been empowered during the crisis.

5.3 STAGES OF DECISION-MAKING

We now turn to the third core part of this chapter. After the extensive descriptions of the characteristics of decision-making in the two previous sections, this section presents in-depth country case studies of the stages of cutback decision-making.

Decision-making on fiscal consolidation and cutback measures was usually not a one-off event, but consisted of a series of decision-making stages. It seems likely that the decision-making over the fiscal cutbacks of the 2010s followed a similar trajectory as in the 1980s in most of the European countries (for an overview of the previous crisis period, see Raudla *et al.* 2013). The first cutback decisions in most countries took place in 2009–2010, and subsequent rounds of further cutbacks followed as the fiscal crisis persisted. In the 2012 update of the 2011 consolidation figures, the OECD (2012: 34) noted that most OECD countries had revised their previous consolidation plans, and had increased the volumes of fiscal consolidation.

At the beginning of the fiscal crisis, the decisions tended to be moderate and temporary, as the actors were unwilling to believe that the crisis and the need to undertake cuts were real. In many European countries, the first cutback plans met with protest and resistance from the political left, trade unions and other affected interest groups. Consequently, in many European countries, cuts were postponed, as the crisis was believed to be over soon (called the 'tooth fairy syndrome' by Levine 1979). Later, the decisions became less hesitant but still addressed rather small adjustments. Consequently, initial rounds of small and incremental cutbacks were undertaken in most European countries by 2010 (with Norway being a clear exception). Governments became aware that the crisis was more severe and persistent. Moreover, one could also argue that the initial (modest) cutbacks were among factors contributing to aggravating the crisis. Other stages of more serious cutbacks have followed, especially in countries hit the hardest by the crisis. This shows that in most European countries, it took several decision-making rounds before the gravity and duration of the crisis was fully comprehended and decisions came to be serious and resolute. In some countries, attempts to set political priorities and to arrive at more targeted cutback decisions were made.

Table 5.5 repeats the scheme of 'stages of decision-making' introduced in Chapter 3 about the 'analytical framework'.

The following country examples illustrate various stages of cutback decision-making in selected European countries. Adhering to the scheme on stages of

TABLE 5.5 Stages of cutback decision-making (repeated from Chapter 3)

Stages of cutback decision-making	Types of cutback measures
Denial. Defend advantages of present situation. Unconvinced of gravity and duration of crisis.	Temporary small measures. Moderate adjustment to status quo. Cuts postponed.
Compliance with the need for cutbacks.	First attempt at serious cutbacks.
Internalised need for cutbacks. Action. Resolute cutback decisions.	First across-the-board and efficiency cuts. Later targeted downsizing and cuts of public tasks. Ultimately fundamental political priority-setting.

cutback decision-making presented in Table 5.5, we pay particular attention to the two following aspects:

- the increasing volume of cutback measures in subsequent stages – from small and moderate to serious and large; and
- the changing type of decision-making in subsequent stages – from incremental and across-the-board to targeted and political priority-setting.

First, we present the example of the Netherlands, where the cutback decision-making indeed followed the pattern describe above: initial postponement of cutback decisions, a first fiscal consolidation package consisting of small and gradual cuts, and later consolidation stages with more serious cutbacks and even first attempts at targeted cuts based on political priority-setting.

Second, we present the case of Slovenia, where fiscal consolidation also consisted of many stages. At first, only modest cutbacks were applied. Later, serious fiscal consolidation was proposed, but voted down in a referendum, leading to early elections that resulted in a right-wing coalition that took drastic and structural measures, though still predominantly of the across-the-board type.

Third, the stages of fiscal consolidation in Lithuania are presented. In Lithuania, the initial cuts were broad-based and across-the-board, but later some targeted reductions in different programme categories were adopted. Despite the large cuts, the changes remained small and gradual, and many of them were legally defined as temporary.

Fourth, we present the Estonian case, where the size of cutbacks did not increase in successive stages, but rather diminished as the cuts were front-loaded: the largest cuts were applied right at the beginning of the crisis. Despite the large size of the cuts, the decision-making was mainly of the across-the-board proportional cuts type.

Finally, we present two examples of countries that had to seek external assistance for bail-outs, Ireland and Iceland. In those countries, there was no room for initial crisis denial, postponement of cuts or temporary measures. The severity of the crisis was quickly recognised by the governments. The conditions for the loan program of the Troika in Ireland, and the loan by the IMF in Iceland, forced governments to immediate and drastic fiscal consolidation. Despite the enormous size of the cutbacks, the decision-making in both countries was predominantly of the across-the-board proportional cuts type.

The Netherlands

In the previous section, the political decision-making about the first stage of consolidation in 2010 was described. Fiscal consolidation in the Netherlands involved three stages.

Stages of cutback decisions in the Netherlands

Fiscal consolidation in the Netherlands involved three stages: the October 2010 coalition agreement, the April 2012 spring agreement and the October 2012 coalition agreement.

In the Netherlands, politically sensitive decisions about cutbacks were postponed until after the 2010 general elections. Although in 2009 it was already clear that the huge costs of the banking bail-outs and the costs of the economic recovery package were to be compensated by major cutbacks, the Christian-Social Democrat cabinet at the time refused to do so in view of the approaching general elections. The first October 2010 consolidation package was the budgetary outcome of the formation of a new multi-party coalition after the May 2010 elections, as described in the previous section. The new Liberal-Christian Democrat coalition, which had a parliamentary minority and was supported in parliament by the right-wing populist Freedom Party, agreed upon an €18 billion cutback package. The fiscal consolidation package was a patchwork of political compromises comprising a variety of small and gradual across-the-board steps.

Because of negative economic and budgetary forecasts, the Liberal and Christian Democrat coalition partners and the supporting Freedom Party in March 2012 started negotiations about an extra €14 billion cutback package. After six weeks, the Freedom Party leader Wilders left the negotiation table, withdrawing his support for the cutbacks and also his support of the coalition cabinet. Early general elections were called. Immediately after the fall of the cabinet, three small opposition parties – the ecologist Green Left Party, the progressive Liberal Party and the Christian Union – took the initiative to reach an agreement on cutbacks necessary to fulfil the European 3 per cent deficit norm, which they surprisingly succeeded to do within a couple of days. Together with the coalition parties, this resulted in the April 2012 five-party agreement on €14 billion of cutback measures to consolidate the 2013 budget. This event was highly exceptional and unique in Dutch political history. Dutch consensual politics invariably lead to eternal deliberations, endless compromise seeking and lengthy decision-making. Now, suddenly, three small opposition parties, in a few days, together in unity, reached a joint agreement on €14 billion of cutbacks. Both the speed and the extent of the decision-making were an incredible accomplishment in the sluggish and lingering Dutch political habits. The cutback package contained several decisions on politically sensitive issues. The pension age would be increased. The Employment Act was to be reformed. The deduction of housing mortgage interests, a vital issue for home-owners long considered a political taboo, was to be restricted. The first signs of targeted cuts were based on political priority-setting.

The September 2012 early general elections resulted in the conservative Liberals (VVD) and the Social Democrats (PvdA) becoming the two largest parties. The two ideologically opposite parties started coalition negotiations, and surprisingly it only took half a month to reach a budget agreement and another month to finalise the October 2012 coalition agreement. One of the main reasons for this quick outcome was a deliberate change in decision-making procedure by the negotiators. Instead of both parties endlessly searching for intricate compromises on every single policy issue, which was expectedly troublesome in view of the two opposing ideologies, the two parties more or less swapped policy issues. In exchange for one issue to be gained by one party, the other party acquired another issue in return. No endless negotiations at the many side tables of the coalition formation by numerous party specialists, but just a quick exchange of cards between the two informers, the two party leaders, and their two adjutants. The two party leaders, Rutte (VVD) and Samsom (PvdA), were both youthful and energetic, and eager to show that they together could break through the usual Dutch political viscosity. Dutch coalition formations normally took ages; both the speed and the extent of the decision-making were again unprecedented. The Budget agreement contained several politically sensitive issues – income-dependent measures for health care insurance were introduced; the deduction of housing mortgage interests was further restricted; the student bursary system was to be abolished and replaced by a loan system; again, attempts at targeted cuts were based on political priorities.

Source: Kickert (2013c)

The Dutch example neatly illustrates the hypothesised scheme of stages of cutback decisions. At first, cutbacks were postponed, and the first cutback stage consisted of a patchwork of small and gradual decisions. Later, more serious attempts were made at spending cuts, not only in the size of the cuts, but also in the type of political decision-making. It became more swift and drastic, and first attempts at targeted cuts based on political priorities were made. Politically targeted cuts reflected some of the fundamental cutback proposals made by the 'reconsideration working groups' in 2010, which at the time had little or no impact on political decision-making (see first section of Chapter 5). These now turned out to have a marked effect on political priorities, although not publicly accredited.

The new 2012 Liberal-Social Democrat coalition had a majority in parliament, but only a minority in the senate, which has the right of consent in legislation. The coalition cabinet therefore had to reach consensus with opposition parties on virtually every major political policy issue.

Slovenia

Stages of cutback decisions in Slovenia

After the Autumn 2008 general elections, a left-wing coalition led by the Social Democrats was formed in November 2008 when the financial crisis peaked and the economy showed signs of downturn. The coalition agreement, which was based on positive economic forecasts, immediately had to be adapted to the imminent crisis.

In December 2008, a first anti-crisis package was devised that chiefly consisted of stimulus measures to boost the economy. The second February 2009 anti-crisis package contained both stimulus measures to recover the economy and reductions in public expenditures. The public-sector cuts consisted of withholding wage increases, a reduction of state employment, a reduction of subcontracting and a reduction of basic salaries. The increase of individual social transfers and pensions was limited. These small and gradual measures were accepted by trade unions and employers. In the April 2009 Stability Program and September 2009 Intervention Act, the government postponed wage settlements for public servants and introduced a wage freeze. Nevertheless, the measures undertaken in 2009 were relatively mild.

Real fiscal consolidation was only undertaken in 2010. In February 2010, the government announced further spending cuts to be realised by efficiency gains. In May 2010, measures were taken to cut public procurement expenditures. The September 2010 Intervention Act announced that spending on wages, pensions and social transfers would be frozen. Actually, it only limited the increases. In April 2011, structural reforms were planned, but although the pension and labour market reforms were approved in parliament, they were voted down in a referendum, and the government was forced to implement only moderate measures.

Because of the government's inability to successfully manage the crisis, which was ongoing and even deepening, its inability to implement structural reforms, its failing dialog with social partners, and low public support, early general elections were held in November 2011, which the incumbent government lost. In February 2012, a new coalition government was formed led by the right-wing Democratic Party. Downsizing the public sector became its priority by combining fiscal austerity with structural reforms. The May 2012 Fiscal Balance Act aimed at major cost-cutting of public-sector salaries and employment, and was based on prior negotiations with social partners. Fiscal consolidation in 2012 became more radical and systematic.

In January 2013, accusations of corruption against leading government politicians somewhat stopped new cutbacks, leading to the restructuring of the government, with a new coalition of mainly left-wing parties formed in March 2013.

Source: Pevcin (2013)

Fiscal consolidation in Slovenia during the period 2008–2012 was managed by two different governments and involved a long series of successive consolidation measures.

Fiscal consolidation decision-making in Slovenia indeed consisted of many stages. Although the first stages comprised some cutback measures, they remained modest. Only in 2010 was serious fiscal consolidation truly addressed. However, the drastic structural reforms proposed by the government were voted down in a referendum. The lack of public and social support forced the government to call early elections, which resulted in a new right-wing coalition. Fiscal consolidation finally became more drastic and structural.

Although the cutbacks in the successive stages became larger and more drastic, there were no indicators that the type of political decision-making shifted from across-the-board and efficiency gains towards targeted cuts based on fundamental political priority-setting.

Lithuania

During the economic boom years in Lithuania, both the ruling majority and the opposition had agreed to massively expand public-sector spending (wages and social security) before the 2008 elections to show their generosity to the voters. The incumbent left-wing government had, for several months, been denying that Lithuania would be affected by the crisis.

Fiscal consolidation in Lithuania consisted of several stages. The timing and contents of the rounds of cutbacks were politically influenced. The fact that, in 2009, two rounds of cutbacks took place within two months was due to the presidential elections. The consolidation decision-making at the end of 2008 was extremely swift. The tax reform was even dubbed 'the night reform' as important decisions were literally made overnight. In Lithuania, the cuts were initially across-the-board, but later some targeted reductions in different programme categories were adopted. Despite the large cuts, the changes remained small and gradual, and many of them were legally defined as temporary. Despite the large size of the cutbacks, major structural reforms did not occur, and the ones that occurred had a fragmented nature and were implemented incrementally.

Estonia

In Estonia, fiscal consolidation was relatively large and front-loaded.

In Estonia, fiscal consolidation took place in several stages. However, the size of the cutbacks did not increase during the successive rounds as the most severe cuts were applied right at the outset. In the period following the three cutback packages of 2008 and 2009, no further consolidation measures were taken. Actually, Estonia withdrew from consolidation and redressed the cutbacks so

Stages of cutback decisions in Lithuania

The October 2008 general elections took place at the height of the financial crisis and the beginning of the economic downfall. The newly formed December 2008 Conservative-Liberal coalition government was immediately confronted with the worsening economic outlook and looming budget deficit. Lithuania, together with the other Baltic states, was among the most severely hit economies in the world, with a GDP decline of 15 per cent in 2009.

The new right-wing government, at the end of 2008, adopted a package consisting of spending cuts, tax increases and measures to restore economic growth, together with a list of long-term structural reforms. The tax reforms were very swiftly drafted and adopted, more or less overnight. More than sixty legislative changes were very quickly adopted in parliament, and more than 100 tax rules were enacted only weeks after their adoption. The firm stance of the Lithuanian government on strict fiscal consolidation was partly explained by its desire to access the Eurozone.

In 2009, three rounds of cutbacks in government expenditures took place. The May 2009 plans involved 6 per cent cuts on state budgets and 16 per cent cuts for county administrations. Sensitive wage reductions for public servants were postponed until after the presidential elections, which were won by someone supported by two of the coalition parties. The second July 2009 round, after the presidential elections, involved more targeted cuts in public-sector wages. The third December 2009 round involved further public-sector wage cuts and cuts in pensions, maternity and unemployment benefits (which were considerably raised in the years before).

The annual budget approved in December 2011 contained a further reduction of all state expenditures. These further cuts were made necessary because, at the end of 2011, authorities had decided to expire the 2009 pension cuts, restoring pre-crisis pension levels. This decision was publicly supported by the Lithuanian president as an anti-poverty measure and promoted by the leading Homeland Union Party as an appeal to its electorate before the upcoming general elections in autumn 2012.

In 2009, some parties left the coalition government so that, during its four-year term, it balanced on the verge of parliamentary minority. It managed to adopt decisions in parliament mainly because of the lack of mobilisation from the opposition. The relative lack of public protest was related to the habit of living in conditions of instability during the last two decades, as well as the relative weakness of trade unions.

Source: Nakrosis *et al.* (2013)

Stages of cutback decisions in Estonia

Estonia was among the first European countries that implemented immediate and radical cutbacks at the outset of the crisis in 2008. Fiscal consolidation in Estonia comprised three stages, that is, three successive negative budgetary supplements in June 2008, February 2009 and June 2009.

In order to prepare for the first supplementary budget, the cabinet opted for across-the-board cutbacks in the first supplementary budget because all ministries defended their own interests in the cabinet. The spending cuts were considerable, though. Expenditures in nearly all policy sectors were cut by 7 per cent. Nearly half of the expenditure cuts were about operational costs, mainly by curtailing personnel expenditures through dismissals, salary cuts, work-time reduction and lay-offs. Operational cuts amounted to considerable lay-offs in ministries, ranging from 10 to 25 per cent.

In preparation for the second supplementary budget, the government again installed an informal budgetary working group, again consisting of Members of Parliament and ministers from each of the three coalition parties. Moreover, an expert committee was established of three economics professors and the deputy Governor of the Bank of Estonia. The second supplementary budget was very rapidly rushed through parliament, placing the opposition parties off-side. An additional 7 per cent cut in operational expenditures was applied, and despite the lay-offs being less than in 2008, civil service salaries were further diminished.

The preparation of the third negative supplementary budget intensified political conflict and tensions. The Social Democrats left the coalition in May 2009, reducing the coalition to a parliamentary minority. The third supplementary budget was approved in parliament due to a bargain of the minority coalition with the Green Party. This third budget introduced major changes at the revenue side, with a number of considerable increases in taxes, excise duties and fees.

Source: Savi and Randma-Liiv (2013)

that the total fiscal consolidation volume dropped from 9.2 per cent in 2009 to 2.6 per cent in 2015 (OECD 2012: 36, 111). Despite the 2008 and 2009 cutbacks having a considerable size, the decision-making was predominantly of the across-the-board proportional cuts type. Although some targeted cuts were applied in the later years of fiscal crisis, the decision-making did not reach a stage of fundamental political priority-setting. The speed of cutback decision-making was high. The supplementary budgets were very rapidly pushed through parliament, even when the coalition became a minority.

Ireland

Ireland was deeply affected by the financial and economic crisis, and more specifically the Eurozone crisis. The collapse in revenue and increase in debt that followed the banking crisis resulted in the state entering an IMF-EU-ECB (Troika) loan programme in November 2010. The cost of bank bail-outs amounted to some 40 per cent of GDP with a deficit of 31.2 per cent in 2010 and state debt increasing by more than 70 per cent. Severe austerity measures were inevitable, as well as being conditions for the Troika's loan programme.

There is no evidence of remarkable crisis denial, postponement of cuts or temporary measures applied. The severity of the crisis was quickly recognised by the government and cemented by the Troika loan programme, leading to a combination of spending cuts and increased taxation. The path of fiscal consolidation followed the usual route of annually increasing volumes (OECD 2012: 160), though. Although the size of the cutbacks was considerable – a staggering 17.9 per cent of GDP, by far the highest fiscal consolidation volume of all European countries we investigated (OECD 2012) – the decision-making seems to have been of the across-the-board type mainly, although the capital cuts were targeted at specific sectors.

The speed of the cutback decision-making was high from the outset of the crisis. There is no evidence that the decision-making became more rapid during later cutback stages. Otherwise, it must be that the acceptance by the general population of the undiminished crisis and cutbacks decreased, and that social agreements with trade unions were made to secure the government's legitimacy, pointing at a gradual slowdown of decision-making.

Iceland

The oversized banking sector in Iceland, whose total assets counted ten times the Icelandic GDP, was hit hard by the global financial crisis in October 2008. The three main banks, representing 85 per cent of the financial sector, fell within days of each other. Due to the size of the banking sector, a domestic bail-out by the Icelandic government was impossible. The government could do nothing but seek assistance from the International Monetary Fund (IMF).

The severe banking crisis in Iceland in October 2008 did not leave room for crisis denial, postponement of consolidation measures or temporary solutions. The cutback decisions were swift and drastic. But despite the enormity of the cutbacks, the decisions were predominantly of the across-the-board proportional type and did not shift in later stages to targeted cuts based on political priorities.

Table 5.6 summarises the stages of cutback decision-making country by country.

Stages of cutback decisions in Ireland

Between July 2008 and spring 2012, Ireland had eight stages of fiscal consolidation: in July 2008, expenditure adjustments (efficiency cuts) of £1 billion were made; in October 2008, the Budget for 2009 (£2 billion); in February 2009, again expenditure adjustments (£2.1 billion); in April 2009, a supplementary budget (£5.4 billion); and in December 2009, 2010 and 2011, the annual budgets for the following years were made, resulting in a total fiscal adjustment of £20.8 billion over the period 2008–2011.

In October 2008, as part of the Budget for 2009, a wide range of taxes was increased to curb the sharp decline in revenues since 2007. The first round of spending cuts relied upon efficiency cuts, moving to across-the-board measures in operational expenditures (e.g. recruitment embargo across all sectors, cuts to public-sector pay as a 'pension levy', pay freeze), and from there to targeted capital cuts particularly affecting the health services, environment and transportation sectors. Capital spending was halved over the 2008–2011 period. Current spending mostly consisted of the public service wage bill. Due to the economic decline and rising unemployment the social security expenditures sharply increased. Public-sector wage increases scheduled for payment in 2009 were cancelled. In 2009, public-sector wages were cut again. But in December 2010, the government agreed with the trade unions (Croke Park agreement) that public-sector employees would not suffer any further direct cuts to their pay, in exchange for cooperation with structural changes. Public-sector employment has seen a marked decline since 2008, mainly realised by voluntary and early retirement. In early 2013, as further savings became necessary, the government renegotiated the Croke Park agreement with trade unions, proposing pay cuts, increased working hours, reductions in overtime pay and restructuring pay grades. The 'Croke Park II' agreement was, however, rejected in a ballot of the public-sector unions.

The February 2011 general elections resulted in a collapse of the conservative Fianna Fáil Party, which had been in power since 1997, and in a large majority coalition of the main centre-right and centre-left parties (Fine Gael and the Labour Party). Despite the participation of Labour in the new government, the stance to retrenchments did not change significantly. The Labour Party assumed the responsibility for the department responsible for the administrative reforms and cost-saving programme.

Source: MacCarthaigh and Hardiman (2013)

Stages of cutback decisions in Iceland

The government's initial response to the banking crisis was to pass an Emergency Act in October 2008 and seek assistance from the International Monetary Fund (IMF). According to the Emergency Act, the Financial Supervisory Authority was granted extraordinary powers to seize insolvent banks and restructure them. The three major banks were nationalised and divided into 'new' domestic banks and 'old' (bad asset) banks, thus keeping the domestic banking system functioning.

The Stand-By-Agreement with the IMF was to secure the external financing of the recovery programme. It was to stabilise the Icelandic currency (Króna), much needed because most company and state debt was in foreign (currency) hands. Second, it was to ensure fiscal sustainability by increasing revenues and cutting government expenditures. Third, the banking sector was to be completely restructured. The IMF programme highly restricted the options available to the Icelandic government.

In January 2009, fierce protests against the government broke out in Reykjavik (the so-called 'pots-and-pans revolution'). The Social Democrats demanded a change in the coalition leadership, where the conservative Independence Party held the reigns, bringing down the coalition and replacing it by a minority coalition of Social Democrats and Left Greens. New elections were called for in April 2009 that resulted in an absolute majority for the two parties, the country's first ever left-wing majority government, with an all-encompassing program of reform aimed at creating a Nordic welfare society in Iceland. The left-wing government was, however, bound by the fiscal consolidations agreed upon with the IMF, consisting of both tax increases and expenditure cuts. The cutback decision-making was swift and drastic. The Icelandic government opted for a prevalence of across-the-board cheese-slicing proportional cuts over targeted ones. The great ambitions of the left-wing government to completely reform politics and society failed to realise. The enormous burden the fiscal consolidation measures agreed upon with the IMF placed upon personal households and debts (e.g. mortgages in foreign currency), dominated the 2013 election campaign. Although a majority of the voters positively evaluated the government's handling of the crisis in a 2013 opinion poll, the Social Democrats and Left Greens suffered a crushing defeat in the April 2013 elections. The IMF program was completed in 2013.

Source: Kristinsson (2013)

TABLE 5.6 Stages of cutback decisions

	BEL	GER	EST	ESP	FRA	HUN	IRL	ISL	ITA	LTU	NLD	SLO	GBR
Temporary small measures	2009	–	–	–	–	–	October 2008	2009	2009	–	February 2009	February 2009	2009
Moderate adjustments	2009–2011	–	–	–	–	–	December 2008	–	2009	–	February 2009	April 2009	2009
First attempts at cutbacks	2009	–	–	June 2008	2010	–	April 2009	2009	2010	–	October 2010	April 2009	2009
Resolute cutback decisions	2012	June 2010	June 2008	May 2010	2012	June 2010	December 2009	2009–2010	2011	December 2008	October 2012	May 2012	2010
Fundamental priority-setting	–	–	–	December 2011	–	–	December 2010	2009	–	–	October 2012	May 2012	2010

European countries passed through different crisis-related decision-making stages at varying paces. As a rule of thumb, countries hit the hardest by the crisis reached the later stages of decision-making faster. The majority of European countries followed a gradual development from crisis denial, to temporary to moderate measures, leading finally to more radical cutbacks (if necessary). With the exception of Germany, virtually no country could escape the measure to freeze hiring and pay, and to set caps on replacements. The latter resembles the responses to the fiscal crisis of the 1980s, when this was typically the first modest step in curbing administrative expenditures. It was only in the later stages of further mounting budgetary deficits that governments were forced to introduce politically much more contested measures of actually reducing wages and employment. Cutbacks were made in several rounds, with the measures increasing in severity.

There were also exceptions to this general pattern. First, the Estonian and Lithuanian governments decisively skipped modest measures and opted quickly after the outset of the crisis for resolute cutbacks. Second, those European countries that had to request financial assistance from the IMF, EU and ECB, such as Iceland, Ireland, Italy and Spain, received the bail-outs and other support on the condition that the public-sector wage bill was reduced, leading to far more than only hiring and pay freeze, that is, to substantial cuts in public-sector salaries and employment. The conditionality of the Troika forced governments swiftly towards radical cutback measures without giving the governments leeway in delaying cuts and slowly introducing more modest cutback measures.

General conclusions of this chapter

In this chapter, we presented the empirical data on the political aspects of fiscal consolidation. As explained in Chapter 2, we concentrated on the political decision-making of governments about consolidation. First, we distinguished different characteristics of the political decision-making, as explained in Chapter 3 about the analytical framework:

- size and speed of the political decision-making; and
- across-the-board versus targeted decision-making.

We presented a survey of these characteristics from the country case studies carried out in the COCOPS project, and presented a number of country examples that illustrated more in-depth the specificity of the political decision-making in several European countries, including the United Kingdom, where large and swift cutbacks occurred; France, where they were to be expected, but did not occur; Estonia, where the cutbacks were huge and immediate; and the three consensual countries, Germany, the Netherlands and Belgium, where swift and large decisions were hardly possible.

Second, our analysis confirmed that centralisation was an overwhelming pattern in all fourteen European countries during fiscal consolidation. In most cases, it was related to the increase in the power of Ministries of Finance on national-level decision-making, and of budgetary units on organisational-level decision-making. This presents an interesting paradox since the prevailing across-the-board cuts should theoretically assume a shift towards decentralised decision-making, but in fact they are coupled with increased centralisation. It is still too early to conclude whether a shift towards centralisation is only a temporary change related to consolidation decision-making or if it leads to a longer-term trend in Public Administration.

Third, we distinguished different stages of the decision-making and observed the following:

- the size and speed of the cutback measures increased in the subsequent stages – from small and slow, to large and swift; and
- the types of decision-making changed in subsequent stages – from incremental and across-the-board, to targeted and political priority-setting.

The empirical analysis confirmed that most European countries indeed passed through such stages, albeit at a varying pace, and with a few exceptions. Countries that had received external financial assistance usually were obliged by the moneylenders to immediately realise hard and swift cutbacks, leaving no room for denial, delay and postponement.

We now turn to the analysis of these empirical observations in the next two chapters, the search for possible explanations of the fiscal consolidation in Chapter 6, and the investigation of the effects of consolidation in Chapter 7.

Part three

Causes and effects of fiscal consolidation

Explanations of fiscal consolidation

In this chapter, possible explanations for the fiscal consolidation undertaken by European governments are considered from three perspectives.

First, the consolidation measures are explained from a financial-economic perspective. Fiscal consolidation was primarily a response to the deteriorating economy and public finances. The measures taken to reduce the budget deficit and curb the further accumulation of state debt therefore primarily depended on the 'financial size' of the economic and fiscal crisis. After presenting an overview of the extent of the economic crisis and of the fiscal crisis, we subsequently consider the 'financial size' of the fiscal consolidation measures in the various European countries, and quantitatively investigate whether consolidation was correlated with the extent of the fiscal crisis. Second, we turn our attention to possible explanations of the governments' fiscal consolidation by means of political factors. As announced in Chapter 3 about the analytical framework, the political factors considered are the state system (unitary, decentralised, federal), the political system (majoritarian, consensus), the government system (one-party cabinet, multi-party coalition cabinet), the political orientation of government (left, centre, right) and the margin of parliamentary majority (grand, simple, minority). In line with the methodological pluralism favoured by the authors, in our explanations we alternate between qualitative case studies and quantitative analysis.

Third, we pay attention to supra-national explanatory factors, that is, circumstances that were beyond the influence of domestic governments. Besides the obvious major influence of the worldwide economic developments on domestic economy and public finances, we pay particular attention to the European influences on the domestic fiscal consolidations, not only the regular influence of the EU Maastricht Treaty ceilings on budget deficit and state debt, but also the influence of the extraordinary circumstances of the Eurozone crisis and bail-outs by the IMF, ECB and EU. As mentioned before, in this book we do not separately investigate the fiscal measures and decision-making at the European Union level, but we do consider those influences of utmost importance.

6.1 ECONOMIC EXPLANATIONS

The 'financial size' of the fiscal consolidation plans of a government obviously depends on the 'financial size' of the economic and fiscal crisis in a country. Countries with larger economic imbalances and deeper deterioration of public finances require larger fiscal consolidation. In other words, economic and fiscal indicators such as GDP growth, gross debt and budget deficit affect the size of fiscal consolidation. In this section, we show that this economic line of argument is not only true in a normative prescriptive sense, but is also empirically valid.

Here, we therefore begin by presenting some macro-economic indicators for the selected countries, in order to characterise the depth of the crisis. From an economic perspective, the economic and fiscal data before and during the crisis indicate the degree of the economic and fiscal crisis, but the economic and particularly the fiscal data after the outset of the crisis are also important indicators of a country's performance in managing the fiscal crisis. Although the influence of a domestic government's fiscal consolidation plan on its GDP growth rate and unemployment can be questioned, gross debt and especially budget deficit can be considered as indicators of a government's consolidation efforts. In Chapter 7, on effects of fiscal consolidation, we pay attention to the latter subject.

Figure 6.1 offers an overview of the GDP growth rate in the selected European countries. Among the countries included in this book, the GDP started to decline in 2006 in Estonia and Hungary when they faced a 3-percentage-point drop after an unprecedented boom following the accession to the EU. The fast economic growth in Central and Eastern Europe was fuelled by cheap credits available through foreign-owned banks, which increased domestic demand and were channelled into real estate, financial services and private consumption. This was accompanied by an overheating of the economy, a soaring current account deficit, high inflation, a housing boom and accelerating wage growth, but slow gains in productivity (Kattel and Raudla 2013). In several Central and Eastern European countries, the domestic bubbles burst already in early 2008, which was further aggravated by negative developments in the external economic environment after the Lehman Brothers' bankruptcy.

After the 2008 banking crisis, which accelerated the economic decline, the low point was reached in 2009, when all the studied countries faced negative growth – more than 14 per cent in Estonia and Lithuania, more than 5 per cent in Germany, Hungary, Iceland, Ireland, Italy and Slovenia, and less than 5 per cent in Belgium, France, the Netherlands, Norway, Spain and the United Kingdom. By 2010, most countries had recovered, with only Iceland, Ireland and Spain still having a negative growth rate. In most of the countries, the GDP increased up to 2011 and then dropped again; in others, the second decrease had started already in 2010.

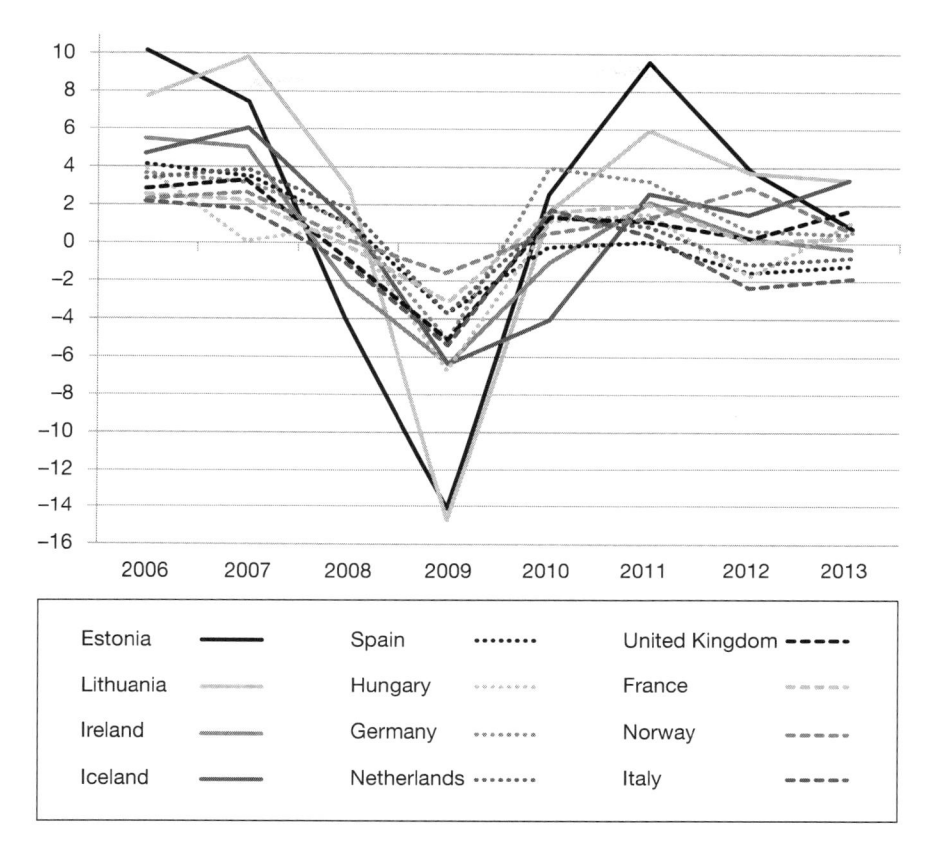

FIGURE 6.1 GDP growth 2006–2013 (per cent of GDP)

In all European countries, the budget surplus/deficit underwent a sharp deterioration in 2008–2009 after the costly bank rescue measures during the banking crisis, and recovered afterwards (see Figure 6.2). During the peak years of the crisis, only Norway retained a general government surplus, as it was only slightly hit by the global financial and economic crisis due to its North Sea gas and oil revenues. The budget deterioration was the most abrupt and steep in Iceland due to the sudden and complete collapse of its overly large banking sector and the consequent collapse of its economy. In Chapter 5, the Icelandic rescue operation with the IMF loan programme was described. The budget deficit deterioration was by far the hardest and deepest in Ireland, which was so severely affected by the financial and economic crisis, and specifically by the Eurozone crisis, that it had to be bailed out by the IMF, EU and ECB. The enormous costs of the Irish bank bail-outs amounted to some 40 per cent of its GDP, causing a staggering deficit of more than 30 per cent in 2010.

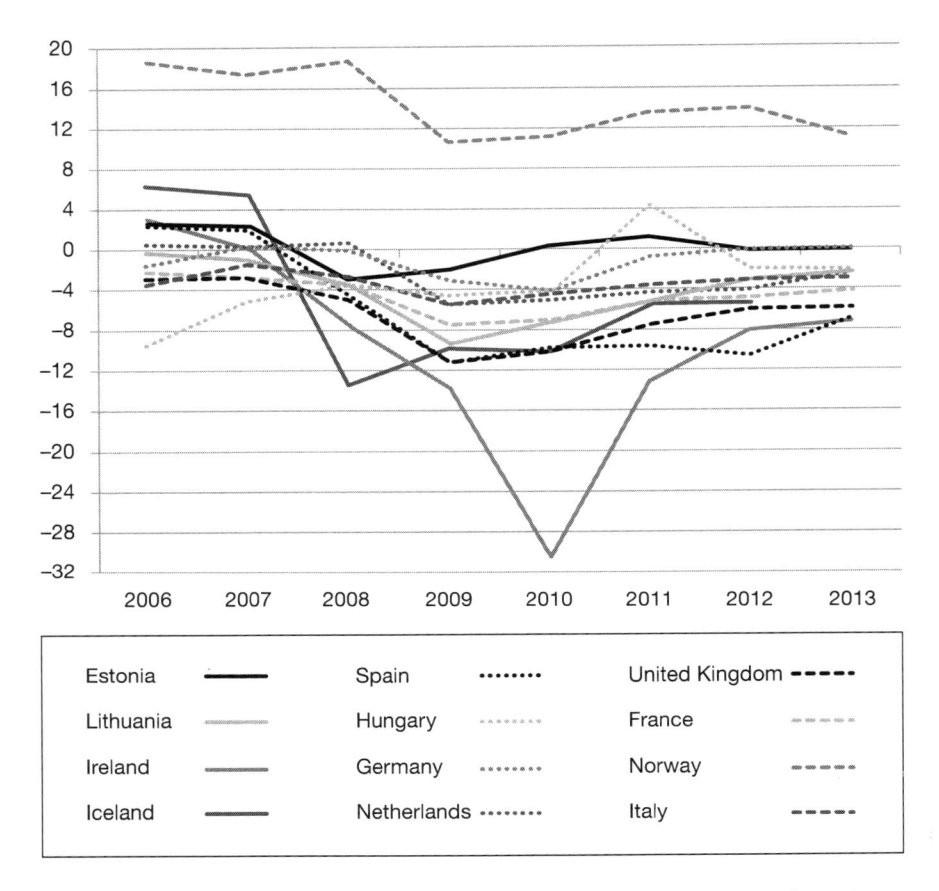

FIGURE 6.2 General government surplus/deficit 2006–2013 (per cent of GDP)

In most of the countries, the government gross debt started to rise from 2007 onwards, and continued to grow up until 2012 (see Figure 6.3). Ireland and Iceland stand out in this respect, as in 2007–2012 the countries' governments' gross debt increased by 93 and 75 percentage points, respectively. The sharp increase in deficit was due to the governments' financial assistance to the banks, which was officially recorded as sovereign debt. Also, the United Kingdom and Spain had a remarkable debt growth of about 45 percentage points, whereas most of the other governments faced a debt growth between 12 and 27 percentage points. Estonia has shown a rather stable trend with the lowest government gross debt in Europe, while Norway, thanks to its oil and gas reserves, has even decreased its gross debt during the period from 55 to 29 per cent.

Table 6.1 presents the volume of the fiscal consolidation plans in the selected countries, as presented in the OECD (2012) survey. The OECD defined fiscal

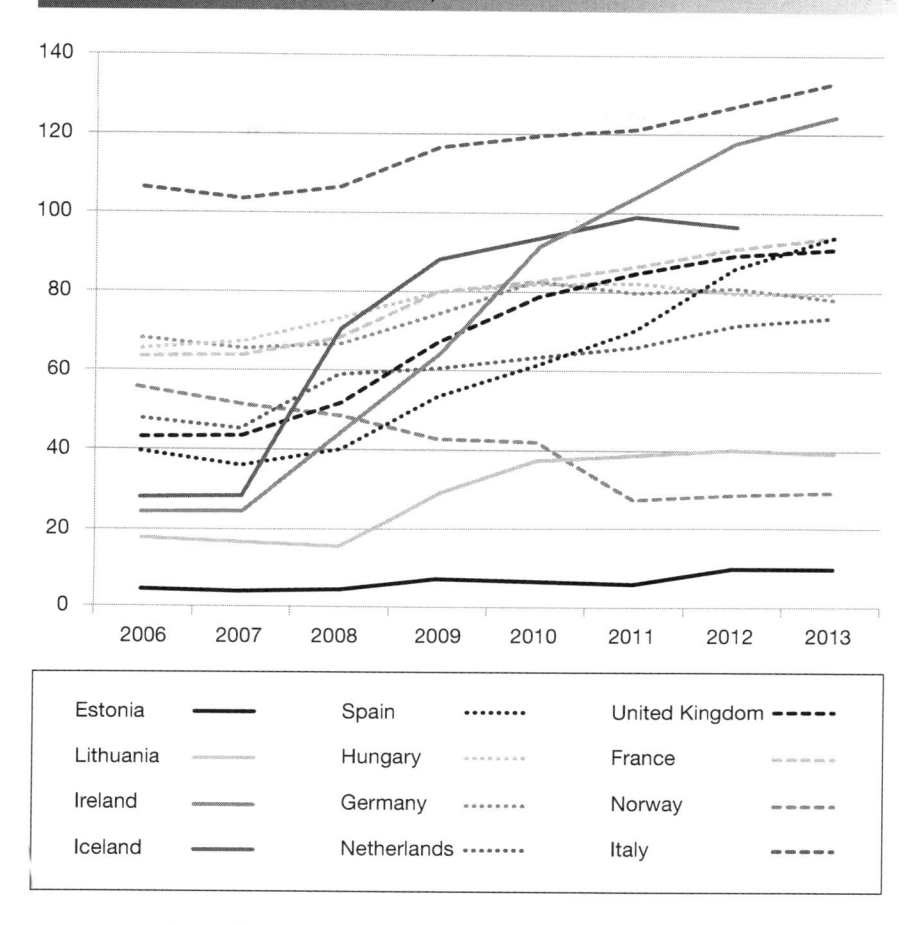

FIGURE 6.3 General government gross debt 2006–2013 (per cent of GDP)

consolidation as 'concrete and active policies aimed at reducing government deficits and debt accumulation', not mere announcements of targets without specific plans. The survey was based on self-reporting by governments, that is, data reported by the various governments in response to a questionnaire sent out to countries in December 2011 by the OECD Senior Budget Officials Group. The timescale of fiscal consolidation plans in most countries was limited to 2015. The data on 2009–2011 refer to implemented consolidation, and the later data about projected consolidation were presented with a cumulative impact over the consolidation period (OECD 2012: 3; some of the missing data had to be recalculated by the OECD secretariat).

The data show that the consolidation plans were generally back-loaded, that is, the measures were annually growing and the maximum consolidation efforts were postponed, with the exception of Estonia, where the consolidation plans were front-loaded, meaning that the maximum effort took place right at the

TABLE 6.1 Fiscal consolidation volumes (per cent of GDP)

	2009 (%)	2010 (%)	2011 (%)	2012 (%)	2013 (%)	2014 (%)	2015 (%)
Belgium		0.4	0.8	3.4	3.8	4.3	
Estonia	9.2	6.4	3.7	3.1	3.1	3.0	2.6
France			1.1	2.5	3.2	3.7	4.2
Germany			0.5	2.0	2.5	3.0	
Hungary		4.1	4.5	7.6	7.6	8.2	8.2
Iceland		3.6	6.2	7.9	8.5	8.9	9.1
Ireland	5.9	8.8	12.8	14.8	16.5	17.6	17.9
Italy			0.9	4.3	5.9	6.1	
Netherlands			0.3	1.0	1.7	2.4	2.9
Spain		2.7		5.7	7.1	7.3	
Slovenia		2.6	3.8	4.5	5.3	6.0	
United Kingdom		0.6	2.8	3.8	5.1	6.1	7.1

Note: Lithuania is not an OECD member, and is therefore not included in this OECD survey. Nakrosis *et al.* (2013) reported that Lithuania had a fiscal consolidation plan of 5.5 per cent GDP in 2011. Figures following the OECD format are not available.

Source: Derived from country profiles in OECD (2012)

outset of the crisis. As mentioned before, the main explanation for this exceptionally swift and drastic consolidation is that Estonia strongly desired access to the Eurozone, and therefore the government clearly and convincingly complied with the EU deficit and debt ceilings. After 2009, Estonia withdrew from consolidation (OECD 2012: 36). So, the 2015 accumulated volume of consolidation in Estonia, in the end, was relatively low.

The data show that the governments' consolidation efforts tended to slowly increase over the period, with the exception of a rather sudden increase in consolidation efforts in 2011–2012 in Belgium and Hungary. In Belgium after the general elections of 2010, the coalition formation lasted eighteen months and the caretaker government was not allowed to take drastic consolidation measures, so the new coalition agreement of November 2011 was the first serious step towards consolidation. In Hungary, the sudden step forward in consolidation can be explained by the landslide victory in the 2010 general elections of the right-wing party FIDESZ, winning a grand parliamentary majority, and therefore capable of pushing through the severe cutbacks it favoured.

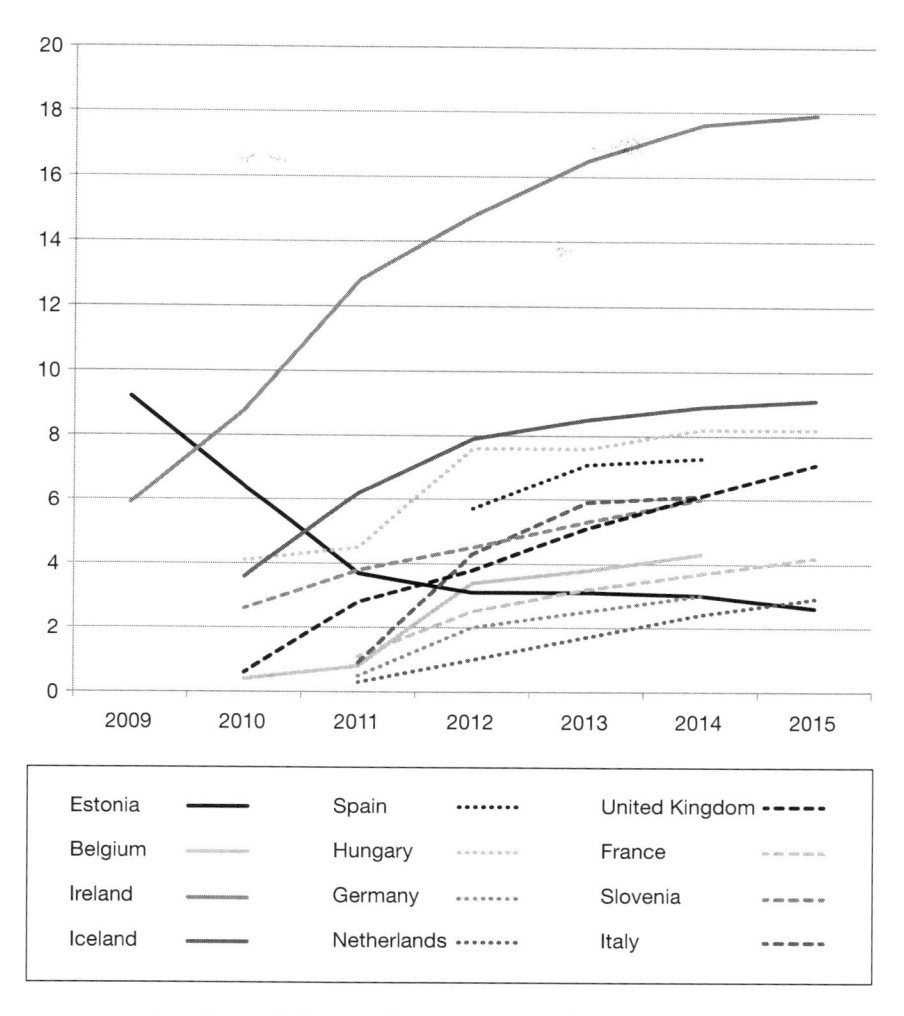

FIGURE 6.4 Fiscal consolidation volumes (per cent of GDP)

Figure 6.5 ranks the countries in order of the volume of their accumulated fiscal consolidation plans in 2015.

The highest consolidation effort took place in Ireland, where the fiscal crisis was so high that it had to be bailed out by the IMF-EU-ECB Troika in November 2010. The costs of the Irish bank bail-outs were enormous, resulting in the highest debt increase and largest deficit of all countries studied. The banking crisis in Iceland resulted in a bail-out by the IMF in November 2008. The costs of the Icelandic bank bail-outs led to an increase of debt and deficit, both second largest in Europe. In July 2012, Spain received a €100 billion ECB loan to rescue its failing banking sector, obligating it to devise drastic consolidation

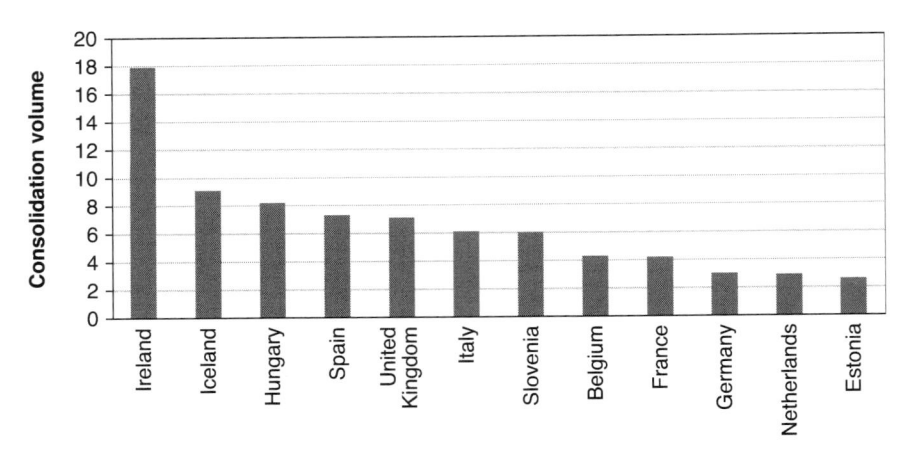

FIGURE 6.5 Fiscal consolidation volumes (per cent GDP)

plans. As mentioned before, the high consolidation volume in Hungary can be explained by the grand parliamentary majority of the right-wing FIDESZ government, enabling it to push through massive cuts. The prime explanation for the high consolidation volume in the United Kingdom was the excessively grown state debt and budget deficit.

The lowest consolidation efforts took place in Germany and the Netherlands. Thanks to the swift economic recovery of Germany, and consequently of the neighbouring and economically connected Belgium and the Netherlands, the deficit and debt increases remained relatively modest. Estonia's accumulated consolidation efforts in 2015 were indeed low, but the Estonian consolidation was front-loaded and amounted to 9.2 per cent in 2009, making that actually the second highest consolidation effort.

Besides some incidental political and electoral explanations for differences between countries, the undoubtedly main explanatory factor for the volumes of fiscal consolidation efforts the national governments took in the fiscal crisis were the fiscal and economic circumstances prior to and during the crisis.

Explanation of fiscal consolidation size

In its international analysis of how the OECD member states restored their public finances, the OECD (2011) distinguished four groups of countries. The first group – named 'consolidation under market pressure' – included countries where consolidation was forced by pressure from international financial (bond) markets, including such European countries as Hungary, Ireland, Greece, Portugal and Spain. The second group – named 'pre-emptive consolidation' – consisted of countries that faced substantial fiscal deficits and announced proactive fiscal consolidation plans, including Estonia, Germany, the

Netherlands and the United Kingdom. The third group – named 'consolidation needed but no plans by 2011' – included countries that had delayed their consolidation until economic recovery became self-sustaining, among others such European countries as France and Poland. And the fourth group – 'low fiscal consolidation needs' – consisted of countries that had a better fiscal position and needed only modest spending restraints, including Finland, Norway, Sweden and Switzerland.

The fast changes in the 'positions' of various countries in relation to fiscal consolidation is well demonstrated in the summaries provided by the OECD, where major differences occurred a year later. For instance, given the different pressures and speed of fiscal consolidation, the OECD, in its 2012 update of the 2011 report, categorised (European) countries into four groups (OECD 2012: 24–5):

(A) Countries with IMF-EU-ECB programmes: Greece, Ireland and Portugal. These countries, in return for their loan programmes, had formally committed to substantial consolidation packages, the largest in the OECD survey.

(B) Countries under distinct financial market pressure: Belgium, Hungary, Italy, Poland, the Slovak Republic, Slovenia and Spain. Long-term interest rates on bonds had increased in these countries, but they had still been able to finance their debt without external loan programmes. In particular, the Italian and Spanish bond interest rates had alarmingly risen, but the financial markets calmed down after ECB interventions in early 2012.

(C) Countries with substantial deficits and/or debt, but less financial market pressure: Austria, the Czech Republic, Denmark, Finland, France, Germany, Iceland, Israel, the Netherlands and the United Kingdom.

(D) Countries with no or marginal consolidation needs: Estonia, Luxembourg, Norway, Sweden and Switzerland. These countries had low deficits, low debts, decreasing long-term interest rates, and hence took no or very limited consolidation efforts.

The governments' responses to the crisis show a fast-moving target. Besides that, scholars, governments and international organisations have increasingly started to question the appropriateness of drastic cutbacks for restoring economic growth. Let us not address this political-economic issue, but focus on the consolidation measures and their effects that have already taken place.

Based on the economic literature, one can hypothesise that fiscal crisis decisions are related to the financial-economic circumstances of a country prior to the crisis. The worse the economic situation was (GDP, GDP growth rate, unemployment, etc.) and the worse the fiscal situation was (budget deficit, state debt, etc.), the more drastic and far-reaching measures had to be taken by the government. In addition, the 'financial size' of consolidation measures grew

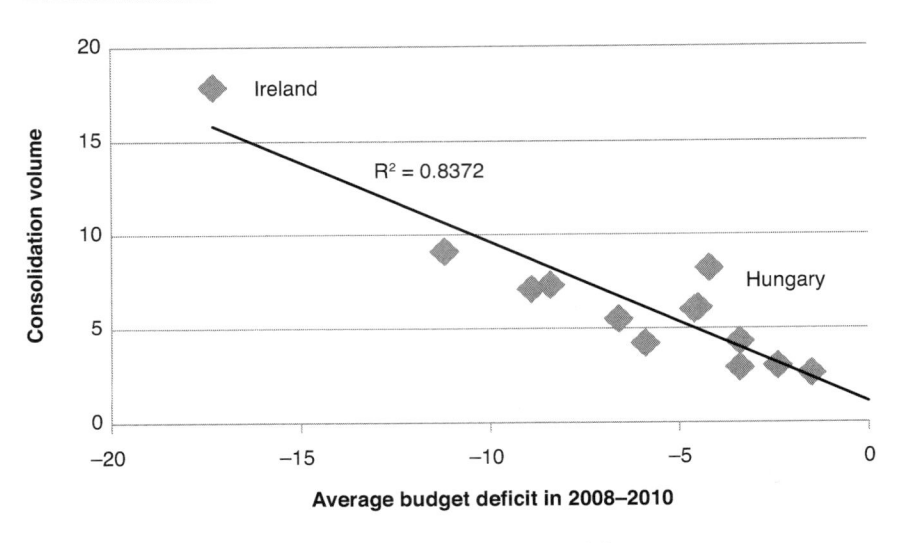

FIGURE 6.6 Consolidation volume – average budget deficit

substantially if a government had experienced a banking crisis and had made substantial costs to rescue banks. The basic economic logic of the fiscal crisis and consolidation is that deterioration of economy and public finances led to an increase of budget deficit and state debt, which forced governments to take fiscal consolidation measures with the aim of decreasing the deficit and debt growth and recovering the economy. Therefore, it can be conjectured that the financial-economic situation prior to the crisis, together with the financial size of the banking and economic crisis, influenced the financial size of the consolidation measures.

Figure 6.6 confirms that the size of the fiscal consolidation plans was indeed related to the state of the public finances in previous years. Figure 6.6 illustrates that the volume of fiscal consolidation is significantly correlated (explained variance of 83 per cent) to the average budget deficits in the preceding period, beginning in 2008 when the banking sector collapsed, the principal trigger of the ensuing global financial-economic crisis. Such correlation is hardly surprising, as the main objective of the consolidations was to bring the excessively grown budget deficits back to the EU ceiling of 3 per cent. In the calculation models that the EU's Budget Directorate uses to determine the volume of consolidation that a government is required to carry out in order to return to the deficit ceiling within a certain period, undoubtedly the deficits over the previous period play a prominent role. The many more variables incorporated in their calculation models may account for the remaining 16 per cent variations in Figure 6.6.

The markedly deviant position of Hungary in the figure might be due to political reasons, as explained before. Ireland also has a deviant position at the extreme upper-left corner. In all other countries, the prior state of public finances clearly and understandably explains for the size of the fiscal efforts to restore the public finances.

6.2 POLITICAL EXPLANATIONS

After considering, in the preceding section, the role of economic and fiscal factors in explaining fiscal consolidation, we now pay attention to possible explanations of the governments' consolidations by means of political factors. We apply the indicators of types of state, politics and government that were derived from the literature on comparative politics and government in Chapter 3 about the analytical framework.

In this section, we only briefly once more introduce the types of state, politics and government, and indicate how these are supposed to influence the fiscal consolidation decisions. A summary of the characteristics of state, politics and government is presented for all European countries studied, distinguishing the same government periods we used in Chapter 5 to characterise the consolidation decision-making. This allows us to directly relate the characteristics of state, politics and government to the corresponding characteristics of decision-making, and hence employ them as explanatory factors. Despite serious methodological limitations of a quantitative analysis of both data sets, such an attempt is carried out. This attempt at rudimentary statistics is then supplemented by illustrating the validity and strength of the explanatory factors with qualitative country examples. Finally, a quantitative comparative analysis is carried out of the correlation between political factors and fiscal consolidation in the selected countries, by using an additional data set, that is, the World Bank (2012) Database of Political Institutions.

State system

States can have a *unitary*, *decentralised* or *federal* structure. Various degrees of decentralisation exist (Italy, Spain) and various degrees of federalism (Belgium, Germany) according to a number of factors such as number of autonomous regions (Spain), authorities and responsibilities of regions (legal and budgetary), fundamental conflicts and political polarisation (Flanders-Wallonia; Madrid-Catalonia/Basque), and degree of instability. Unitary states are supposedly more capable of pursuing comprehensive and coherent policies than decentralised or federal states.

Political system

In *majoritarian* political systems, one single party wins a parliamentary majority at the general elections and forms a single-party government. In multi-party *consensual* political systems, no single party obtains a parliamentary majority. Parliamentary decisions are reached by compromises between a number of parties. According to Lijphart's (1977, 1984) theory of consensus democracy, in such a system, political stability is maintained because the leaders of the different political parties reach pragmatic compromises and control their rank and file. The usual pattern is lengthy multi-party deliberation, consultation and compromising. The stability and complexity of consensual politics depend on various factors such as the number of parties, the number and degree of ideological differences, political polarisation (Flemish versus Walloons in Belgium, the early 2000 surge of right-populist anti-Muslim parties), and the degree of instability (frequent government turnovers and early elections). Supposedly, majoritarian systems are able to reach decisions more easily and quickly.

Government system

A basic distinction is that between the majoritarian system with a *single-party government* (France, Spain, United Kingdom until 2010) and the consensual system with a *multi-party coalition cabinet*. A single-party government allegedly is better capable to take swift and drastic decisions than a multi-party coalition government. A further sub-distinction within single-party governments is that between a cabinet system (Spain, United Kingdom) and a presidential system (France). A further sub-distinction within multi-party coalition governments can be made between a grand (more than two-thirds) parliamentary majority (Germany 2006–2010, Hungary since 2010), a simple (minimal winning, more than half) majority, and a parliamentary minority (less than half) coalition (Estonia 2009–2011, Netherlands 2010–2012, Lithuania 2011–2012). Minority governments tend to face major problems in making decisions and upon implementing hard and unpopular decisions.

Political orientation of government

Political decisions of governments, and especially decisions on fiscal policy, can be related to the political-ideological orientation of a country's government (Cusack 1999, 2001). Conservative and Liberal parties tend to advocate quicker and more drastic balancing of the books than Socialists, Social Democrats or progressive Liberals. *Right-wing* governments (Estonia since 2009, Hungary since 2010) supposedly are more inclined and better capable of taking swift and drastic fiscal consolidation decisions than *left-wing* governments.

   Table 6.2 summarises these characteristics of the state, politics and government systems in the countries studied, with the same distinctions between government periods that we used in the previous chapter (until 2013).

Here, we now employ these characteristics of state, political system and government as explanatory factors for the characteristics of cutback decision-making by governments, as summarised in Table 5.2 and duplicated here in Table 6.3.

Notice that these two tables are less adequate for quantitative analysis as the variables only assume a limited number of values. Correlating size of cutbacks (small/moderate/large), speed of cutbacks (slow/swift) or targeted versus across-the-board cuts, with type of government (single party/coalition) or margin of parliamentary majority (grand/normal/minority) only yields indistinctive and hardly informative frequency tables, as the following examples show.

The frequency counts for decentralised and federal states are low mainly because its sample totals were low. Nonetheless, the frequency counts vaguely indicate that large cutbacks occurred more often in unitary states than in decentralised or federal ones, while moderate and small cutbacks occurred to a lesser extent. Likewise, most of the samples were coalition governments (twenty out of twenty-four), hence hardly allowing for any conclusions about correlations.

In Table 6.5, too, the frequency counts vaguely indicate that swift cutbacks occurred more often in unitary states than in decentralised and federal ones, while slow cutbacks occurred to a lesser extent. Again, the very small sample of single-party governments (four out of twenty-four) hardly allows for any conclusions. The fact that single-party governments more often took slow decisions than swift seems rather counterintuitive.

The frequency counts for targeted or across-the-board cuts are totally indistinctive as to type of government and hardly any better as to margin of parliamentary majority. Here, too, the main explanation rather seems the low total counts of grand and minority samples.

Remember, furthermore, that in Chapter 5, we concluded that the three variables 'size of cutbacks', 'speed of cutbacks' and 'targeted or across-the-board cuts' were almost one-to-one correlated, so that, from a statistical perspective, the three variables should rather be combined to one single covariate variable. In the next section, we carry out a statistical analysis of the single and well-defined quantitative variable 'volume of consolidation'.

Acknowledging the serious empirical-methodological limitations of a quantitative analysis of the data presented in Tables 6.2 and 6.3, we now proceed with a qualitative analysis of these two tables by looking at the country examples.

The assumption in comparative political science research – that *unitary states* are better capable to take swift, drastic and uniform decisions than *federal states* – is confirmed in the cases of Belgium and Spain, but rejected in the case of Germany. As illustrated before, Belgium is an example of the high complexity of a federal state hindering resolute political decision-making. Besides a federal government, Belgium has three 'regional' governments and three 'community'

TABLE 6.2 State and government characteristics

	Belgium		Estonia			France	Germany	
	(–2011)	(2011–)	(2007–2009)	(2009–2011)	(2011–)	(2007–2012)	(–2009)	(2009–)
Unitary/decentralised/federal	Federal	Federal	Unitary	Unitary	Unitary	Unitary	Federal	Federal
Single party/coalition	Coalition	Coalition	Coalition	Coalition	Coalition	Single	Coalition	Coalition
Left-wing/centre/right-wing cabinet	Left-centre-right	Left-centre-right	Right-centre-left	Right-centre	Right-centre	Right	Centre-left	Centre-left
Grand/normal/minority	Grand	Grand	Normal	Minority	Grand	n/a	Grand	Normal

	Hungary	Italy			Ireland		Iceland	Lithuania
	(2010–)	(2006–2008)	(2008–2011)	(2011–2012)	(2008–2011)	(2011–2013)	(2009–)	(2008–2012)
Unitary/decentralised/federal	Unitary	Decentralised	Decentralised	Decentralised	Unitary	Unitary	Unitary	Unitary
Single party/coalition	Coalition	Coalition	Coalition	Coalition	Coalition	Coalition	Coalition	Coalition
Left-wing/centre/right-wing cabinet	Right-centre	Centre-left	Centre-right	Non-political	Centre-right	Centre-left	Left	Centre-right
Grand/normal/minority	Grand	Normal	Normal	Grand	Normal	Normal	Normal (minority from 2011)	Normal-minority

(2010–2012)	Netherlands (2012–)	(2008–2011)	Slovenia (2012–2013)	(2004–2011)	Spain (2011–)	(–2010)	United Kingdom (2010–)	
Unitary/decentralised/federal	Unitary	Unitary	Unitary	Unitary	Decentralised	Decentralised	Unitary	Unitary
Single party/coalition	Coalition	Coalition	Coalition	Coalition	Single	Single	Single	Coalition
Left-wing/centre/right-wing cabinet	Centre-right	Right-left	Left	Right	Left	Right	Left	Right-centre
Grand/normal/minority	Minority	Normal	Normal	Normal	n/a	n/a	n/a	Normal

TABLE 6.3 Characteristics of cutback decision-making by central government

	Belgium		Estonia			France	Germany	
	(–2011)	(2011–)	(2007–2009)	(2009–2011)	(2011–)	(2007–2012)	(–2009)	(2009–)
Small/moderate/large cuts	Small	Moderate	Large	Large	Small	Moderate	Small	Moderate
Swift/slow	Slow	Slow	Swift	Swift	Slow	Slow	Slow	Swift
Targeted/across-the-board	Across	Across	Across	Across	Targeted	Across	Across	Targeted

	Hungary	Italy			Iceland	Ireland		Lithuania
	(2010–)	(2006–2008)	(2008–2011)	(2011–2012)	(2009–)	(2008–2010)	(2010–2012)	(2008–2012)
Small/moderate/large cuts	Large	Moderate	Moderate	Large	Large	Moderate	Large	Large
Swift/slow	Swift	Slow	Slow	Swift	Swift	Slow	Swift	Swift
Targeted/across-the-board	Targeted	Across	Across	Targeted	Across	Across	Targeted	Across

	Netherlands		Slovenia		Spain		United Kingdom	
	(2010–2012)	(2012–)	(2008–2011)	(2012–2013)	(2004–2011)	(2011–2013)	(–2010)	(2010–)
Small/moderate/large cuts	Moderate	Large	Small	Moderate	Large	Large	Small	Large
Swift/slow	Slow	Swift	Slow	Swift	Slow	Swift	Slow	Swift
Targeted/across-the-board	Across	Targeted	Targeted	Across	Targeted	Targeted	Across	Targeted

TABLE 6.4 Frequency counts size of cutback decisions

Size of cutbacks	Type of state		Type of government	
Large	Unitary	9 out of 11	Single party	2 out of 11
	Decentralised	2 out of 11	Coalition	9 out of 11
	Federal	0 out of 11		
Moderate	Unitary	5 out of 8	Single party	1 our of 8
	Decentralised	1 out of 8	Coalition	7 out of 8
	Federal	2 out of 8		
Small	Unitary	3 out of 5	Single party	1 out of 5
	Decentralised	0 out of 5	Coalition	4 out of 5
	Federal	2 out of 5		

TABLE 6.5 Frequency counts speed of cutback decisions

Size of cutbacks	Type of state		Type of government	
Swift	Unitary	10 out of 12	Single party	1 out of 12
	Decentralised	1 out of 12	Coalition	11 out of 12
	Federal	1 out of 12		
Slow	Unitary	6 out of 12	Single party	3 out of 12
	Decentralised	3 out of 12	Coalition	9 out of 12
	Federal	3 out of 12		

governments (the Flanders regional and Flemish community government are merged).

Belgian federal government is responsible for the relatively high state debt, but has no authority over the expenditures by sub-national governments, which have no incentive to curb their spending as their federal financing is legally determined.

Germany also is a federal state where the central government's decisions are influenced by the regional (Länder) governments, represented in the senate (Bundesrat). But that was not the reason that Germany only took moderate

TABLE 6.6 Frequency counts targeted or across-the-board decisions

Targeted or across-the-board	Type of government		Grand, normal or minority	
Targeted	Single party	2 out of 11	Grand majority	3 out of 10
	Coalition	8 out of 11	Normal majority	6 out of 10
			Minority	0 out of 10
Across-the-board	Single party	2 out of 11	Grand majority	4 out of 12
	Coalition	10 out of 11	Normal majority	7 out of 12
			Minority	2 out of 12

Federal, regions and communities in Belgium

Belgium's federal government has the authority over most taxes and social security.

The three 'regions' – Wallonia, Flanders and the Brussels capital region – have authority over what the Belgians call 'soil'-related affairs: planning, economy and employment, agriculture, environment, nature, water, public works and transport.

The French-, Flemish- and German-speaking 'communities' have authority over so-called 'person'-related affairs: education, welfare, sports, media and culture.

Regions and communities have modest incomes of their own, and are predominantly financed by federal government.

Source: Kickert (2012c)

---

cutback measures in 2009. Germany's swift economic recovery tempered its fiscal problem so that drastic spending cuts became unnecessary.

The reason why the Spanish Socialist Zapatero government started preparing a cutback programme was not related to its state structure, but more or less externally enforced by the Eurozone leaders when the fiscal sustainability of Spain lost international credibility. The federal state structure had consequences for the government's fiscal consolidation. National government in Spain is responsible for social security, but the autonomous communities take care of social welfare, health and education. The rising regional government expenditures during the crisis led the right-wing Rajoy government to impose cutback measures upon regional government as part of a budget stability agreement.

The political science assumption that *single-party* governments are better capable to take swift and drastic decisions than *multi-party* coalitions is not confirmed by our data on cutback decision-making. In the United Kingdom, the single-party Labour government under Prime Minister Brown refrained from making harsh cutback decisions. It was the 2010 Conservative-Liberal Democrat Cameron-Clegg coalition cabinet that took drastic and swift cutback decisions. The main reason for Labour's refusal to be clear and specific about future spending cuts, which everyone knew were predictable and inevitable, were the approaching May 2010 general elections. The new government would have taken drastic cutback measures and quite quickly, no matter whether it was a Conservative-Liberal Democrat coalition or a Labour majority.

Another counter-example of the assumption is France. The French single-party government under the right-wing President Sarkozy did not take drastic cutback decisions, but kept hesitating between economic stimulus measures and spending cuts.

And the reason that the Spanish single-party left-wing government under Prime Minister Zapatero prepared drastic cutbacks was the pressure of the EU and ECB, as explained before.

Multi-party coalition governments in both Estonia and Lithuania were capable of taking swift and radical cutback measures.

The assumption in political science that *minority coalition* governments are less capable of taking swift and drastic decisions than *grand coalitions* is partly confirmed and partly rejected. The Estonian coalition government lost its parliamentary majority in 2009 because the Social Democrats could not endorse new cutbacks and left the coalition, but the new right-wing minority coalition was able to decide swiftly on major consolidation measures. It did not call early elections, and won a grand majority at the regular general elections afterwards.

By contrast, the centre-right minority coalition in the Netherlands fell because the supporting right-wing populist Freedom Party refused to endorse the extra cutbacks in 2012, and it had to call early elections. In Denmark, which, contrary to the Netherlands, does have a long tradition of minority coalitions, a similar centre-right minority cabinet, supported by a similar right-populist party as in the Netherlands, reached agreements with the populist party to take drastic cutback decisions, and moreover did so right before approaching general elections (Kickert 2013a).

The landslide victory of the right-wing government in the 2010 Hungarian general elections, resulting in a grand parliamentary majority, enabled it to push through severe cutback measures.

On the other hand the Christian-Social Democrat grand coalition in Germany postponed unpopular decision-making about fiscal consolidation and cutbacks until after the general elections.

The political science assumption that *right-wing governments* are more inclined and capable of taking swift and drastic cutback decisions than *left-wing governments* is not confirmed by our data. The only right-wing government that took drastic cutback measures was the Hungarian government. The left-wing government in Iceland and centre-left government in Ireland undertook drastic and immediate cutbacks, as did the left-wing Spanish government. It is doubtful, however, whether the political colour of these governments played a decisive role in those decisions. The external pressure by the IMF on Iceland, and by the IMF, EU and ECB on Ireland and Spain, rather seems to explain the harsh decision-making, no matter whether it were left-wing or right-wing governments.

Electoral cycle

In most European countries (with the exception of Denmark, Estonia and Lithuania), governments did not have the political courage to take and implement harsh unpopular cutback measures in sight of forthcoming general elections. The difficult decisions were deferred to the next office holders. In many countries, this meant that the first round of fiscal consolidation decisions coincided with the formation of a new coalition cabinet, which, in multi-party consensual politics, normally is a process of lengthy and delicate deliberations and consultations with many different actors, intricate compromise and consensus searching, which hardly leaves any room for fundamental political priority-setting. Consensual politics, especially during coalition formations, is usually not swift, centralised and coherent, but rather slow, multi-actor complex, incremental and resulting in compromises between many different interests, often leading to incoherent patchwork agreements.

Quantitative comparative analysis

In this section, we supplement the previous qualitative analysis of the relations between fiscal consolidation and government characteristics with a quantitative comparative analysis. Tables 6.2 and 6.3 were less adequate for quantitative analysis, as the output variables assumed only two or three values (small/moderate/ large; slow/swift), which only resulted in indistinctive and hardly informative frequency counts. Let us now employ the well-defined and measurable variable of volume of fiscal consolidation, as calculated by the OECD (2012). Another methodological argument for this choice is that we concluded in Chapter 5 (see Table 5.2) that the three variables 'size of cutbacks', 'speed of cutbacks' and 'targeted or across-the-board cuts' were almost one-to-one correlated, so that, from a statistical perspective, the three variables should rather be combined to one single co-variate variable. An extra argument would be to rather employ the single and well-defined quantitative variable 'volume of fiscal consolidation' (see Figure 6.5).

Moreover, instead of the less adequate data on politics and government in Table 6.2, we employ two well-defined and measurable variables, that is, the political orientation of a government and its margin of parliamentary majority. These quantitative data are drawn from the World Bank (2012) Database of Political Institutions. First, the political orientation of governments, which the World Bank defined in terms of economic policy, is well suited for our purpose. Right parties are defined as Conservative, Christian Democratic or right-wing. Left parties are Communist, Socialist, Social Democrat or left-wing. (Right-wing is denoted as 1, centre is 2 and left-wing is 3. A centre-right coalition is denoted as 1.5 and a centre-left one as 2.5. A right-centre-left coalition is denoted as 2.) Second, the margin of parliamentary majority of government (less than 0.50 is minority, more than 0.50 is simple (minimal-winning) majority and more than 0.66 is grand majority).

The OECD (2012) and World Bank (2012) data that we employ are combined in Table 6.7.

TABLE 6.7 Government characteristics and consolidation

	Consolidation volume (% GDP)	Government right-centre-left	Government margin majority
Belgium	4.3	2	0.64
Estonia	2.6	2	0.59
France	4.2	1	0.57
Germany	3.0	1.5	0.61
Hungary	8.2	1	0.68
Iceland	9.1	3	0.53
Ireland	17.9	2.5	0.68
Italy	6.1	1.5	0.54
Lithuania	5.5	1.5	0.56
Netherlands	2.9	1.5	0.46
Slovenia	6.0	3	0.48
Spain	7.3	3	0.48
United Kingdom	7.1	1.5	0.55

Source: OECD (2012) and World Bank (2012)

Political orientation of government (right/centre/left)

The political science assumption is that *right-wing* governments tend to take harder and swifter fiscal consolidation and cutback measures than *left-wing* governments. The World Bank data on political party orientation are based on the party's economic policy. Figure 6.7 illustrates that the theoretical assumption is not confirmed (linear correlation R^2 is merely 0.15). The left-wing government in Iceland and left-centre government in Ireland actually took drastic fiscal consolidation measures. The right-wing Hungarian government took relatively hard measures, but the French government did not. Figure 6.7 vaguely indicates that centre-right and centre governments consolidated less.

The explanation for the deviation from the assumption is to be found in the specificity of the political circumstances in the various countries. The landslide victory of the right-wing FIDESZ government in the 2010 general elections enabled it to push through severe cutbacks, thus confirming the assumption. The right-wing French government and President Sarkozy, however, refrained from drastic cutback measures. Although the right-wing President Sarkozy was Minister of Economics and Finances before and had initiated reforms in public finances, and therefore strict and severe fiscal policy was to be expected from this president, the fiscal consolidation was half-hearted. The primary explanation why the left-wing governments in Spain, Iceland and Ireland, contrary to the common assumption, took large consolidation measures, was their dependence on the IMF, EU and ECB loan programmes. Whatever their political orientation, they had no choice but to carry out the prescribed and imposed cuts. The left-wing Zapatero government was punished in the early elections for its proposed cutback measures, but the succeeding right-wing Rajoy government could do nothing but

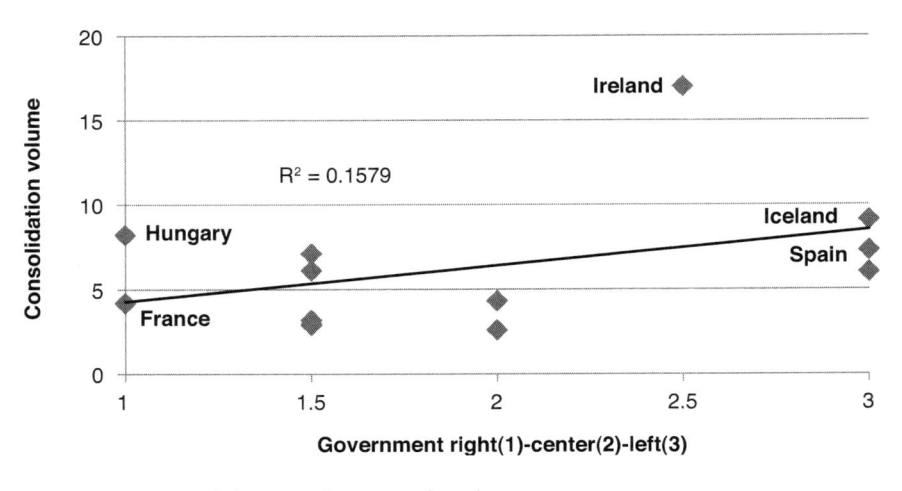

FIGURE 6.7 Consolidation volume – political orientation

continue these. The fact that the broad left-centre-right coalition in Belgium, and the centre-right minority coalition in the Netherlands, only managed to take moderate cutback measures does uphold the political science assumption that multi-party coalition governments tend to take less and slower actions. The reverse assumption that single-party governments are better able to take hard and swift actions was not sustained in the French and British case, though.

Margin of parliamentary majority of government

Another political science assumption is that the higher the parliamentary majority, the better a government is able to take hard and swift action. Governments with a *parliamentary minority* are seriously hampered in taking bold action, and governments with a *grand two-thirds majority* are hardly hindered by political opposition. Figure 6.8 more or less supports these assumptions.

In Hungary, the grand parliamentary majority of the FIDESZ government enabled it to push through bold measures. The opposition was fragmented and lame, so the government could act unrestrained. In Ireland, the two-thirds parliamentary backing of the government certainly contributed to its readiness and capability to carry out unpopular drastic cutback measures that were required by the IMF-EU-ECB Troika.

The centre-right minority coalition in the Netherlands, supported by a right-wing populist party, in 2010, took only moderate consolidation measures, but the main explanation for that was economic. The Dutch public finances and economic circumstances did not require larger cutbacks. When another round of cutbacks came to be necessary in 2012, the populist party withdrew its support for the coalition, and so it fell and had to call early elections.

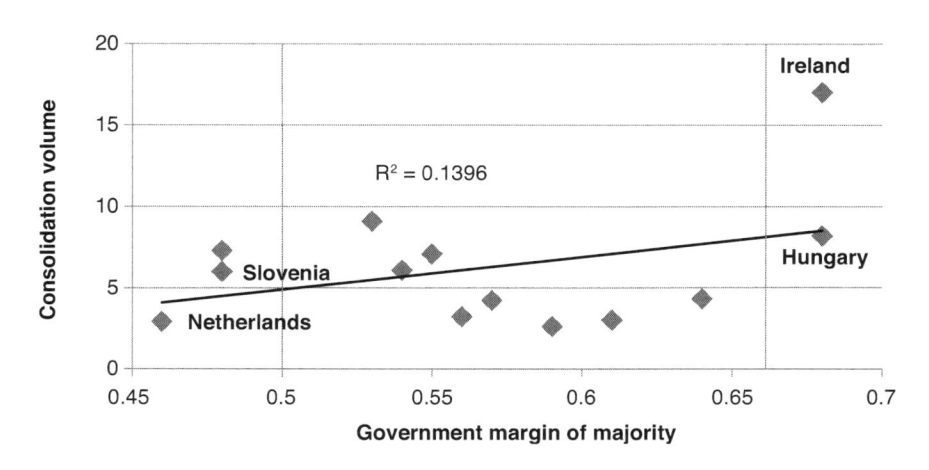

FIGURE 6.8 Consolidation volume – margin government majority

Figure 6.8 does not reveal any linear correlation (R^2 is only 0.13) with the volume of fiscal consolidation for the normal winning majority (between 0.50 and 0.66) cases. Higher degrees of majority for that in-between range did not lead to higher consolidation measures. The political assumption only holds for the minority and grand majority cases.

6.3 SUPRA-NATIONAL EXPLANATIONS

Developments in the worldwide economy clearly affected the state of economy and public finances. The increase of industrial exports to East Asia, especially China, highly contributed to the swift economic recovery of Germany (export industry) and therefore, indirectly, to the economic recovery of surrounding countries with strong economic relations with Germany, such as Belgium and the Netherlands.

The influence of the European Union on the domestic fiscal consolidation decisions should also not be underestimated, especially for countries that were (or wanted to become) Eurozone members. The EU Treaty of Maastricht placed ceilings on budget deficit (3 per cent of GDP) and state debt (60 per cent of GDP). In virtually all European countries, the EU pressure to keep within the deficit limit was influential, thus forcing governments to cut back. Apart from the EU formal excessive budgetary procedure that obliges Eurozone members to keep within that limit and allows the EU to impose large fines on states that do not conform to the rules, the influence was also indirect and political. At the outset of the crisis, in many countries, the strictness of the budget ceiling was politically disputed, usually by left-wing and populist parties. The growing Eurosceptic attitude following the Eurozone crisis, and especially the widely contested bail-out of the failing Greece, which Western European tax-payers were not particularly eager to pay for, contributed to the political disputes about alleged 'dictates from Brussels'.

In many Western European countries, left-wing parties were less inclined to swift and drastic spending cuts than right-wing parties. Though usually recognising the necessity for fiscal austerity because of the undeniable economic and fiscal crisis, Socialist and Social Democrat parties in Britain, Denmark, France, Germany and the Netherlands commonly advocated moderate instead of drastic cutbacks, and to spread out the cuts over a longer period. Yet, the primary fiscal objective was still to bring the budget deficit back to the EU ceiling.

On the other hand, Estonia provides an interesting example of a country where the fiscal consolidation was caused by the Estonian government's predominant political priority to join the Eurozone. This goal tied the government to strictly adhere to the above-mentioned criteria of the Maastricht Treaty.

In Belgium, after eighteen months of coalition formation, finally, at the end of 2011, the newly formed coalition announced an €11.3 billion budget reduction. That figure was claimed to be directly derived from the EU budget requirement. Blaming external pressure from the EU as the main cause of the retrenchment increased its political rigour. This was no longer domestic Belgian politics, where everything is always open for wheeling and dealing, but an externally imposed 'fait accompli'.

The Italian Prime Minister Berlusconi provided the example of an outright refusal to bend to the dictates from Brussels. After the European Central Bank (ECB), in 2011, massively bought up Italian state bonds to ease the widening yield spread and therewith assist the Italian government's fiscal policy, the ECB sent a letter with recommendations about Italian fiscal tightness, which outraged Berlusconi as foreign interference in sovereign domestic affairs. His public refusal to obey the strict fiscal rules did not contribute to his trustworthiness abroad.

Blaming budget cuts on 'dictates from Brussels', and thus shifting the blame for highly unpopular harsh cutback decisions, has repeatedly been applied by the Greek and Portuguese governments. In those countries, the fiscal cuts were indeed externally prescribed and imposed. Countries such as Greece, Iceland, Ireland, Latvia and Portugal that received financial assistance (bail-outs) from the IMF, the ECB and the EU had to comply with strict and specified conditions on fiscal reform and cutbacks.

It is important to note that the Troika holds an 'orthodox' view in addressing the crisis (Dellepiane 2012). This involves a general understanding that fiscal consolidation should start early and be imposed quickly in a front-loaded strategy to restore market confidence in a government's ability to manage its public finances. A government must implement a 'cold shower', or fiscal shock treatment (Pisani-Ferry 2007). With such an ideology in the background, it is not surprising that countries following the requirements of the Troika's loan programmes were forced quickly to the serious cutbacks, without letting them go through long phases of crisis denial and postponement of cuts.

Two of the countries investigated here, Iceland and Ireland, were explicitly bailed out. The bail-out of the Icelandic banking sector occurred before the Eurozone crisis erupted, and the loan programme was not provided by the IMF-ECB-EU Troika, but by the International Monetary Fund (IMF).

European trust in Berlusconi

The 24 October 2011 television interview when Chancellor Merkel and President Sarkozy, being asked whether they were reassured by the Italian leader's reform efforts, just tellingly smiled at each other, was broadcast worldwide.

Source: YouTube

Iceland bail-out

The October 2008 worldwide financial crisis led to an almost immediate collapse of the Icelandic banks; relative to economic size, the largest banking collapse experienced by any country in history. In November 2008, a $5.1 billion sovereign debt package was enacted, of which $2.1 billion came from the IMF and the remaining $3.0 billion from a group of Nordic countries in order to stabilise the currency and ensure fiscal sustainability and the functioning of domestic banks. In return, the Icelandic government agreed on a drastic austerity program.

Source: Kristinsson (2013) and Wikipedia: Icelandic Financial Crisis, accessed 20 March 2014

Icesave

Icesave was the name under which the second largest Icelandic bank Landsbanki had become active in Britain and the Netherlands through Internet banking. Icesave offered substantially higher interest rates than domestic banks. In October 2008, Icesave counted some 300,000 clients in Britain with a total deposit of £4.5 billion, and about 100,000 in the Netherlands with a deposit of €1.7 billion.

In October 2008, the global financial crisis caused Icesave to go bankrupt. Bank accounts were frozen and clients could not withdraw money. Lansbanki announced to its Icesave clients that they had to apply for the national deposit guarantee system. The British and Dutch national banks refunded their domestic Icesave clients to the guaranteed maximum of £50,000 and €100,000, respectively.

The British and Dutch Ministries of Finance and both national banks immediately started negotiations with the Icelandic authorities to ensure that Iceland would meet its obligations to repay the guaranteed savings. The November 2008 agreement between Iceland, Britain and the Netherlands was rejected by the Icelandic parliament in August 2009. The International Monetary Fund (IMF) immediately blocked its loan programme credits. Parliament accepted a new version of the agreement in December 2009. After protests from the Icelandic population, the President of Iceland refused to sign the Act and the government announced a referendum. In the March 2010 referendum, 98.5 per cent of the population rejected the savings refund agreement. In December 2010, a new agreement was reached, which, in February 2011, was accepted by the Icelandic parliament, but the president once again refused to sign, and in another referendum the population again rejected the agreement.

The case was then brought before international justice. In January 2013, the Court of the European Free Trade Association (EFTA) ruled that Iceland was legitimate in its refusal to compensate the British and Dutch savers.

Source: Kristinsson (2013) and Wikipedia: Icesave dispute, accessed 20 March 2014

Despite the fact that the Icelandic government was completely bound by the fiscal consolidations agreed upon with the IMF, it demonstrated resistance to external pressure, such as in the diplomatic dispute about the repayment of foreign deposit insurances of the Icesave bank.

Together with Greece and Portugal, Ireland belonged to the first receivers of financial assistance by the IMF, EU and ECB Troika when, in 2010, the Eurozone crisis broke out. The cost of the bank bail-outs amounted to a staggering 40 per cent of GDP with a budget deficit of 32 per cent in 2010 and state debt increasing by more than 70 per cent, by far the worst state of public finances in Europe. The government could do nothing but seek assistance from the EU and IMF. In Chapter 5, the stages of political decision-making in Ireland have been outlined. Here, the stages of the Irish financial crisis are summarised.

Table 6.8 summarises the external influences on European governments in managing the crisis.

Irish bail-out

The financial and economic crisis hit Ireland hard. Ireland had a disproportionally large banking sector and a property price bubble that already burst in 2007. The government swiftly responded with the October 2008 Emergency Budget. The government issued an unlimited bank guarantee to the six main Irish-based banks, which was to cost much more than the government had estimated, and resulted in the EU-IMF intervention in late 2010. In April 2009, the government established a National Asset Management Agency (NAMA) to take over large loans from the banks, enabling them to return to normal liquidity.

The costs of the bank rescues, NAMA and government deficits enormously increased the Irish national debt. With Ireland's credit rating falling due to the estimated banking losses, the six banks' guaranteed depositors and bondholders cashed in during 2009–2010. With bond yield spreads on Irish government debt rising rapidly, and government help for banks rising to 32 per cent of GDP, the government was obliged to seek assistance from the EU and IMF.

In November 2010, the European Union, International Monetary Fund and the Irish state agreed to an €85 billion rescue deal. The deal included €10 billion for bank recapitalisation, €25 billion for banking contingencies and €50 billion for financing the Budget. In return, the government agreed to reduce its budget deficit to below 3 per cent by 2015. This implied an unprecedented and massive austerity programme. The terms of the fiscal consolidation plan were worked out by the Troika and Ireland.

Ireland officially exited from the bail-out in December 2013.

Source: MacCarthaigh and Hardiman (2013) and Wikipedia: Irish Financial Crisis, accessed 20 March 2014

TABLE 6.8 Supra-national influences

	BEL	GER	EST	ESP	FRA	HUN	IRL	ISL	ITA	LTU	NLD	SLO	GBR
Impact of worldwide economy on swift recovery	Yes	Yes	Yes	Yes	No	No	Yes	Yes	No	Yes	Yes	Yes	No
EU budget deficit influence none/small/large	Large	Small	Large	Large	Small	Large	Large	n/a	Large	Large	Large	Large	Large
IMF, ECB and EU conditionality	No	No	No	Yes	No	Yes	Yes	Yes	Yes	No	No	No	No

Conclusions of this chapter

In this chapter, we have explored possible explanations of the fiscal consolidations. In line with the two main perspectives employed in this book, we followed both an economic perspective and a political one.

After a brief overview of the economic and fiscal crisis in the selected countries, in terms of the Eurostat data about GDP growth and budget surplus/deficit, an overview was presented of the volume of fiscal consolidation plans in the various European countries as presented by the OECD (2012) in its survey. Based on these data, we tested the hypothesis that fiscal consolidation decisions in a country were primarily related to the financial-economic circumstances of a country prior to the consolidation. Not surprisingly, it turned out that the volume of fiscal consolidation was indeed clearly correlated with the average budget deficits in the preceding period.

Subsequently, we turned to possible political explanatory factors, such as the type of state, politics and government in a country. Although the country examples amply illustrated the importance of such political factors in the government's fiscal decision-making, a quantitative statistical analysis proved harder to carry out. The qualitative data collected from the country case studies hardly allowed for meaningful quantitative analysis, and only generated indistinctive and hardly informative frequency tables. To carry out a more meaningful statistical analysis, we subsequently employed the well-defined and measurable variable 'volume of fiscal consolidation' from the OECD (2012) survey, and correlated that with the well-defined and measurable variables 'political orientation of a government' and 'margin of parliamentary majority of a government' from the World Bank (2012) Database of Political Institutions. The political assumption that right-wing governments tend to take larger cutback decisions than left-wing governments was statistically not confirmed in the thirteen countries. The assumptions that governments with a grand parliamentary majority are better capable to take larger cutback decisions than governments with a mere parliamentary minority was moderately supported by the statistics.

Finally, attention was paid to supra-national explanatory factors, especially the major European influence on domestic fiscal consolidation decisions by the European governments. The influence of the EU Maastricht Treaty ceilings on budget deficit and state debt, as well as the influence of the extraordinary circumstances of the Eurozone crisis and bail-outs, were illustrated with country examples, confirming them to be of major importance.

Chapter 7

Effects of fiscal consolidation

In this chapter, we consider the effects of the fiscal consolidation measures taken by European governments. We concentrate on the three types of effects that were introduced in Chapter 3 on the analytical framework. The first type of effect that we consider is the economic and fiscal one. Fiscal consolidation was primarily aimed at the reduction of the budget deficit and debt accumulation, and the recovery of economic growth. Here, we investigate whether such effects of fiscal consolidation have in fact been achieved. The second type of effect we address is the political effect of consolidation. Throughout this book, we followed both the economic and political perspective on consolidation. And the third type of effect we consider here is the effect of fiscal crisis on Public Administration and management.

As in previous chapters, here, too, we alternate between methodological modes. The fiscal and economic effects are shown in a quantitative and statistical manner. The political effects are investigated by looking at the qualitative country studies. Finally, the effects of consolidation on Public Administration and management are shown both by qualitative country examples and by the results of the COCOPS public executives' survey (Hammerschmidt *et al.* 2013).

Effect measurement is not identical to evaluation. As mentioned in Chapter 3 about the analytical framework, we try to avoid the methodological pitfalls of the normative exercise of evaluation. Though well aware that practitioners, politicians and policy-makers are above all interested in the question of successfulness, we argued in Chapter 3 that it is still too early to assess the success of fiscal consolidation. The fiscal crisis is not yet over by some long way, and new rounds of consolidation and cutbacks are to be expected in several European countries. Moreover, we raised the question of the methodologically problematic choice of criteria for success or failure of fiscal consolidation. Is it only about restoring public finances? What about economic recovery and employment? And what about the political and social aspects of success? Many consolidation and cutback measures were socially, publicly and politically disputed.

In this chapter, we refrain from normative evaluation and restrict ourselves to the more neutral measurement of effects. It is only in Chapter 8 that we cautiously address the tricky issue of alleged success and failure of consolidation.

7.1 ECONOMIC EFFECTS OF FISCAL CONSOLIDATION

From an economic perspective, the main intended effects of fiscal consolidation are, first, a reduction of budget deficit and debt accumulation, and second, a recovery of the economy, that is, restoring economic growth. As repeatedly mentioned before, it is common wisdom in economics that the recovery of domestic public finances and economic growth depends on many more variables than the government's fiscal consolidation efforts alone. The restoration of public finances can be much more affected by economic recovery than by consolidation. The theory of public finances teaches us that economic growth normally increases state revenues and decreases state expenditures. And it is quite contested that public expenditure cuts and tax revenue rises do contribute to economic growth, to put it mildly. Moreover, in relatively small and internationally open economies, domestic economic growth is highly dependent on the international economy.

Furthermore, our country case studies finish in 2013, and the data about budget deficit and GDP growth in 2013, while fiscal consolidation in most countries only started in 2010, leaving too little time for the measurement of effects. Many government consolidation plans explicitly mentioned longer timescales for fiscal recovery, with time spans ranging to 2015 or beyond (OECD 2012: 35).

Despite these and other limitations, and our consequently low expectations, we now proceed with the comparative effect measurement.

Fiscal and economic effects of consolidation

Figures 7.1 and 7.2 about the fiscal and economic effects of the consolidation plans actually confirm the limitations just mentioned. Figure 7.1 relates the volume of consolidation plan of a country (volume of accumulated fiscal consolidation in 2015; OECD 2012; see Table 6.1) to the subsequent reduction of the budget deficit; in other words, the growth of the budget surplus. Because in all studied countries the budget deficit was at its lowest point in 2009, we measured the recovery since then (comparable Eurostat data ended in 2012).

Figure 7.1 illustrates that there is only a weak correlation (the explained variance is merely 33 per cent) between the consolidation efforts and budget deficit decline in the thirteen countries. The figure shows a paradox at the right-hand side: both the country with a modest consolidation effort (Lithuania,

5.5 per cent of GDP) and the one with the far highest effort (Ireland, 17.9 per cent of GDP) achieved the highest reduction of budget deficit. A more detailed look at the underlying data reveals that Ireland suffered its worst deficit in 2010 (30.8 per cent of GDP) and, related to that low point, actually managed to reduce the deficit in 2012 by 23.2 per cent. A more detailed analysis also shows interesting evidence for Estonia. In Figure 7.1, the Estonian fiscal consolidation effort was the lowest (2.6 per cent of GDP in 2015) but, as we indicated before, Estonia front-loaded its fiscal effort in 2009 (9.2 per cent of GDP), which was the second highest volume of all studied countries. Estonia formed a paradoxical example of very high consolidation effort and low deficit reduction in 2009, but the accumulated consolidation remained rather low. A comment upon the Lithuanian deviation is that its figure of fiscal consolidation effort is not derived from the OECD (2012) survey but from Nakrosis *et al.* (2013), and is therefore actually incomparable.

Figure 7.2 relates the volume of fiscal consolidation to the subsequent economic recovery. As the highest GDP decline in all countries occurred in 2009, we measured the GDP growth since then (on the basis of Eurostat data on GDP growth in 2009–2012). Figure 7.2 illustrates that there is no positive correlation (the explained variance is a mere 18 per cent) between the consolidation efforts and the recovery of economic growth in the studied European countries. Moreover, the correlation paradoxically looks inverse: the higher the consolidation effort, the lower the economic recovery. Figure 7.2 shows a paradox at the right-hand and top side: the countries with the lowest consolidation effort (Estonia) and a modest effort (Lithuania) reached the most economic growth, and the one with the highest effort (Ireland) achieved hardly any growth. A more detailed analysis of the underlying data modifies the picture for Estonia. When we take the front-loaded consolidation effort of

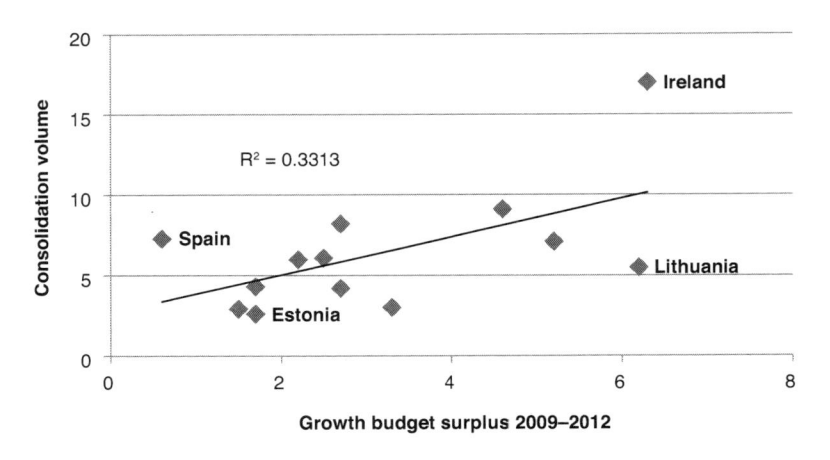

FIGURE 7.1 Consolidation volume – budget deficit reduction

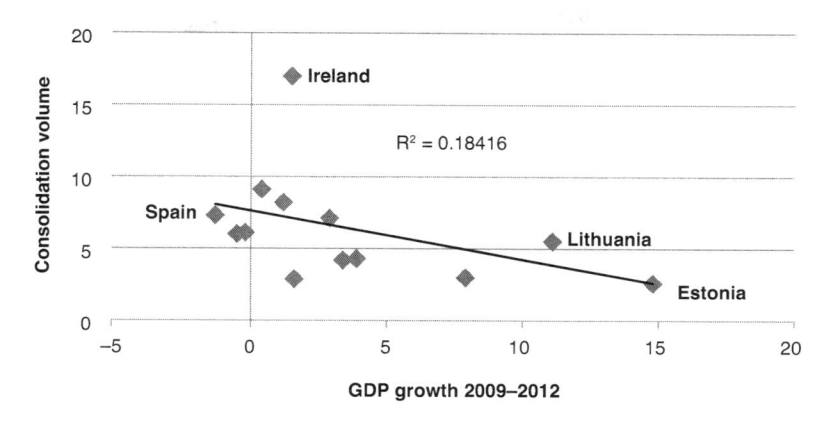

FIGURE 7.2 Consolidation volume – economic recovery

Estonia (9.2 per cent in 2009) into account, Estonia would transform into an example of high consolidation effort and high economic growth. A comment to the Lithuanian case – apart from the aforementioned remark that its figure on fiscal consolidation volume does not derive from the OECD (2012) review – is that Lithuania suffered the deepest economic decline of all countries (14.8 per cent GDP decline) in 2009, from which it swiftly recovered. Estonia suffered the second deepest economic decline (14.1 per cent) in 2009. Both Baltic states, after a period of strong economic growth, suffered a sudden and deep decline and enjoyed a quick recovery.

Apparently, the fiscal and economic effects of fiscal consolidation rather deviate from the 'mainstream' expectations in the thirteen-country comparison. Let us now try another perspective and see whether the effects might be related to political factors.

Effects of politics and government on fiscal and economic performance

Although neither theoretically grounded nor empirically verified, a popular assumption is that the political orientation of a government influences its fiscal and economic performance. A right-wing government allegedly tends to put more emphasis on fiscal tightness than a left-wing government, which was refuted in the example of the right-wing French President Sarkozy, and inversely by the left-wing Spanish Prime Minister Zapatero. Moreover, more emphasis on fiscal consolidation does not necessarily lead to factual successful consolidation.

Figure 7.3 relates the reduction of the budget deficit (surplus growth) in a country to the political orientation of its government (right-wing (1), centre (2) and left-wing (3); World Bank 2012; see Table 6.4). Figure 7.3 illustrates that there is no correlation ($R^2 = 0.0041$) between the political orientation of governments and the reduction of the budget deficit. Centre-right governments (denoted as 1.5) display about the same variation in deficit reduction as centre-left (2.5) and left-wing (3) governments. Ireland and Lithuania were the most successful in reducing their budget deficits, and Spain the least.

Figure 7.4 relates the GDP growth in the period 2009–2012 in a country to the political orientation of its government. Figure 7.4 illustrates there is no correlation ($R^2 = 0.0983$) between these two variables. The figure shows that centre-left and left-wing governments were less successful at economic recovery (rise in GDP growth) than centre (Estonia) and centre-right ones (Lithuania and Germany), and that the latter were more successful than right-wing governments (France and Hungary). However, we have argued before that other variables, such as developments in the worldwide economy, might more validly explain GDP growth.

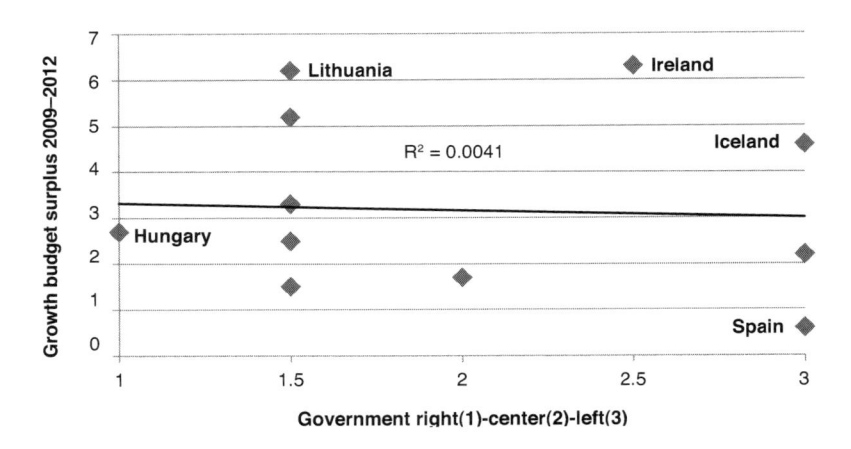

FIGURE 7.3 Budget deficit reduction – political orientation

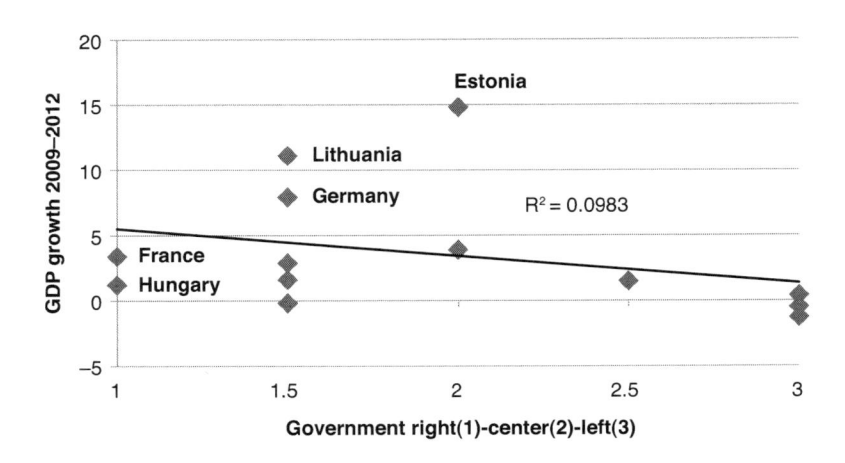

FIGURE 7.4 Economic growth – political orientation

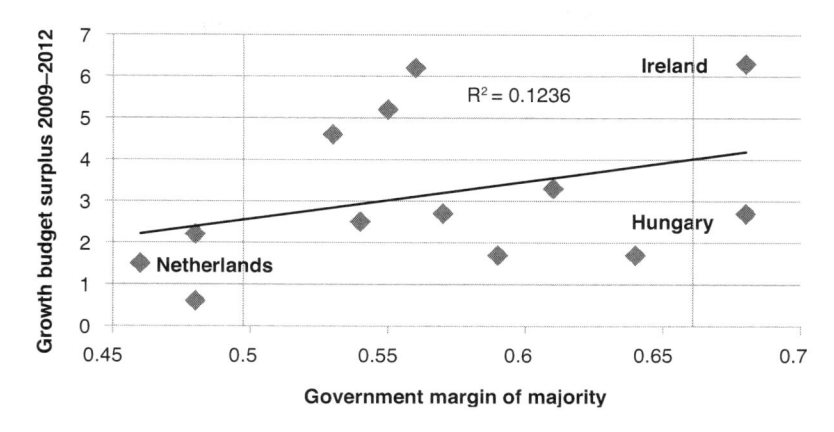

FIGURE 7.5 Budget deficit reduction – margin government majority

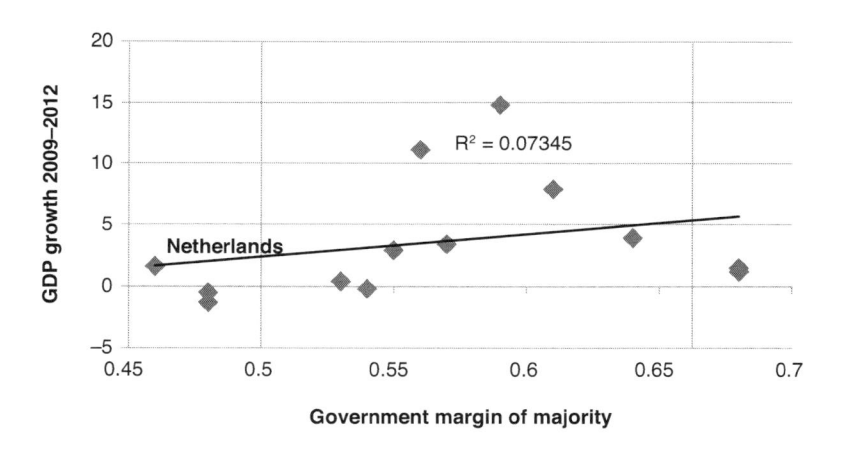

FIGURE 7.6 Economic growth – margin government majority

Neither is there any theory-grounded and empirically verified relationship between margin of parliamentary majority (minority or grand) and fiscal or economic performance. Figures 7.5 and 7.6 indeed illustrate that neither the variation in budget deficit reduction (surplus growth 2009–2012), nor that in economic recovery (GDP growth 2009–2012), correlate with the parliamentary margin (minority or grand) of governments, with the exception of the minority coalition in the Netherlands. The Dutch minority government performed poorly both in deficit reduction and in economic recovery. The grand majority government in Hungary was, however, not more successful in reducing the deficit, and neither Hungary nor Ireland were successful in economic recovery.

The statistics confirm the low expectations we had about the effect measurements. The fiscal effects of consolidation could only be shown to a limited degree, and the economic effects could not be substantiated. As expected, the fiscal and economic effects of the political variables were even less impressive.

7.2 POLITICAL EFFECTS OF FISCAL CONSOLIDATION

In Chapter 2, the political aspects of fiscal consolidation were discussed. Several types of political effects were distinguished. First, the effects of consolidation and cutbacks on voters, that is, the electoral effects. The governments' cutback decisions are unpopular and can therefore lead to a loss of the incumbent government at the next general elections. Here, we start by presenting a quantitative and qualitative analysis of the electoral effects. Subsequently, we pay attention to other political effects, such as political opposition in parliament and public opposition outside parliament. In countries that were most severely hit by the crisis and were compelled to devise drastic and harsh cutback packages, public protests and demonstrations and social unrest resulted in more than the ousting of the government-in-office.

Electoral effects

Table 7.1 presents data from the COCOPS country studies about the electoral effects of the governments' fiscal consolidation plans in the thirteen countries. The third column indicates whether the general elections (second column) were lost by the incumbent government. The fourth column denotes whether the general elections were early calls, and the fifth column indicates whether the call for early elections was related to the fiscal consolidation plan of the government. The sixth column indicates whether a coalition government was reduced to a parliamentary minority due to the withdrawal of one or more coalition parties, and the last column indicates whether that walkout of parties from the coalition was related to the fiscal consolidation. The bottom row of the table presents the summary counts of the electoral effects.

General elections in all but one case (Estonia in 2011) resulted in a defeat of the incumbent government. Whether the economic and fiscal crisis, and particularly the fiscal consolidation plan of the government, were the main causes for the electoral losses is doubtful in some cases. The 2007 general elections in Estonia took place before the financial banking crisis broke out, and the governments that were newly elected in 2008 in Lithuania and Slovenia were confronted with the very beginning of the financial crisis. The 2010 elections in Belgium were dominated by the Flanders-Wallonia controversy, and solving the fiscal crisis was only the finishing priority of the eighteen months of coalition formation.

TABLE 7.1 Electoral effects of fiscal consolidation

	General elections	Incumbent government lost election	Early elections	Related to cutbacks	Coalition turns to minority	Related to cutbacks
Belgium	2010	Yes	Yes	No	Yes	No
Estonia	2007	Yes (2009)	No		Yes (2009)	Yes
	2011	No	No			
France	2007	Yes	No			
	2012	Yes	No			
Germany	2009	Yes	No			
Hungary	2010	Yes	No			
Iceland	2009	Yes	Yes	Yes	Yes	Yes
Ireland	2011	Yes	Yes	Yes		
Italy	2011	Yes	Yes	Yes		
Netherlands	2010	Yes	Yes	Yes		
	2012	Yes	Yes	Yes	Yes	Yes
Lithuania	2008	Yes	No (2009)			
	2012	Yes	No			
Slovenia	2008	Yes	No			
	2011	Yes	Yes	Yes		
Spain	2012	Yes	Yes	Yes		
United Kingdom	2010	Yes	No			
Frequency counts		All but 1	8 out of 18	All but 1	4 times	3 times

Source: COCOPS country studies

In the eight cases where governments had to call early elections, only the Belgian case was not related to the fiscal crisis. The complex and unstable Belgian political system frequently results in the fall of governments and early elections. Although Belgium, in 2010, was confronted with a severe fiscal crisis, that was not the hot political issue for the coalition breaking up. The breaking point was the Flemish-French language problem in the electoral district Brussels-Halle-Vilvoorde, which also dominated the long-lasting coalition formation.

In four countries, the coalition government faced one or more parties leaving the coalition, which therefore fell back to a parliamentary minority. As just mentioned, in Belgium that was not related to cutbacks. In all other cases, it was. When the Estonian coalition turned into a minority government in 2009, it did not call early elections. In all other cases, the governments did. In Estonia, the centre-right minority coalition was not defeated (the only case out of seventeen), but actually gained a grand majority at the 2011 general elections. This was largely due to the fact that most cutbacks took place in 2009, and at the time of the general elections in 2011, the country had already restored economic growth.

Despite such an exception, it seems plausible to conclude from these data that the electoral effects of governments' fiscal consolidation decisions were indeed significant.

Qualitative case studies

The frequency counts only provided an overall insight into the electoral effects of the fiscal crisis and consolidation. More in-depth explanations are to be found in the specificity of the country cases. Table 7.2 presents a summary of the electoral and governmental course of affairs in the thirteen countries, based on the COCOPS country studies (for more political details on elections and governments, see the Appendix with country summaries).

Political effects: public protest and social unrest

The adjective 'political' has a more encompassing meaning than only 'electoral'. As discussed in Chapter 2 on the political effort of government, other political effect variables can be considered, such as party-political opposition inside parliament and public and social opposition outside parliament, that is, public protest and social unrest. We distinguished the following types of opposition a government's cutback decision can face:

- Political opposition in parliament. Sort and degree of opposition, walkout of parties, fall of coalition.
- Public opposition. Protests, demonstrations, unrest. Media coverage.
- Social opposition. Employers, employees, trade unions, interest groups, pressure and action groups.
- Administrative opposition. Resistance to (operational) consolidation measures by civil servants.

TABLE 7.2 Fiscal consolidation and elections: country cases

Country	General elections	Sitting government lost election	Relation to fiscal consolidation
Belgium	2010	New coalition formation took eighteen months	Flemish-Walloon politics dominated elections and coalition formation. Economic crisis was mild. Moderate fiscal cuts in coalition agreement.
Estonia	2007	New right-centre -left coalition	June 2008 first cutback plan. February 2009 and June 2009 next cutbacks. Social Democrats could not support second 2009 cuts and left coalition in May 2009. Minority centre-right government continued. No early elections.
Estonia	2011	Centre-right coalition	Centre-right coalition won grand majority (74%).
France	2007	Sarkozy (UMP) new president	Although Sarkozy was advocate of budget discipline, and France seriously hit by crisis, government hesitated between cutbacks and economic stimulus.
France	2012	Sarkozy (UMP) lost against Hollande (PS)	Bad economic and fiscal shape of France. Disappointment over Sarkozy achievements. Hollande advocate of economic stimulus instead of cutbacks. Top income tax increases.
Germany	2009	CDU/CSU-SPD replaced by CDU/CSU-FDP	Economy soon recovered after the crisis. Moderate cutbacks taken after the elections. Chancellor Merkel pursued cautious and strict fiscal policy.
Hungary	2010	MSZP (left) replaced by FIDESZ (right)	Right-wing FIDESZ won grand majority. Advocate of severe cutbacks (to prevent foreign (IMF) interference in domestic politics). In 2011, Kalman plan for structural cuts. In 2012, Kalman plan 2.0.

continued . . .

TABLE 7.2 Continued

Country	General elections	Sitting government lost election	Relation to fiscal consolidation
Iceland	2009	Social Democrat-Left Green coalition	2008 banking crisis. 2009 bail-out by IMF. Pots and pans revolution. Population lost trust in government. Coalition partners left, interim minority government. April 2009 early elections. Labour-Green won majority. First ever left-wing majority government.
Ireland	2011	Fianna Fáil replaced by Labour-Fine Gael (grand) coalition	Eurozone crisis. November 2010 bail-out by Troika. Hard fiscal conditions imposed. Fundamental changes took place in politics.
Italy	2008	Berlusconi (PdL) with Lega Nord wins elections	Alternation between centre-left group under Prodi and centre-right group under Berlusconi.
Italy	2011 (no elections)	Berlusconi replaced by Monti government	Eurozone crisis. Fiscal policy of Berlusconi lost credibility. Berlusconi ousted. Replaced by technocrat Monti government.
Lithuania	2008	New conservative-Liberal coalition	New government in 2008. Immediate anti-crisis plan. Three rounds of cutbacks in 2009. Next cuts at end of 2011.
Lithuania	2009	Presidential elections	Minor budget cuts in 2009 before presidential elections, major cuts afterwards. In 2009, coalition partners left government due to cutbacks. Early elections were not called.
Lithuania	2012	New centre-left coalition government	Centre-right replaced by centre-left government.
Netherlands	2010	CDA-PvdA-CU replaced by VVD-CDA	In elections, economy and budget less important than populist anti-Muslim rhetoric. Cutbacks (€18 billion) in new (minority) coalition agreement.

continued . . .

TABLE 7.2 *Continued*

Country	General elections	Sitting government lost election	Relation to fiscal consolidation
Netherlands	2012	VVD-CDA replaced by VVD-PvdA	Minority government fell when supporting populist party refused extra (€14 billion) cutbacks. Spring agreement about cuts. Early elections. New coalition endorsed €14 billion cuts.
Slovenia	2008	New centre-left social-Liberal (SD) coalition	New government in December 2008 made immediate anti-crisis plan. In February 2009, second plan with spending cuts. In 2009 and 2012, four rounds of cutback plans. May 2011 referendum voted down reforms. Early elections November 2011.
Slovenia	2011	New centre-left (SDS) coalition	In December 2011, cutback plan approved in new parliament, before new government installed. May 2012 cutback plan. January 2013, accusations of corruption halted cuts. New left-wing coalition government in March 2013.
Spain	2011	Zapatero (SPOE) replaced by Rajoy (PP)	Double-dip economy. Soaring bond yields. Bad economic and fiscal shape of Spain. First cutbacks. Zapatero lost confidence of population. Protests and demonstrations. Zapatero called early elections, which he lost.
United Kingdom	2010	Labour replaced by Tory-Lib Dem	Bad economic and fiscal shape of Britain. Labour postponed cuts, Tories advocated major cuts. New Tory-Lib Dem coalition immediately took unprecedented cuts.

Source: COCOPS country studies

An important source of possible social unrest in European countries was the marked increase in unemployment since the outbreak of the financial and economic crisis. Not only did unemployment rise substantially, but youth unemployment rates reached an alarming level, particularly in Southern European countries. The 2013 World of Work report by the International Labour Organisation (ILO 2013) warned about the alarmingly rising (youth) unemployment rates, accompanied by widening income inequalities. According to the ILO, the worsening employment and income situation has intensified the risk of social unrest since the start of the global crisis, especially in Cyprus, Czech Republic, Greece, Italy, Portugal, Slovenia and Spain.

In our sample of countries, particularly the ones hardest hit by the crisis faced substantial public protests, demonstrations and social unrest. We give a brief account of the public protests in Iceland, Ireland and Spain.

Iceland is a small country with only 319,000 inhabitants and a small economy dominated by fisheries, hydroelectric power and some tourism, and in recent times a booming banking sector. The fierce protests that broke out after the global financial crisis completely wiped out the Icelandic banks were unprecedented. Violent riots broke out and police used tear gas. The protests resulted in the first ever left-wing majority government in Iceland.

Public protests in Ireland were nationwide and widespread. Nearly every segment of society was affected by the severe economic recession and the cutback measures. Students demonstrated against rising fees, pensioners demonstrated against withdrawal of medical cards, workers called sit-ins and strikes against factory closures, everyone was protesting.

Although the severity of the economic and fiscal crisis in Ireland was undeniably exceptional, one should realise that these forms of students, pensioners and workers protests and demonstrations could be witnessed in many more European countries that were confronted with economic decline and firms going bankrupt, with unemployment rising and cutback measures in pensions, social security, health, housing and more leading to the customary response of protest and demonstration.

In Spain, the social unrest and public protest assumed an extraordinary form. The gigantic youth unemployment in Spain implied such an existential threat to a complete younger generation that immense public protests spontaneously broke out all over Spain. The protests of the young Facebook generation were organised through social media and took place outside the regular political system. The 15-M Movement explicitly accused the existing political system and parties.

Radical consolidation measures in both Estonia and Lithuania did not cause massive protests. Whereas Lithuania experienced only one violent protest against fiscal consolidation in 2009, the harsh and massive consolidation measures in Estonia the same year were accepted with 'silent response' by societal groups and civil servants alike. In Estonia, this has been explained by the underdeveloped civil society and weak unions (Raudla 2013; Savi and Randma-Liiv 2013), and in Lithuania by the relative instability and change in the society during the past two decades, which had fostered the 'culture of patience' (Nakrosis *et al.* 2013).

Our country studies did not contain enough quantified information about aspects of public protest and social unrest to carry out a comparative analysis.

Public protest in Iceland: pots and pans revolution

After sporadic protests since October 2008 against the government's handling of the financial crisis, in January 2009, massive protests broke out at the parliament in Reykjavik. No banker, politician or official had accepted responsibility for the banking crisis. The protesters demanded the resignation of government officials and early elections. The protests turned into riots, with thousands of people violently clashing with the police. Rioters threw eggs, rocks, paving stones and smoke bombs at the parliament building (Althingi). The police used tear gas to disperse the violent demonstrators. As demonstrators were banging pots and pans and blowing horns, the protest became dubbed the 'kitchenware (pots and pans) revolution'.

The protests more or less stopped when the Prime Minister of the right-wing Independence Party announced his resignation. In February, the Social Democratic Alliance formed a new minority coalition with the Left-Green Movement. The April 2009 general elections resulted in a gain for both parties, resulting in a parliamentary majority. The big loser was the Independence Party, which had been in power for eighteen years. The first ever left-wing majority coalition in Iceland was formed.

In view of the fierce protests and demonstrations, the new government decided that Iceland's citizens should be actively involved in creating a new constitution. In November, a National Forum was organised in the form of an assembly of 1,500 Icelandic citizens, randomly sampled from the national population registry and evenly distributed over the country and gender. After parliament accepted the Constitutional Act, a new National Forum 2010 was installed of 950 random participants, which produced a document that would be the basis for constitutional changes. In October 2010, twenty-five people of no political affiliation were elected into the Constitutional Council. In July 2011, the draft was presented to parliament, which decided to organise a referendum on the proposal. Only months before the April 2013 elections, the government decided not to pass the draft through parliament.

Source: Kristinsson (2013) and Wikipedia: Icelandic financial crisis protests, accessed 20 March 2014

Public protest in Ireland

The Irish economy entered severe recession in 2008. The unemployment rate rose dramatically. Due to the burst of the housing bubble, both sales and property values collapsed.

The Emergency Budget of October 2008 caused a public outcry over the proposed withdrawal of medical cards for elderly and the return of university fees. A series of demonstrations of pensioners, teachers and students followed. Even within the ranks of the ruling coalition government, coalition members rebelled against the proposals.

Sit-ins and strikes occurred. In January 2009, workers at the Waterford Crystal plant in Kilbarry were told they would lose their jobs. The workers began a sit-in that continued for almost two months. Later, many sit-ins took place in firms over issues such as lay-offs.

In February 2009, 120,000 people protested on the streets of Dublin, and 13,000 civil servants went on strike over a proposed pension levy.

In December 2009, the government reached an agreement with public-sector unions (Croke Park agreement) that the public sector would not face further pay cuts, nor lay-offs.

In November 2010, the European Union, International Monetary Fund and Irish state reached an agreement about an €85 billion rescue deal. Afterwards, a 'March for a Better Way' was held in Dublin, organised by the Irish Congress of Trade Unions, and attended by 50,000 people, in protest against the Troika deal.

In November 2010, between 25,000 and 40,000 students demonstrated in Dublin against a proposed increase in university registration fees, further cuts to the student maintenance grant and increasing graduate unemployment and emigration levels.

In early 2011, with approaching general elections, no major protests took place. In February 2011, the coalition government of Fianna Fáil and the Green Party lost the election and were replaced by a coalition of Fine Gael and the Labour Party.

Students became increasingly concerned about the Labour Party promise made before the election that it would oppose increased tuition fees. In November 2011, thousands of students, parents and families demonstrated in Dublin. Student protests and demonstrations went on into 2012.

Source: MacCarthaigh and Hardiman (2013) and Wikipedia:
Irish financial crisis, accessed 20 March 2014

Public protest in Spain: 15-M Movement

The economic crisis hit Spain hard with one of the highest unemployment rates in Europe, 21.3 per cent in 2010, and youth unemployment at 43.5 per cent, the highest in Europe. The September 2010 plan of the government to reduce unemployment and revive the economy was rejected by the trade unions and a general strike was called, the first in a decade in Spain. The government went on with economic reforms, and in January 2011 the retirement age was increased from sixty-five to sixty-seven. Although major trade unions had agreed, minor ones rejected the plan and demonstrations were held in Madrid.

Before the local and regional elections, on 15 May 2011, massive demonstrations and protests broke out in many Spanish cities, most notably Madrid. The relatively young and social network-organised protesters from 'the lost generation' condemned the existing political system and the two main ruling parties. The so-called 15-M Movement rejected politics, capitalism, banks and corruption, and above all attacked the massive youth unemployment. Millions of Spaniards participated in these protests. The Puerta del Sol in Madrid and Plaça Catalunya in Barcelona were occupied. After the police cleaned out the places, responses were called for via social media such as Facebook and Twitter, leading to mass demonstrations in many cities. Tens of thousands camped out on the Puerta del Sol in Madrid and other places. Police attempts to clean up occupied places led to violent clashes with demonstrators, notably in Barcelona. In Madrid, the police refrained from clashes. The protests were criticised by politicians across the country, 'legitimate force to restore order' was called for, and some denounced an attempted 'coup d'état'.

In June 2011, the 'Indignant People's March' was organised. In eight separate routes from various directions in Spain, activists marched through rural areas upon Madrid, uniting on 23 July at the Puerta del Sol after a month long walk under the banner 'Welcome Dignity'. A 'book of the people' was deposited at the Congress of Deputies.

Source: Kickert and Ysa (2014) and Wikipedia: 2011–2012 Spanish protests, accessed 20 March 2014

Likewise, we miss systematic data on administrative resistance to cutbacks. A recent cross-country investigation of budget cuts and social unrest in Europe during a 100-year period (Ponticello and Voth 2011) revealed a clear correlation between fiscal retrenchment and social unrest. Especially, expenditure cuts result in public protests; tax revenue rises much less so. The cross-country study also showed that the social unrest and protest not only related to economic decline and budget cuts, but also to the type of state and politics. Growing media attention did not strengthen the effect of cutbacks on the level of unrest, and retrenchments that led to social unrest were quickly redressed (Ponticello and Voth 2011).

After all, the measurement of the political effects of fiscal consolidation yielded more substantiated results than the economic effects measurement. The electoral effects of the governments' fiscal plans turned out to be significant. Governments were indeed almost always punished in general elections for their consolidation plans. In more than half of the cases, governments had to call early elections. In many cases, coalition governments lost their parliamentary majority due to consolidation plans. These significant results were further explained and illustrated with country summaries. Finally, we widened up the concept of political effects from only electoral to include public protests and social unrest, and showed what happened in the three countries where the severity of the crisis most clearly had wider political effects.

7.3 EFFECTS OF FISCAL CRISIS AND CONSOLIDATION ON PUBLIC ADMINISTRATION

In this section, we will first look at the effects of the crisis on administrative reform. Has the fiscal crisis and consolidation led to particular administrative reform initiatives? Have certain reforms been emphasised or turned back during the crisis? Or has the fiscal crisis merely led to the enhancement of already existing administrative reforms? In answering these questions, the outcomes of the COCOPS country studies will be used.

Second, we take a look at the effects of the crisis on public management. Has the fiscal crisis led to changes in public management patterns? These questions will be analysed by means of the COCOPS executive questionnaire (Hammerschmidt *et al.* 2013). So, once more, we alternate the qualitative country examples with the quantitative results from the COCOPS questionnaire.

Administrative reforms

In this section, the impact of fiscal consolidation on Public Administration is addressed. As mentioned in Chapter 1, the previous financial-economic crisis in the 1980s resulted in a major reform movement in Western administrations, called new public management (NPM). The question arises whether the current financial-economic crisis will again lead to a specific administrative and managerial reform trend. Has the current crisis only caused temporary short-term changes? Alternatively, can we expect more fundamental changes in Public Administration? It is much too early to draw major conclusions, as the fiscal consolidation decision-making in many European countries only started in 2010, and the stage of resolute cutback decision-making was only reached in 2012 in several countries. Consequently, long-term impacts on Public Administration are still far away; however, short-term impacts of the cutbacks are beginning to appear, and it is possible to trace preliminary tendencies.

As concerns the impact of the crisis on administrative reform, four groups of countries can be distinguished. First, in some countries such as Iceland, Ireland, Hungary and the United Kingdom, there was a clear impact of the crisis on reforms in Public Administration. Second, in other countries such as Italy, there was a clear impact that, however, resulted in unsuccessful reforms. Third, in quite a number of other countries, such as Belgium, Estonia, France, Germany and the Netherlands, the relation between the crisis and administrative reforms was less clear: managerial cost-efficiency reforms were already ongoing. The crisis was not the cause of these reforms, but certainly reinforced them. Fourth, in Lithuania, Slovenia and Spain, the crisis only led to minor administrative reforms. Finally, Norway is left out of this overview as it was only very mildly affected by the crisis, which did not have any implications on ongoing administrative reforms (Lægreid 2013).

Clear impact of crisis on reforms in Public Administration

The bank crash and economic collapse in Iceland was a window of opportunity for fundamental political and administrative reforms. The new left-wing government set out to end the patronage and clientelism-based politicisation of administration. Leadership and coordination were strengthened, political nominations limited and professionalism increased.

The enormous financial and economic crisis in Ireland opened the way for political and administrative reforms. Political leadership, coordination and control were strengthened, and the rationalisation of public service agencies was carried through.

In Hungary, the new conservative government, backed with a two-thirds majority, embarked on drastic reforms. The primary aim of the reforms was to strengthen the political control of administration, not only by strengthening political leadership and central control, but also by outright politicisation of recruitment. Although the Hungarian government introduced tight and hard fiscal policy and severe budget cuts, it is doubtful whether politicisation of the administration helped to manage the crisis.

Unlike Iceland and Ireland, the United Kingdom was not under external pressure to conduct hard cutbacks and deep reforms. The severe economic and fiscal crisis prompted the new Cameron-Clegg government to make unprecedented and unequalled cutbacks, also on its administration. Major administrative reforms were taken, some even larger and deeper than in some bailed out countries.

Iceland: fundamental reform of politics and administration

The economic collapse following the October 2008 banking crash led to massive public protests in 2009 (pots and pans revolution) against the Conservative-Social Democrat government, bringing down the coalition and leading to early elections, which resulted in the first ever left-wing (Social Democrat-Left Green) majority government in Icelandic history, with an over-arching reform programme – not only administrative reforms, but also tackling moral problems of greed, hubris and corruption. Politics and administration were to be fundamentally changed. The new government promised to create a Nordic welfare society in Iceland. The people had very high expectations for this new government, which was tightly constrained by the IMF loan programme conditions its predecessor had agreed upon.

The public sector used to be highly patronage- and clientelism-based, and was long dominated by the conservative Independence Party and the rural Progressive Party. Clientelism implied strong ministerial involvement in administrative affairs, a myriad of politicised boards and committees, and an active involvement of parliament in running the executive. The left had traditionally been weak and divided. From 1991 to 2008, the Social Democrats had been a partner in coalition governments dominated by the conservative Independence Party.

The massive protests had led to the instalment of a special inquiry commission into the bank crash. The 2010 report of that commission had an important impact on the political and administrative reforms. The report concluded that political leadership, effective coordination and professionalism were lacking in administration. As a result, the coordination within and between ministries was strengthened, the Prime Minister's role increased and political appointments of top officials limited. The fragmented nature of the Icelandic government, where informal personal and political ties used to be the main method of coordination, was to be ended. Depoliticisation and professionalisation of administration was an important objective of the reforms. The impact of the crisis was to increase centralisation and strengthen administrative procedures and professionalism.

Gradually, the left-wing government lost control in parliament, even over its own members. Disagreements with Left Green over foreign policy issues (Icesave guarantees, EU membership, etc.) weakened its credibility. In August 2012, it became a minority government, and in April 2013 it suffered a crushing defeat in the general elections. In the eyes of the voters, the great expectations and promises of the left-wing government had not been delivered.

Source: Kristinsson (2013)

Ireland: major administrative reforms

The collapse in revenues and debt increase that followed the banking crisis resulted in a bail-out by the IMF-EU-ECB Troika in late 2010. The crisis in Ireland forced a number of sweeping and unprecedented state retrenchment and reform measures. A new coalition of centre-right (Fine Gael) and centre-left (Labour) holding a large parliamentary majority was elected in 2011 on a mandate promising fundamental political and administrative reforms.

The new government, in 2011, created a new Department of Public Expenditure and Reform, combining the decision-making power of both the Finance and Prime Minister's departments, thus not only increasing the fiscal discipline but also strengthening the central control over the bureaucracy and standardising the accountability across the public service. Also, a cabinet super-committee (Economic Management Council) to manage the Troika loan programme was created.

Another notable measure was to decrease the number of public service agencies, which had grown in the past decade into a complex organisational 'zoo'. Agencies were to share back offices, to merge or to be reabsorbed into the parent departments. With small budget and staff bodies, that proved to be easy; with the larger ones, more problematic. The reform mandate of the new 2011 government led to a renewed 'rationalisation' of state agencies, with plans for new performance frameworks, financial management systems, annual reviews and improvement of agency-department agreements. Considerable emphasis was placed on 'shared service centres', combining back office functions such as procurement and property management.

Furthermore, the new government proposed to reshape the 'public service bargain', that is, the trade between loyalty and competency of bureaucrats to their political masters, in return for security of tenure and a sufficient level of remuneration. In Ireland, public-sector pay was severely and unilaterally cut by governments, as were the conditions for public-sector employment, a break with over twenty years of 'social partnership', the tripartite consultation mechanisms over pay and the labour market. In 2011, a 'Croke Park Agreement' was reached between government and trade unions on banning further pay cuts and lay-offs. An attempt in 2013 to renegotiate a social agreement with the trade unions to include pay cuts, increased working hours, reductions in overtime and premium pay, and reform of employment grades in the public sector was initially rejected in a trade unions ballot. A subsequent deal was later agreed on by the majority of unions following concessions.

Source: MacCarthaigh and Hardiman (2013)

Hungary: strengthening political control of administration

After the landslide victory by nationalist-conservative party FIDESZ over the Socialist Party (MSzP) in the April 2010 elections, the new Conservative-Christian Democrat coalition government, under Prime Minister Orban, had a more than two-thirds parliamentary majority. The new right-centre government engaged in far-reaching administrative reforms that were primarily aimed at strengthening the political control of administration. Eight integrated 'super-ministries' were created, and the Prime Minister's office was restructured into a Ministry of Public Administration and Justice with a broad portfolio. A new Local Government Act aimed to severely reduce the tasks and responsibilities of local governments. The aim of the Orban government to enforce the political control over administration also led to stricter hierarchical and political control of the recruitment of top officials. The Ministry of Public Administration and Justice – an expansion of the former Prime Minister's office – received the right to veto any appointment of public managers, and the new civil service regulation explicitly established 'political loyalty' as an employment criterion, thus introducing elements of a 'spoils system' in the Hungarian administration. The aim to enforce political control expanded beyond the scope of administration, and also involved constitutional weakening of the Constitutional Court, the Budgetary Council, some Ombudsmen and a new media supervisory authority. The two-thirds majority also enabled the government to reform the election system in favour of the parties in power.

Source: Hajnal (2013)

United Kingdom: major administrative reforms

The British government announced the 'Public Bodies Reform Programme' in order to reduce the number and costs of arm's-length bodies. As part of this initiative, civil servants across sixteen departments reviewed 904 public bodies, of which it was suggested that a total of 496 should be dissolved, merged with others or substantially reformed. This change reduced the managerial autonomy of public bodies and presented evidence of an attempt to re-centralise in response to fiscal pressure. Central control was also increased over local governments and each public service, particularly regarding capital projects. In addition, reorganisations of executive agencies were carried out: some executive agencies had their executive agency status rebuked, and they became subordinate units of departments (e.g. UK Border Agency, Job Centre+). The British government also introduced the 'Operational Efficiency Programme' for all departments targeted at saving in back-office operation, equipment, IT reforms and collaborative procurement, as well as increased cost saving in the public-sector estates.

Source: James and Nakamura (2013)

Clear impact of the fiscal crisis on administration but reforms unsuccessful

In Italy, administrative reforms were clearly driven by economic and managerial efficiency motives enhanced by the crisis, but the government lacked the political will and power to drive them through. Moreover, the hiring and pay

---

Italy: reforms unsuccessful and hindered by cutbacks

After decades of inertia, an administrative reform became possible at the beginning of the 1990s because of the currency crisis and the collapse of the old party system. Consequently, a radical and comprehensive programme of NPM reforms was introduced throughout the entire bureaucracy. However, these grand aims were confronted with serious implementation problems as successive governments were politically unwilling to drive through these reforms, and the formal-legalistic tradition of administration remained in contrast to the economic-managerial nature of the reforms.

After the 2008 financial crisis, a new administrative reform programme was devised by the minister of Public Administration and Innovation to revitalise the implementation of performance management, a key component of previous NPM reforms. However, the severe austerity measures taken since 2010 to freeze hiring and pay and to cut higher salaries deprived the performance management reform of the incentives to realise it. The fall of the Berlusconi government and its replacement by the technocratic Monti government did not lead to new administrative reforms. Under EU pressure, all efforts were focused on public expenditure reduction and cutback management. The EU distrusted the effectiveness of successful reforms in the Italian administration.

Another noteworthy reform of Italian Public Administration was the reform of provincial government. Riding on the popular dissatisfaction with the costs of fragmented provinces, successive governments addressed the efficiency and coordination problems. The economic and fiscal crisis further enhanced the need for efficiency gains. The centre-left Prodi government (2006–2008) lacked the cohesion to arrive at a reallocation of the workforce across different levels of government. The centre-right Berlusconi government (2008–2011) was a coalition of the People of Freedom Party advocating the abolition of provinces and the Northern League advocating the devolution of tasks to provinces, especially the northern ones governed by them. When the fiscal crisis reached its height in 2011, the abolition of (small) provinces became part of the austerity agenda of the government. The new Monti government, in 2011, tried to bypass the complex constitutional route of reform to decentralise provincial powers to regions and municipalities.

Source: Ongaro *et al.* (2013)

freeze did not motivate the administration to cooperate. And because the EU disbelieved in the possibility of reforms in Italian administration, it primarily focused on fiscal consolidation and budget cutbacks.

In Spain, public-sector reform was mainly austerity-driven and the fiscal austerity was externally imposed by the EU and ECB. Spain needed to convince Europe (and the international financial markets) of its fiscal credibility if it wanted to keep counting on European support. The domestic inclination and sincere commitment for structural reform is doubtful, though. The public sector is the heartland of Spanish political patronage and clientelism, so the chances for successful reform look dim there.

Spain: structural reforms unsuccessful

The Socialist Zapatero government initially denied the crisis and campaigned 'for full employment' in the March 2008 elections, which he won, but not with absolute majority. In November 2008, Zapatero launched a 'plan for stimulating the economy and employment' that included an extra €8 billion for public investments by local governments, meant for municipal construction and building projects that quickly generated employment. This plan was widely considered a prime example of patronage and clientelism. The first announcement by Zapatero of spending cuts in May 2010 was conceived under pressure by the Eurozone leaders, in return for ongoing European support on the international financial markets. Despite these first cutbacks comprising public employees' salary reductions (besides hiring freeze, replacement caps, etc.), they did not involve structural reforms in the public sector. Right after the November 2011 elections, the new centre-right Rajoy government announced labour reform, public-sector cuts, and cuts in health and education (the latter being the responsibility of autonomous regions). In September 2012, Rajoy presented a 'national reform programme', which, besides fiscal cutbacks, included structural reforms in the labour market, public sector, health and education. A 'commission for reform of Public Administrations' (state, regional, local) was installed. It was no coincidence that this reform programme was published right after the June 2012 bail-out of the Spanish banking sector. Again, austerity was externally imposed, and presumably structural reforms were also part of the external loan conditions. Moreover, the substantial cuts in health and education involved a 'budgetary stability agreement' between national government and the autonomous regions. In other words, the Rajoy government imposed fiscal cutbacks upon the regions. All in all, these were not the best preconditions for widely shared and genuine readiness and commitment for structural reforms.

Source: Kickert and Ysa (2014)

Relations between fiscal crisis and administrative reform less clear: reforms already ongoing

Administrative reforms in France were designed before the crisis erupted in 2008, but were clearly related to fiscal problems and aimed at budget cutbacks.

Administrative reforms aimed at increasing managerial efficiency were introduced in Belgian federal and Flemish administration long before the crisis.

France: reforms designed before the crisis

Structural reforms of the French administration were not the result of the 2008 financial crisis; they had already been designed in 2007. After the 2007 election of President Sarkozy, who was minister of Economics and Finance before and was sensitive to budgetary problems, a General Public Policy Review (Révision Générale des Politiques Publiques; RGPP) was launched to 'rethink the state' in the context of the fiscal problems. The aim was to reduce the size of government and to increase managerial effectiveness and efficiency of the bureaucracy. The RGPP reviews were an exercise in cutback management, in line with the 2001 budgetary procedure reform (Loi organique relative aux lois de finance; LOFL) that had introduced NPM-type instruments such as performance management, and following the widespread introduction of semi-autonomous executive agencies (opérateurs de l'Etat, établissements publics, etc.) during the 1990s and early 2000s.

A drastic reorganisation was carried out: the number of ministries was reduced, large meta-ministries were created, and intra-ministerial mergers took place. The territorial state administration was also reformed by merging twenty-three regional directorates into eight, corresponding to the new meta-ministries, and merging the dozen directorates at the 'department' level. Although not directly related to the 2008 crisis, these reforms were still linked to fiscal problems and aimed at cutbacks.

The 2008 crisis led to an extended use of managerial instruments. In 2010, the 'strategic steering' of semi-autonomous agencies was introduced by means of performance contracts, clear objectives, measurable indicators and annual reports, and by rationalising the relation between parent ministries and agencies (tutelage). The 'strategic steering' reform included cutbacks in operating and personnel costs of agencies. In addition to that, the use of public-private partnerships also sharply increased after the 2008 crisis.

Source: Bezes and LeLidec (2013)

Belgium: reforms long before the crisis

One of the major recent administrative reforms was the 2001 'Copernicus' reform of the organisation structure and personnel policy of federal administration. The aim was to move from a Weberian bureaucracy to a customer-oriented administration and increase the managerial capacity of civil servants. Besides this federal reform, in 2000, a structural and cultural reform was launched in the Flemish administration to improve its policy-making capacity, among other things by making a distinction between policy-making departments and executive agencies. These two major public management reforms in Belgian administration occurred during a period of no fiscal crisis, suggesting that such reforms are more perceived as a luxury for good times than as a need in bad ones.

It is important to note that Belgium underwent a much more fundamental state reform in the transformation of the unitary state into a federal state with three regions and three communities. This fundamental state reform has been carrying on for decades, recently in the fifth stage reform in 2003 and the sixth stage in 2011. The latter involved an amendment of the Public Finance Act for regions and communities, which was one of the reasons why the coalition formation took so long.

Source: Troupin *et al.* (2013)

Managerial reforms in the Dutch administration were also introduced before the crisis. Managerial modernisation has a long tradition in Dutch civil service (Kickert 2000). Managerial cost-efficiency gains and expenditure cuts have been carried out for decades, long before the crisis erupted, but were later clearly reinforced by the fiscal crisis.

Netherlands: ongoing managerial reforms

The major recent civil service reforms have been unrelated to the fiscal crisis. The 2003 reform programme had no budgetary cutback targets. The 2007 reform programme explicitly focused on cutbacks both in the budget of and the personnel in central administration, but was launched before the crisis. Technical-operational improvements in management and administration, such as housing, salary administration, personnel services and shared service centres, were aimed at increasing cost-efficiency and related to budgetary retrenchments, but managerial modernisation had already been taking place for a long time in Dutch administration. The fiscal crisis was not its cause, but enhanced its necessity, and therefore fuelled its further implementation. In 2010, this technical-operational and managerial type of reform was continued in the subsequent 'compact government' programme, which was related to the cutback package announced by the new government at the time. In 2012, the new cabinet announced the continuation and completion of this latter reform programme.

As in Dutch politics, changes in administration were small, gradual and incremental rather than swift, drastic and fundamental. Public management reform was less politically sensitive and visible, which probably contributed to its successful implementation.

In addition, both the new 2010 and 2012 governments launched far-reaching plans for territorial reform. The existing thirteen provinces were to merge into five regions, and municipalities were to increase their size to 100,000 inhabitants.

Source: Kickert (2013c)

In Estonia, administrative reforms aimed at cost-efficiency gains had already been taking place since the early 2000s, long before the crisis hit. The crisis offered the government the opportunity to carry out further-reaching reforms that were prepared but voted down before.

Estonia: reforms reinforced

Estonian Public Administration reforms have been carried by cost-efficiency motives since the early 2000s, and cost-efficiency continued to be one of the aims of reform even during the years of economic boom. This had to do with anti-state attitudes among the citizens, fuelled by consecutive right-wing governments. In this regard, the goal of more cost-efficiency during the years of the fiscal crisis was nothing new in the government rhetoric. However, the general retrenchment environment helped the government to carry out reforms that were turned down earlier. Most importantly, the parliament passed a new Public Service Act in 2012 that had been rejected already twice before, in 2002 and 2009. According to the new Act (implemented in 2013), one-quarter of civil servants (e.g. staff in the ICT, personnel, accounting and public relations departments) lost their civil service status and became employed according to the private-sector Employment Act. Seniority pay and public service pensions were abandoned, and the existing (limited) job security was equalled with that in the private sector. Although this reform was prepared before the crisis hit, it is possible to argue that the crisis situation paved the way for its approval within the coalition and in the parliament. Similarly, the crisis only indirectly affected the other ongoing administrative reforms, such as the establishment of shared service centres and mergers of government agencies (nine mergers took place at the peak of the crisis in 2008–2010).

Source: Savi and Randma-Liiv (2013)

Germany: ongoing minor reforms

The German federal government launched an administrative reform program in 2010, after the introduction of its austerity package. The reform programme covered three areas of activity: optimising organisation, human resources and ICT. The key focus of the reform was the further development of shared service centres in order to increase the efficiency of administration. To a large extent, all these undertakings presented an incremental continuation of the previous reform trajectory. The most important changes that were implemented in response to the crisis concerned budgeting and fiscal governance: the introduction of a debt brake into the constitution, and the establishment of a new top-down budgeting procedure on federal government level, which granted the minister of Finance more power to curb excessive spending of other ministers.

Source: Osterheld *et al.* (2013)

The German government continued implementing relatively minor managerial reforms during the years of fiscal crisis. While the crisis had a clear impact in introducing changes in budgeting procedures and fiscal governance, the ongoing Public Administration reforms were unrelated to fiscal consolidation.

Crisis resulted in minor administrative reforms

In Slovenia, the crisis only led to minor administrative reforms. No systematic reform programme was formulated by the government. Some minor cutback measures were taken in public-sector pay, some ministerial reorganisations took place, and some budgeting instruments were introduced.

Similarly, in Lithuania, no major structural reforms of administration took place during the crisis period. Only some minor reforms and reorganisations were carried out.

Slovenia: minor reforms

Before the crisis, a real inclination towards achieving greater efficiency and costs savings in the public sector did not exist. Economic, and particularly fiscal, pressures changed this attitude, yet only minor changes had happened by 2013. In early 2012, public-sector downsizing became the real issue for the first time since the country was established (in 1991, Slovenia split from Yugoslavia to become an independent democratic state), as the public-sector debt had doubled during three years. Consequently, the new government started planning and implementing fiscal austerity measures combined with structural reforms in certain policy fields (e.g. welfare), but not systematically addressing Public Administration itself. The 'rationalisation' of Public Administration did not include systemic administrative reform plans, but was limited to simple cutback measures such as wage freeze, reductions in the costs of business trips of public servants, reductions in civil servants' holidays and so on.

Despite the lack of a general administrative reform agenda, the new 2012 government substantially changed the mechanisms of the decision-making process by considerably reducing the number of ministers to twelve, and by transferring the central role in fiscal consolidation from the Minister for Development and European Affairs (without portfolio) to the ministry of Finance.

In addition, by adopting the austerity and interventionist measures, government also limited the autonomy of public organisations, in particular the ones belonging to the state administration, as special permits became necessary to hire personnel and mandatory retirements were introduced. This indicates that more centralised modes of functioning of public organisations were established, and the government effectively introduced more control on those organisations, in particular relating to their costs.

The government introduced programme and performance budgeting for the first time during the period of 2008–2011, but they had prepared the plans to introduce that instrument before the crisis.

Source: Pevcin (2013)

Lithuania: minor reforms

The Lithuanian government abolished county administrations as separate legal entities; however, this fundamental reform was already planned before the crisis hit. In addition, Lithuania carried out some organisational reforms (including the abolition of county administrations) and some efficiency measures during the crisis. Although parliament revised the existing civil service legislation in a few areas (e.g. the performance appraisal of civil servants and the status of the Civil Service Department) in 2010–2012, the most important decisions of remuneration, motivation and result-oriented system in the civil service were not made. Major structural reforms did not occur in Lithuanian Public Administration in the period 2008–2012. However, Lithuania's response to the global crisis contributed to the centralisation of authority and decision-making in policy areas. The reduction in the number of appropriation managers, the absorption of semi-autonomous agencies into parent ministries or the assignment of the agencies to ministerial policy areas increased the authority of ministers to politically control government expenditure and agency performance.

Source: Nakrosis *et al.* (2013)

Table 7.3 summarises the relations between the fiscal crisis and administrative reforms in the countries studied.

The country studies showed that new administrative reforms – triggered fully or at least partly by fiscal crisis – were planned in the majority of selected European countries, and implemented in half of them. It can also be conjectured that in many countries, the crisis gave a boost to the administrative reforms that were initiated prior to the crisis. The crisis had negative effects (through cancellation, postponement or hindrance) on existing reforms in only a handful of cases. It also occurred from the country studies that a great majority of European countries are in the process of carrying out larger or smaller administrative changes, which were started earlier and/or were unrelated to crisis.

The impact of the fiscal crisis on administration was most straightforward and encompassing in the countries that had to carry out the most radical cutbacks. At one end of the continuum, the ongoing administrative reforms in Norway had no link to the financial crisis. The severity of the fiscal crisis helps to explain the introduction of large-scale administrative reforms in Ireland and the United Kingdom, but also more modest reforms in Hungary, Iceland and Lithuania. The only exception in this pattern is Estonia, which was among the countries hit the hardest by the crisis, but which did not initiate new administrative reforms. In a number of European countries, the impact of austerity upon Public Administration was less evident. In most cases, these countries were hit only modestly by the crisis, where less drastic, mainly managerial efficiency-oriented reforms were made. In these countries, administrative reforms, cost-efficiency measures and operational-managerial reforms were normal 'modernisation' practice already long before the fiscal crisis. The expenditure cutbacks resulting from the current crisis did not cause such reforms, but in several cases enhanced their necessity. In Belgium and France, the important administrative reforms had already taken place before the outbreak of the crisis. In the Netherlands, cost-efficiency reform and cutback programmes in national administration existed before the crisis. In Estonia, a few structural reforms were implemented during the crisis, but the crisis served as a window of opportunity to put in place changes planned earlier. It is characteristic to these countries that the crisis boosted the necessity for ongoing reforms but the already existing reform paths were not altered. These countries thus show only a weak and indirect link between the crisis and administrative reform.

Explaining the cross-country similarities and differences requires the consideration of both internal and external factors in which the reform process unfolds. Our analysis shows that Public Administration has been strongly affected in countries that were obliged to ask for foreign financial assistance, as shown by the cases of Hungary, Iceland and Ireland where the foreign assistance and/or bail-outs were conditioned not only upon severe budgetary cuts, but also upon administrative reforms. The impact of the Troika on administrative

TABLE 7.3 Relations between fiscal crisis and administrative reforms in Europe

	GBR	IRL	HUN	LTU	ESP	SLO	ISL	FRA	ITA	EST	GER	NLD	BEL	NOR
New reforms planned	+	+	+	+	+	+	+	+	+	−	−	−	−	−
New reforms carried out	+	+	+	+	+	+	+	−	−	−	−	−	−	−
Crisis boosted existing reforms	+	+	+	+	+	−	−	+	−	+	+	+	−	−
Cancellation of existing reforms	+	+	−	−	−	−	−	−	+	−	−	−	−	−
Postponement of existing reforms	+	−	−	−	−	−	−	−	−	−	−	−	−	−
Crisis hindered existing reforms	−	+	−	−	−	−	−	−	+	−	−	−	+	−

reforms has, however, varied from one country to another. The most substantial external influence over domestic reforms was detected in Ireland and Iceland, where the Troika conditionality was extended over the cutbacks and also affected Public Administration reforms. However, it should be noted that the Troika conditionality pushed for some reforms, whereas other administrative reforms were initiated 'voluntarily' by domestic governments. In Southern European countries such as Italy and Spain, the Troika imposed strict budgetary reforms only, as it did not believe in the success of ever-failing administrative reform plans. It was the same distrust of Europe in effective administrative reform in Greece that caused the Troika to also only focus on budget reform. Our study thus shows that domestic decision-making is less 'isolated', and the role, power and authority of the international institutions has to be considered more than ever before.

The existing literature shows that the impact of a crisis may range from restoring the status quo to using the crisis for incremental or radical change (Boin *et al.* 2008). Structural change (reform) embodies change *of* the system, whereas the incremental change takes place *within* the system, which leaves its basic structure intact. According to the empirical information presented earlier, structural reforms were supported by limited empirical evidence. Large-scale and systemic structural reforms were carried out only in Ireland and the United Kingdom. In the cases of Hungary, Iceland, Lithuania and Slovenia, a few structural reforms took place but these addressed individual aspects of administrative systems rather than being overwhelming and systemic reforms of Public Administration. In eight remaining countries in our sample, structural administrative reforms were not implemented during the recent crisis. This allows us to conclude that the European governments' responses to crisis predominantly followed a combination of straightforward cutbacks and incremental change by thus working towards stability rather than structural change. The crisis intensified the pressure to reform Public Administration to some extent, but these pressures did not translate into large-scale structural reforms and/or specific reform trajectories in the majority of European countries.

Analysing the contents of reforms indicates that several European countries showed some tendencies towards centralisation – strengthening of central (financial) control over public agencies and local governments, search for improved coordination in the centre of government, rationalisation of public-sector organisation (mergers of agencies), improvement of regulatory capacities, and downsizing back-office functions via creation of shared service centres. This presents an interesting comparison to the previous global crisis in the 1980s. Both crises induced similar aims in administrative reforms – increasing cost-efficiency and cost-effectiveness. On the one hand, the crisis of the 1980s contributed to the occurrence of the NPM approach by involving a widespread introduction of models and techniques from the private business sector carried by the tools aiming at deregulation and decentralisation. On the other hand, the preliminary effects of the 2008 crisis show the opposite direction, where the crisis rather contributes to the post-NPM practices through a more systematic attention paid to centralising initiatives and coordination. One could argue that this shows path dependency of the whole-of-government reforms that have been very popular across Europe over the past decade.

Changes in selected public management patterns

Our aim is not only to identify possible administrative reforms related to the crisis, but also changes in patterns of public management occurring during the budget cuts and in the immediate years following the cutbacks. In this section, we switch our methodological spectacles from qualitative case studies to include the quantitative findings of the COCOPS survey about the effects of the fiscal crisis on a number of aspects of public management.

As Figure 7.7 indicates, fiscal consolidation increased the attention governments pay to performance management. In addition, to achieve cuts on government spending, downsizing back-office functions was applied more often than downsizing the front-line staff directly involved with delivering public services. In this regard, citizens were put first vis-á-vis civil servants. Increase in the fees and user charges of public services were rather modestly applied during the fiscal consolidation.

When looking at the impact of the crisis on the *relevance of performance information*, the respondents from all countries agreed with the claim that the use of performance information during the crisis-time budgeting and

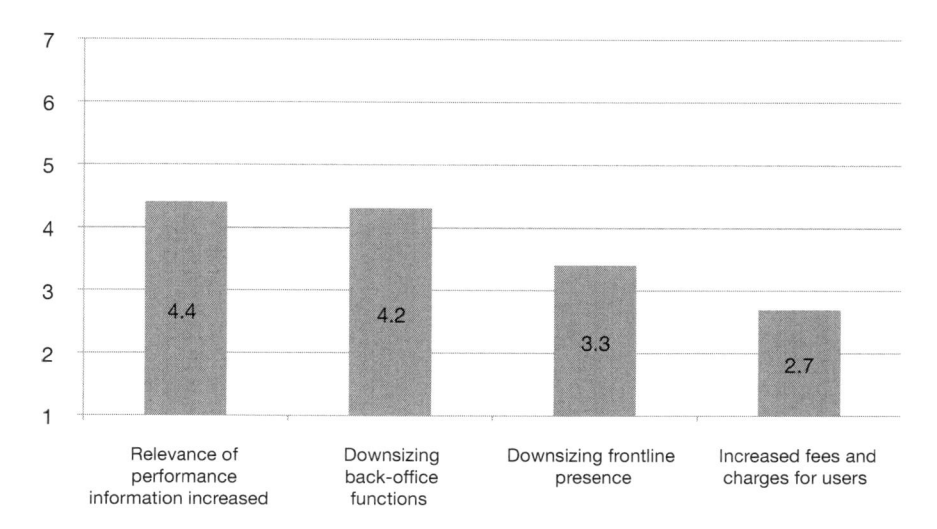

FIGURE 7.7 Changes in public management (1 = not at all; 7 = to a large extent)

decision-making processes increased (Figure 7.8). The increase in the relevance of performance information was considered the highest in Ireland, the Netherlands, Lithuania, the United Kingdom, France, Iceland and Italy. The rest of the countries reported slightly smaller but still rather significant increase in the use of performance information. Performance information is taken into account in the downsizing process as it is believed to enable prioritisation and rationalisation of cutback decision-making.

One of the aims of the survey was also to find out if the crisis affected any organisational functions. In order to achieve cuts on government spending, *back-office functions* were downsized quite frequently (Figure 7.9). In fact, the

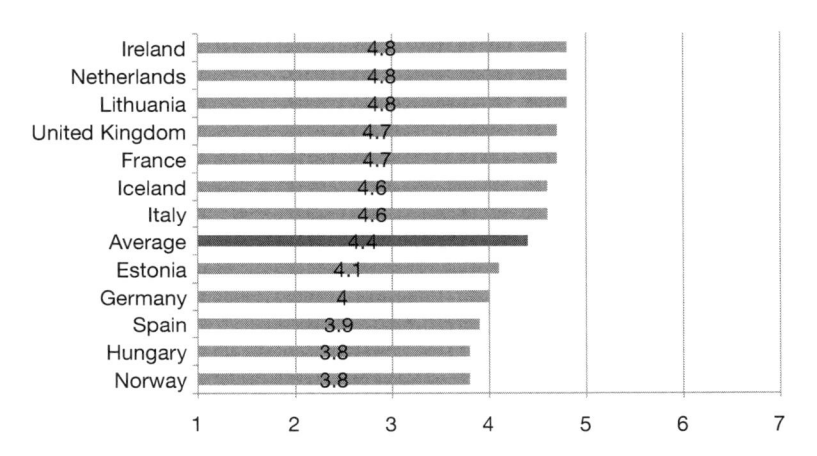

FIGURE 7.8 Perceived increase in the use of performance information (1 = not at all; 7 = to a large extent)

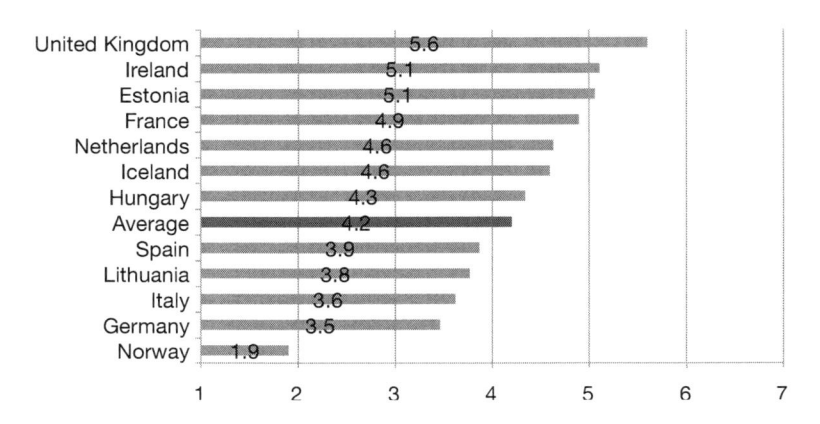

FIGURE 7.9 Perceived downsizing back-office functions (1 = not at all; 7 = to a large extent)

United Kingdom, Ireland and Estonia carried out reforms targeted at downsizing back-office functions and creating shared service centres. In addition to these three countries, the public executives from France, the Netherlands and Iceland also claimed that, during the cutbacks, the back-office functions were downscaled extensively. On the other hand, in Norway, the respondents confirmed the opposite.

Reducing front-line presence during the fiscal crisis seems not to have been a measure applied very often (Figure 7.10). Only in Ireland, reductions in the front line played a greater role during the time of fiscal consolidation. In the Netherlands, Hungary, the United Kingdom and Lithuania, reducing front-line presence was seen as a tool to cope with the crisis to a lesser degree, and Norway traditionally ranks the lowest also in this scale.

Although the fiscal stress may trigger the governments to increase service fees, *increasing the fees and charges of public services* was not a popular measure applied in European countries (Figure 7.11). In all countries but Spain, Ireland, Hungary and the United Kingdom, the respondents estimated that increases in fees or charges were not common during fiscal consolidation.

To sum up the selected changes in public management during the fiscal crisis, as measured in the COCOPS survey, we can conclude the following. First, the impact of the crisis on the relevance of performance indicators was markedly perceived in Ireland, the Netherlands and Lithuania, while the experience of other European countries also supported this trend, though to a somewhat lesser degree. Second, a majority of the respondents from the United Kingdom, Ireland and Estonia claimed that during the cutbacks, the back-office functions were downsized to a great extent, while other European countries except Norway also followed this general shift in public management. Third, the fiscal

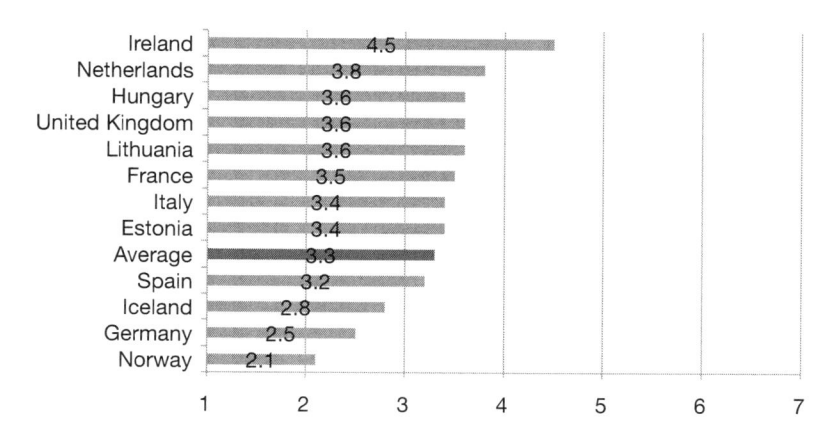

FIGURE 7.10 Perceived reduction of front-line presence (1 = not at all; 7 = to a large extent)

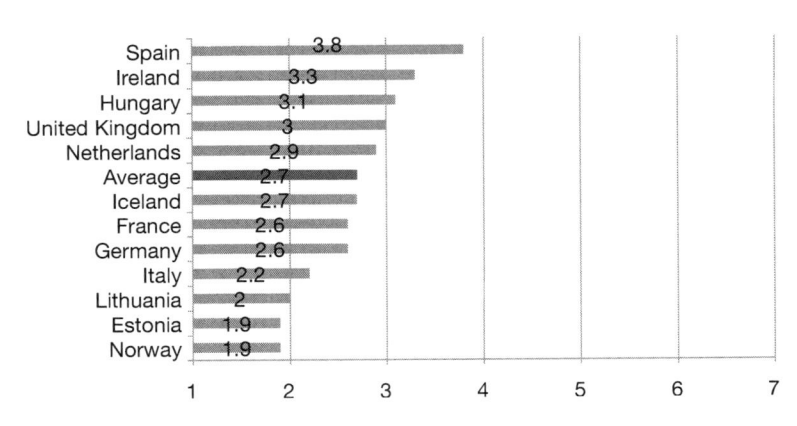

FIGURE 7.11 Perceived increase in the fees and user charges for public services (1 = not at all; 7 = to a large extent)

crisis did not have a remarkable influence on the front-line presence and on the size of fees and user charges for public service. Still, the hardest hit countries can also be distinguished here, as Ireland made the most use of cutting the front-line presence while Spain stands out for increasing fees and user charges for public services.

Admittedly, the questions in the public executives' survey only covered a small and restricted number of aspects of public management, and the outcomes were sometimes mixed and ambiguous, but it delivered a useful quantitative general addition to the qualitative specific results from the country case studies that could not possibly be generalised.

General conclusions of this chapter

In this chapter, we considered three types of effects of the fiscal consolidation. The first type of effect was the fiscal and economic effect of fiscal consolidation plans of European governments, that is, the reduction of budget deficits and the recovery of economic growth. Because both restoring public finances and restoring the economy depend on many more variables than domestic fiscal consolidation efforts alone, our expectations about finding significant relationships were low. The statistical correlations confirmed our low expectations. The correlation between fiscal consolidation efforts and budget deficit reduction could only vaguely be shown, and its correlation with economic recovery could not be substantiated.

The second type of effect we addressed was the political effect of fiscal consolidation. The electoral effects of the governments' fiscal plans turned out to be significant. Incumbent governments almost always lost general elections because of consolidation plans. In almost half of the cases, early elections were called, and in several cases coalition governments lost their parliamentary majority due to consolidation plans. Furthermore, we widened up the concept of political effects from only electoral to include public protests and social unrest, and presented clear examples of such wider political effects in Iceland, Ireland and Spain.

The third type of effect we considered was the effect of the fiscal crisis and consolidation on Public Administration and management. The impact of the crisis on administration was the strongest in countries that had received financial assistance upon the condition of budgetary and administrative reforms. In other countries, the impact of the crisis upon administration was less evident. In some countries, administrative reforms were carried out before the crisis; in other countries, ongoing reforms were enhanced by the fiscal crisis; and in yet another group of countries, the crisis only led to minor administrative reforms. The tendency of European governments thus seems to treat the immediate symptoms rather than the long-term underlying causes of crisis. Short-term fiscal targets tend to dominate over systematic analysis of shortcomings in the operation of administration. The response to the crisis displayed many elements of continuity rather than change vis-à-vis the reform trends and tools that had already been evolving before the crisis. Several European countries witnessed an intensification, rather than reversal, of existing public-sector reform trends. This intensification placed further pressure on governments to cut public-sector personnel, wages and pensions rather than starting structural reforms. Thus, the crisis seems to have promoted pre-programmed responses, and not necessarily new ways of behaviour. In sum, the European experience shows that the 2008 crisis has not automatically translated into administrative changes, which would radically alter the existing reform trajectories by correcting previous governance failures and creating longer-term conditions for recovery and sustainable growth.

Part four

Conclusions and discussion

Chapter 8

Conclusions and discussion

In this book, a comparative analysis has been carried out on how fourteen large and small countries in Western, Eastern and Southern Europe have responded to the fiscal crisis in the period 2008–2012. In this concluding chapter, we now finally get back to the main research questions addressed in this book, and see what conclusions can be drawn. The three main research questions addressed in this book were:

- How did European governments respond to the fiscal crisis, what fiscal consolidation measures were taken, and how did the decision-making take place?
- How can the similarities and differences between consolidation measures and decision-making processes be explained from both an economic and a political perspective?
- How have the fiscal crisis and consolidation affected the restoring of public finances and economy, what were the political effects, and what were the effects on Public Administration and reform?

The analytical framework used in this book was derived from these three research questions. For the sake of conceptual clarity, we repeat the outline of the analytical framework that was presented in Chapter 3.

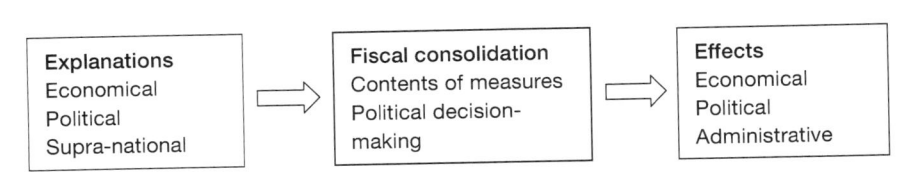

FIGURE 8.1 Outline of the analytical framework

Conclusions

How did European governments respond to the fiscal crisis? This first main research question was addressed along two lines, that is, an economic and a political one. Both in the chapters about fiscal consolidation and in the chapters about explanations and effects of consolidation, these two lines were constantly followed. We looked at the economic aspects of fiscal consolidation, an undeniably essential aspect of that budgetary activity. Both authors not being economists, but administrative scholars, our economic analysis remained restricted and unpretentious. Our special interest (and expertise) was in the political aspects – the politics of consolidation and the political effort of governments to manage the fiscal crisis. That is why, in Chapter 2, special attention was devoted to the conceptual exploration of the political aspects of consolidation. We were seeking for a sort of political equivalent of the well-defined and clear economic variable 'volume of fiscal consolidation', a sort of 'volume of political effort' of a government. After some conceptual contemplations, we chose to interpret this 'political effort' in terms of political decision-making. So, besides investigating the economic volume and contents of fiscal consolidation measures, the second line of investigation we focused upon was the political decision-making by a government leading up to the consolidation measures.

The political decision-making efforts of a government were subsequently conceptualised into the variables 'types of decision-making', 'centralisation of decision-making' and 'stages of decision-making'. Types of decision-making were derived from the basic distinction between across-the-board (cheese-slicing and proportional) cutbacks, on the one hand, and targeted (selective) political priority-setting on the other, and further refined and elaborated. As for centralisation of decision-making, we looked at the shifts in the importance of Ministries of Finance and budget-planning units, as well as politicians versus civil servants, in the government decision-making process. Stages of decision-making were derived from the theories of organisational change, with the usual denial and resistance at first. Fiscal consolidation in most countries also started with politicians denying the need for cutbacks, delaying and postponing them, before they recognised the gravity and duration of the crisis and finally took serious cutback decisions.

So, that is basically what chapters four and five on fiscal consolidation were about. Chapter 4 gave a description and analysis of the economic aspects of consolidation measures. Chapter 5 provided a description and analysis of types and stages of decision-making. Let us now address the question that came out: What were the main conclusions from these analyses?

Content of fiscal consolidation measures

The general overview of the economic aspects of the consolidation measures we started with in Chapter 4 was based on the OECD (2012) cross-country report on fiscal consolidation, following the normal economic distinction between expenditure and revenue measures, and the further subdivision of expenditures into operational, programme and investment cuts. The OECD survey was illustrated by country examples drawn from our COCOPS case studies. As we were particularly interested in the cutback measures targeted at Public Administration, we looked specifically at the operational expenditure cuts to reduce the costs of administration itself. We presented a considerable number of country examples of the varying scope and form of cutbacks in administration. Virtually all countries took measures to freeze payment and hiring (caps on replacement rate), but politically more sensitive measures to really cut payment and lay off staff were not widely taken, but only in countries most severely hit by the crisis, especially the bailed out countries where these drastic measures were prescribed and imposed by the Troika. We then supplemented these qualitative and specific country data with the quantitative results of the COCOPS public-sector executives' survey (Hammerschmidt *et al.* 2013). Most findings of the questionnaire confirmed the data from the country case studies about the wide use of pay and hiring freeze, and the rare use of pay cuts and lay-offs.

Political decision-making about fiscal consolidation

In Chapter 5, data about the political decision-making were collected from both the qualitative country case studies and the quantitative outcomes of the COCOPS public executives' survey. But, undeniably, the first core part of this chapter was the extensive and thick descriptions of the political aspects of governmental decision-making in a number of countries. The focus was on three characteristics of the political decision-making. First, types of decision-making, including the size and speed of the political decision-making, as well as across-the-board versus targeted decision-making. A number of country examples illustrated more in-depth the specificity of the political decision-making: the large and swift cutback decisions taken in the United Kingdom in 2010; France, where large and swift cutbacks were to be expected under president Sarkozy, but did not occur; the huge and immediate cutbacks in the relatively unknown Estonia; and the impossibility of large and swift cutback decisions in consensual countries such as Germany, the Netherlands and Belgium.

Second, the characteristic 'degree of centralisation' was analysed by means of the COCOPS questionnaire's results. The analysis demonstrated that centralisation was an overwhelming pattern in all fourteen European countries during fiscal consolidation. In most cases, it was related to the increase in the power of Ministries of Finance on national-level decision-making, and of budgetary units on organisational-level decision-making. In addition, the increase in the power of politicians was perceived by the public-sector executives during the crisis decision-making. Qualitative country examples further illustrated the increase in power of central decision-making bodies.

The third core part of this chapter consisted of the extensive and thick descriptions of the stages of cutback decision-making. The focus was on the following:

- whether the size and speed of the cutback measures increased in subsequent stages; and
- whether the type of decision-making in subsequent stages changed from incremental and across-the-board cuts to targeted and political priority-setting.

A number of country examples illustrated that many European countries passed through such patterns, albeit in varying ways and with exceptions. At first denial, delay and postponement of cutbacks, then the initial small and gradual cuts, and only later more serious cutbacks. One exception for the gradual cutback pattern was Estonia, where radical cuts were applied immediately at the outset of the crisis, and which withdrew from consolidation and decreased the cutbacks in later stages. Another exception was the countries that were bailed out with external loan programmes, such as Iceland and Ireland. The conditions for the loans forced governments to take immediate and drastic fiscal consolidation measures. There was no room for initial crisis denial, delay and postponement. The targeted political priority-setting decisions, however, remained exceptional. Even resolute, large and serious cuts were predominantly of the across-the-board type.

Explanations of fiscal consolidation

How can fiscal consolidation be explained? This second main research question was also addressed from both an economic and political perspective. As fiscal consolidation was the response of governments on the deterioration of domestic public finances and economy, it was obvious that the primary explanation for the volume of fiscal consolidation was to be found in the financial-economic circumstances of a country prior to the consolidation. No wonder that the volume of fiscal consolidation appeared to be positively correlated with the average budget deficits in the preceding period.

It proved more difficult to statistically validate possible political explanatory factors, such as the type of state, politics and government. The qualitative country examples plainly illustrated the importance of such political factors for explaining a government's fiscal decision-making. A quantitative analysis of the data collected from these country case studies, however, proved hardly meaningful, and only generated indistinctive, with hardly informative statistics. In order to yet carry out a meaningful statistical analysis of political explanatory factors, we therefore utilised other well-defined and measurable data sets, that is, the OECD (2012) data on 'volume of fiscal consolidation' and the World Bank (2012) data on 'political orientation' and 'margin of parliamentary majority' of a government. The political assumption that right-wing governments tend to take larger cutback decisions than left-wing governments was statistically not confirmed in the clear majority of the countries. The assumption that governments with a grand parliamentary majority are better capable of taking larger cutback decisions than governments with a mere parliamentary minority was moderately supported by the statistics.

In this book, we investigated how national governments handled their domestic crisis. We did not investigate the joint multi-national decision-making in the European Union, which is a totally different level of analysis, and incomparable to the domestic level – a completely different type of study, from which we abstained. However, that did not mean that the influence of Europe on the ways in which national government managed their domestic fiscal crisis was to be neglected. On the contrary, ample attention was therefore also paid to supra-national explanatory factors, especially the major European influence on domestic fiscal consolidation decisions by the governments. The influence of the EU Maastricht Treaty ceilings on budget deficit and state debt, and the influence of the extraordinary circumstances of the Eurozone crisis and bailouts, were illustrated with country examples, which clearly confirmed that these explanatory factors were of major importance.

Effects of fiscal consolidation

What were the effects of the fiscal crisis and consolidation on public finances and the economy, what were the political effects, and what were the effects on Public Administration? The formulation of this third main research question indicates that, here too, we followed both an economic and political perspective, as well as an administrative one.

From an economic perspective, the main intended effects of fiscal consolidation we looked at were, first, the fiscal effects, that is, the reduction of budget deficit and debt accumulation, and second, the economic effects, that is, the recovery of economic growth. The statistical correlations confirmed the economic theoretical prediction that restoring public finances and economic growth depend on many more variables than domestic fiscal consolidation efforts alone. The correlation between fiscal consolidation and budget deficit reduction was low, and the correlation with recovery of economic growth non-existent. The statistics even produced paradoxical outcomes: both countries with high and low consolidation efforts achieved good fiscal results, and countries with low and modest consolidation efforts both achieved good economic recovery, while the country with the highest consolidation effort achieved hardly any growth. The quantitative analysis was hardly impressive, to put it mildly.

The measurement of the political effects of fiscal consolidation generated significant outcomes. The electoral effects of fiscal consolidation appeared to be disastrous for the incumbent governments. They nearly always lost the general elections after having carried out or planned for fiscal consolidation. Cutback plans of a government in several cases led to early elections being called. Moreover, in some countries, coalition governments lost their parliamentary majority because one or more coalition partners walked out due to the cutback plans. Subsequently, we widened the concept of political effects from electoral to include public protest and social unrest, and presented examples of widespread and fierce protest and unrest in the three countries that were most severely hit by the crisis, Iceland, Ireland and Spain.

The effects of the fiscal crisis and consolidation on administration were evidenced with extensive country examples. Various groups of countries could be distinguished. First, in countries such as Iceland, Ireland and Hungary, which in return for receiving financial assistance had to comply with reforms, there was a clear impact of the crisis on reforms in Public Administration. In addition, the UK government undertook substantial administrative reforms in response to crisis. In Italy, however, because the EU distrusted the possibility of successful reform in the Italian administration, it exclusively focussed on budgetary reform. In another group of countries such as Lithuania and Slovenia, the crisis only led to minor administrative reforms. And in yet another group of countries such as Belgium, Estonia, Germany, France and the Netherlands, the relation between the crisis and reforms was less clear: managerial cost-efficiency reforms were initiated before the crisis and were ongoing. The crisis was not the cause of that reform, but certainly reinforced its necessity. All in all, the country studies indicated that the fiscal crisis did not cause fundamental administrative reforms (with a few exceptions such as Ireland and the United Kingdom). Neither did it cancel ongoing reforms, but rather contributed to the modernisation efforts that were already underway before the crisis hit. The effects of the fiscal crisis on a number of aspects of public management could be shown by means of the COCOPS public executives' survey, thus supplementing the qualitative country case studies with quantitative analysis. The results of the survey indicated the increase of performance management during fiscal consolidation, and the cutback of back-office rather than front-office functions.

Clusters of countries

Notwithstanding the many differences between European countries, their responses to the fiscal crisis, their decisions, and the effects of the crisis and consolidation seem to reveal some kind of clusters. Countries can be distinguished according to the size and extent of the fiscal crisis. The one extreme includes countries that were not or were hardly hit by the global economic crisis and experienced hardly any need for consolidation. The other extreme involves countries that were so severely hit by the crisis that they had to be bailed out and the outside financial assistance was conditioned upon severe austerity and reform. Most of the European countries fall in between these two extremes. Somewhat like the clustering by the OECD (2012: 24) into the four categories: (a) countries with a loan programme from the IMF, ECB and EU; (b) countries with increasing long-term interest rates on state bonds; (c) countries with substantial deficits and/or debts, but less pressure on debt interest rates; and (d) countries with no or marginal consolidation needs, we arrive at five clusters of countries.

First, thanks to its North Sea gas and oil revenues, *Norway* was only very indirectly affected by the worldwide crisis. Norway neither experienced a banking crisis, nor an economic nor a fiscal one. Apart from relatively modest measures to stabilise the financial sector, there was no necessity for fiscal consolidation and significant expenditure cutbacks. The crisis had no impact on the functioning of Norwegian administration. Not surprisingly, Norway was hardly ever mentioned as a country example in this book.

Second, several European countries were hit so hard by the crisis that they were forced to seek external financial assistance. From our selection of countries, this concerned *Iceland, Ireland, Italy* and *Spain*. The crisis in these countries was severe, and fiscal consolidation was imperative. The Icelandic and Irish governments were unable to domestically solve the crisis and had to be bailed out by the IMF and the Troika, respectively, which, in turn, led to externally prescribed and imposed fiscal cutbacks and administrative reforms.

Although Italy and Spain were not bailed out like Iceland and Ireland, they were deeply affected by the Eurozone crisis erupting in 2010, leading to dangerous levels of bond interest rates, and they received financial assistance from the EU and ECB, leading to conditions of austerity and reform measures. Besides the ECB buying up endangered Italian and Spanish state bonds, the Spanish banking sector was bailed out by the EU, ECB and IMF. Hard and immediate fiscal consolidation was required.

A similar feature in these countries is a relatively swift and centralised decision-making process triggered by the Troika conditionality, which led to radical cutback measures (e.g. lay-offs, pay cuts) and substantive programme cuts, also in public services. The bailed out countries did not have the time to move from crisis denial via small and moderate to radical cuts, but were forced to apply severe austerity measures much more quickly than most of the other European countries. Moreover, the conditionality also involved influence over policy reforms, thus also affecting programme cutbacks and Public Administration reforms.

Third, a cluster of continental European countries can be distinguished where the relatively modest size of the economic crisis led to relatively moderate economic recovery packages, and which show similar decision-making patterns and a similar approach to consolidation measures. This group of countries first includes those neighbouring and economically connected to *Germany*, *Belgium* and the *Netherlands*. They highly benefitted from the swift economic recovery of the German economy. These governments were at first reluctant to applying consolidation measures – in all of these countries, the retrenchment and cutback decisions were postponed until after the 2010 general elections, and hence coincided with the multi-party deliberations and negotiations about a new coalition cabinet. In Germany, that coalition formation was relatively swift; in the Netherlands, it took three to four months; but in the highly complex Belgian consensus politics, it took eighteen months to form a new coalition cabinet. Similarly, the *Slovenian* government at first denied the severity of the crisis, and only later applied small consolidation measures and moved to more substantial cutbacks as the crisis grew deeper. Although *France* had a single-party cabinet and right-wing president, and the energetic Sarkozy as a former Finance Minister, a known advocate of austerity and reform who put fiscal consolidation high on the agenda, in actual practice the cutback decision-making was only half-hearted.

As for consolidation measures, governments of this cluster opted for 'milder' cutback instruments such as hiring freeze or pay freeze instead of 'hard' cuts such as lay-offs and pay cuts. Germany could only apply hiring freeze due to its civil service regulation. In this group of countries, the fiscal crisis did not have a direct link to administrative reforms. For example, the fiscal crisis did not affect state and administrative reforms in Belgium. In the Netherlands, the already existing managerial reform programme in central administration was not caused by the crisis, but the financial squeeze enhanced its necessity.

The fourth cluster of countries involves the Baltic states of *Estonia* and *Lithuania*. These Baltic countries implemented substantial fiscal consolidations during the early stage of the crisis. These small countries were among the first ones hit by the crisis. Instead of denying and postponing cuts, which was clearly characteristic to the countries belonging to the third cluster, the Baltic governments applied immediate and radical cutbacks as early as 2008 and subsequently carried out several rounds of substantive cuts. While in the earlier phases of the crisis across-the-board cuts were applied, as time progressed the cuts became more targeted. Cutbacks included not only hiring and pay freeze, but also cuts in public-sector personnel and pay. The hard and immediate approach was facilitated first by the relatively underdeveloped civil society unable to mobilise major protests, second by very weak unions, with trade union density the lowest in Europe, and third by the missing tenure in the civil service regulation, which allowed for pay and personnel cuts. Public administration reforms were not substantially affected by the crisis.

Finally, the *United Kingdom* seems to represent a unique case. A majoritarian single-party cabinet refuted the alleged assumptions of swift and drastic decision-making. The Labour government under Prime Minister Brown explicitly refused to take cutback decisions in view of the upcoming elections. It was the Cameron-

Clegg two-party coalition cabinet that took unprecedented and unequalled massive cutback decisions. Yet, notwithstanding the massive fiscal consolidation measures, the economy and public finances remained in bad shape.

The politics of fiscal consolidation

Throughout this book, we followed two perspectives, an economic and political one, both in our approach of the core concept of fiscal consolidation, as well as in our treatment of the causes and the effects of consolidation. It is unthinkable to neglect the economic aspects of the fiscal crisis and of the governments' response, fiscal consolidation. After all, that is primarily about budget deficits, expenditures and revenues, and how to balance those basic economic entities. The authors not being economists, our treatment of these essential aspects remained quite modest, and some economists might say superficial. However, we certainly paid more than obligatory lip service to this vital economic perspective. On the other hand, we did not conceal that, candidly, our main focus of interest was the political aspect of fiscal consolidation, which has been a much less investigated perspective of the fiscal crisis, consolidation and budget cutbacks: the politics of fiscal consolidation. So, what came out? Did politics matter in fiscal consolidation? Did it matter as much as economics?

The answer is undoubtedly and clearly 'yes'. Our investigation of the political decision-making by national governments revealed that politicians repeatedly deviated from the rational and objective solutions that economists provided. Rational-comprehensive decision-making based on explicit political priorities, the very definition of rationality, proved to be the very rare exception. Politicians did not follow the rational-objective economic recommendations that were copiously provided by economic professors, economic think tanks, research institutes and more, and even negated the really influential economic advice of authoritative organisations such as the OECD. The exception may be the advice by the economists at the European Commission's Budget-Directorate, who provided not entirely optional 'recommendations' to national governments on how to reduce their deficit to the prescribed 3 per cent. Not listening to them was risking severe punishment. Apart from that exception, the general picture was that politicians were hardly pursuing an economic rationale. Or, to rephrase it more politely, that political aspects were paramount in comprehending and explaining why governments did what they actually did.

The further and deeper we investigated the way national governments responded to the domestic fiscal crisis, the more apparent it became how vital and influential the political circumstances were for real comprehension. The type of politics and government, but also the more intricate details of the coalition cabinets, the political parties in the coalition, the opposition, the electoral cycle, the public opinion and protest, and more; the further and deeper one digs, the more political details surface that offer more and better explanations of the political complexity of reality, an experience one especially comes across when investigating the political decision-making in a foreign country. As a non-native outsider-researcher, not knowledgeable in the 'ins and outs' of 'politics as usual' in a foreign country, each next step in such a country study uncovers new knowledge and insights about what really happened and why – the abundant wealth of highly interesting and relevant details of the in-depth country case studies, referred to earlier in this book.

That wealth of details, however, also poses a serious methodological problem, that is, the uniqueness of abundant in-depth details of a particular government's political decision-making. The country case studies admittedly provided many insightful explanations of a government's fiscal decision-making, but the very nature of these unique insights and explanations made them, by consequence, unsuitable for generalisations in an international comparative sense. National uniqueness excludes international generalisation, and unfortunately that was exactly the deception we stumbled into. We had a faint hope that the relatively large number of country case studies (fourteen) would permit us to perform some comparative statistics. Our attempts at multiple case study statistics, however, proved unsuccessful. Our conceptualisation of political decision-making into the three different characteristics 'size of cutback decisions', 'speed of cutback decisions' and 'across-the-board versus targeted cuts' turned out to be statistically strongly correlated variables. Our attempt to statistically correlate these characteristics of cutback decision-making with the explanatory variables 'state structure', 'single-party or coalition government', 'political orientation' and 'grand, normal, minority' only generated indistinctive and hardly useful statistics. A quantitative statistical analysis of the data collected from the country case studies, after all, proved hardly possible, nor relevant. Despite the considerable amount and valuable contents of the country case studies, they did not allow for international generalisation. The well-known disadvantage of the qualitative case study method, as we mentioned in the introduction, was confirmed. Our faint hope to combine the qualitative method with the quantitative statistics proved in vain. We could only alternate between the two methodological approaches: qualitative analysis of in-depth country studies and quantitative statistics based on other data sets.

The question of whether politics mattered in fiscal consolidation could most certainly be answered affirmatively. But apparently, it is hard to provide such an affirmative answer by means of empirically and methodologically sound statistics that are based on generalised political science theories.

Discussion

However interesting an international comparative explanation of the similarities and differences in national fiscal consolidation decisions may be from a scientific point of view, practitioners, politicians and policy-makers always ask the inevitable question: Did fiscal consolidation work? Was it successful? Which country did better, and why? What were the success and failure factors? As mentioned in the introduction and discussed in Chapter 3, these are methodologically tricky questions, which is why we avoided a normative evaluation and restrained ourselves to a more neutral effect measurement (in Chapter 7). Here, in the final discussion section, we get back to that issue and explicitly address and discuss the question of the effectiveness and successfulness of the fiscal consolidation decisions in the various countries.

Effect measurement and evaluation

In Chapter 7, we addressed the effects of fiscal consolidation, and started with the fiscal and economic effects. The volume of fiscal consolidation was used as an independent variable, and budget surplus/deficit and economic growth as dependent variables in analysing the actual effects of the fiscal consolidation on the improvement of public finances and the economy.

A number of methodological questions arise from the quantitative statistical analysis. First, it has to be specified what variables are used as the independent (explanatory) ones. From an economic viewpoint, the financial size (volume) of the fiscal consolidation measures seems most appropriate to consider, which is a well-defined variable that can accurately be measured. From a political perspective, however, the political effort of a government's decisions might include other variables, such as the political sensitivity of various measures in specific policy sectors. For example, cutbacks in social security issues such as pension age and unemployment benefits usually were socially, publicly and politically highly contested.

Second, the dependent variables have to be specified. For public finances, the budget surplus/deficit and gross debt seem proper indicators. For the economy, the GDP, GDP growth rate, employment and inflation seem adequate indicators. Still, the question remains as to what exactly is specified as successful.

Third, comes the methodological question of the supposed 'causal' relationships between the variables – the attribution problem. As we have repeatedly mentioned and illustrated in Chapter 7, the domestic public finances and economy are dependent on many more variables than the fiscal consolidation measures of a national government alone. For example, the recovery of both public finances and the economy in Germany was less the effect of fiscal consolidation than of the worldwide economy. And the British economy and public finances remained in bad shape although the 2010 fiscal consolidation measures were huge and severe.

This brings us to the main methodological question, that is, the normative one of evaluation. What are the criteria for success or failure of the fiscal consolidation measures? It seems reasonable to measure the success of fiscal consolidation in terms of decrease of budget deficit and debt accumulation. But the ultimate criteria for success are the recovery of the economy, and especially employment. As stated in Chapter 3, the citizens of a country are not interested in sophisticated economic variables, but in their own private economic circumstances, that is, first of all, work and income. But then again, are the political and social aspects of success and failure not likewise important? Public protests and social unrest cannot be neglected at a time when declining trust in government is an increasingly important challenge in most Western countries.

One might even argue that fiscal consolidation is absolutely the wrong thing to do in badly hit economies. After all, economic recovery plans normally consist of fiscal stimulus measures, that is, the very opposite of fiscal austerity and cutbacks. Is fiscal austerity not only hindering economic recovery, then? Obviously, here, we enter the political-economic, and largely ideological, debate about the rightfulness of fiscal austerity. Left-wing Socialists consider the current austerity and cutbacks measures to reflect the ideological choices of ruling interests and classes that dominate governments, and consider this current 'austerity orthodoxy' as misconceived, dysfunctional and causing largely unnecessary pain and damage to the population. We rather abstain from the political-ideological debate. The authors do not presume to possess the moral right to condemn or justify fiscal consolidation; we have just provided an empirical analysis of what actually happened. Apparently, the normative question of success or failure of consolidation is not only a methodological, but also an ideological minefield.

Success or failure of decision-making

In order to avoid the methodological pitfalls of questionable 'causal' relations between fiscal consolidation with fiscal and economic success, an alternative is to assess the cutbacks in terms of decision-making. Did the decision-making result in swift, large and drastic consolidation measures? Alternatively, were they only small, slow and gradual deviations of the 'status quo ante'? Were the decisions targeted and selective, or just across-the-board and cheese-slicing? Were the decisions based on fundamental political priority-setting? Alternatively, were they rather the outcome of incremental, pragmatic political compromising? Throughout this book, these characteristics of decision-making have been applied.

Such an analysis of the governments' decision-making in the various European countries undoubtedly leads to a negative conclusion. Fundamental political priority-setting has been the exception rather than the rule. Examples of politically sensitive decisions to make targeted cuts could be found in certain areas of social security, such as pension systems and unemployment benefits.

These examples of breakthrough of political stalemate, which by implication are fundamental political decisions, were mostly implemented by cautious compromise measures, involving a multi-year gradual path of small annual adjustments of the existing pension age or unemployment benefit period. Should a fundamental political decision, which is incrementally implemented, be evaluated as a success or failure?

However, the seemingly unsuccessful, incremental and compromising decision-making in the consensual democracies with their multi-party coalition governments revealed some characteristics that could well be called a success. The Belgian example showed that, though apparently the country during an eighteen-month coalition formation period neither had a government nor a parliamentary-approved budget, the caretaker government successfully managed to undertake major cutback measures. Notwithstanding the complex political system, which normally renders political decision-making virtually impossible, and the abnormal situation of eighteen months of political deliberations and negotiations about a new coalition, Belgium took fiscal consolidation measures to reduce its budget deficit, which, in view of the circumstances, might well be assessed as an incredible success.

Another example is the Netherlands, where apparently the attempt at fundamental priority-setting in 2010 by the 'reconsideration working groups' of top officials, which was an escape of the government's political responsibility in the first place, was completely ignored by politicians during the 2010 election campaign and disregarded in the political deliberations about the new coalition formation and agreement. However, in the years to follow, several of the proposals made by the 'reconsideration working groups' surfaced in political compromises about increasing the pension age, reducing the unemployment benefit period, reducing the tax-deductible house-mortgage interests, reducing the number of provinces by mergers and increasing the inhabitant size of municipalities, privatising the student bursary system, etc. So, in due time, fundamental priority-setting appeared to successfully break through.

On the other hand, the decision-making in majoritarian democracies with single-party governments did not more clearly lead to successful outcomes. In France, the energetic and decisive President Sarkozy and his single-party government did not succeed to take swift and drastic cutback decisions. The government for a considerable period of time hesitated between cutback and economic stimulus measures. The policy was framed in the neologism 'ri-lance', a combination between the two words 'rigueur' (rigour) and 'relance' (stimulus). Fundamental priority-setting did not take place. The new Socialist President Hollande publicly declared his preference for economic stimulus over cutback measures. In Spain, the single-party Zapatero govern-ment neither succeeded to take drastic cutback decisions. When the Spanish government, pressured by the Eurozone leaders, prepared for expenditure cutbacks, the public protest and social unrest became so intense that early elections were called.

In the United Kingdom, swift and drastic decision-making on fiscal consolidation took place in 2010. Although the May 2010 general elections did not yield an absolute majority for one party for the first time in thirty-six years, and a coalition was formed between the ideologically distant Conservative and Liberal Democrat Parties, the decision-making was quick and far-reaching. The new cabinet was formed within a couple of days after the elections and immediately announced a drastic retrenchment package, worked out in the June 'Emergency Budget', and within four months finalised the details in the October 'Spending Review', which was remarkably rapid, as the preceding Labour government had refrained from making a 'Spending Review' in 2009 so that ministerial budgets were not specified.

So, the evaluation of governments' decision-making, after all, does not necessarily lead to an overall negative assessment. Even in terms of drastic and swift decision-making, and political priority-setting, countries that, at first sight, might qualify as 'failure', at a second look, and from a different perspective, reveal certain features of 'success'. The overall picture, however, yet remains that European governments hardly succeeded in making targeted selective decisions based on political priority-setting. Europe did not successfully 'manage' the crisis, but rather 'muddled through'.

This general conclusion is also exemplified when looking at the impact of fiscal crisis on administrative reforms. Our analysis shows that Public Administration was strongly affected in countries that were obliged to ask for foreign financial assistance, as shown by the cases of Hungary, Iceland, Ireland and Spain, where the foreign assistance and/or bail-outs were conditioned not only upon severe budgetary cuts, but also upon administrative reforms. Also, the severity of the crisis was reflected in major administrative reforms carried out in the United Kingdom. In the rest of the studied European countries, the crisis boosted the necessity for ongoing reforms, but the already existing reform paths were not altered. These countries thus showed only a weak and indirect link between the crisis and administrative reform.

The crisis intensified the pressure to reform Public Administration to some extent, but these pressures did not translate into large-scale structural reforms and/or specific reform trajectories in the majority of European countries. Short-term fiscal targets tended to dominate over systematic analysis of shortcomings in the operation of administration. Thus, the crisis seems to have promoted pre-programmed responses, and not necessarily new ways of behaviour. Despite the limited evidence of 'big bang' administrative reforms in Europe, all countries studied implemented efficiency savings in their administrations by looking at further possibilities for rationalisation of administrative processes and increasing productivity in individual public-sector organisations.

Europe in the global context

This book was about Europe. We investigated how European governments responded to the global economic and fiscal crisis. On the basis of that empirical material, it is scientifically unwise to make statements about other countries. Nevertheless, an undoubtedly burning question on the lips of many readers from outside Europe, as well as inside Europe, is how Europe performed compared with other parts of the world. Here, in the final discussion section, no longer chained by scientific rigour, we allow ourselves to make some observations beyond Europe, first about the United States, and second about Asia. Europe is now widely considered the 'sick old man of the world', particularly by Asians observing how the European Union had so much trouble in handling its own Eurozone crisis. Let us now see how Asia managed the global financial and economic crisis. We start with the third largest economy in the world, Japan, and subsequently turn our attention to the largest democracy on earth, India, and the upcoming economic superpower, China.

Fiscal consolidation in the United States of America

The prime example of majoritarian democracy, the United States of America, did not succeed in swift and drastic fiscal consolidation.

Congress was strongly divided about the rise of public debt and budget deficit. In 2010, the divided Congress decided to extend the tax cuts from the previous Bush administration for two years. In 2011, Congress passed the Budget Control Act, which authorised an increase in the debt ceiling in exchange for $2.4 trillion in deficit reduction in the coming 10 years, half of which to be specified in legislation, and the other half, $1.2 trillion of spending cuts, to be determined by a bipartisan group of senators and representatives known as the 'Super Committee', officially called the 'United States Congress Joint Select Committee on Deficit Reduction'. The 'Super Committee' consisted of an equal number of members from the House and the Senate, and was equally divided between Democrats and Republicans. In November 2011, the committee concluded that it had not been able to reach a bipartisan agreement.

Due to the fierce political fight between the Republican-led House and the Democrat-led Senate, Congress failed to enact legislation appropriating funds for the fiscal year 2014, and this budget impasse caused the United States federal government to shut down from 1 to 16 October 2013. Some 800,000 federal employees were furloughed, and another 1.3 million were required to work without knowing when payment would arrive. Government operations resumed after Congress passed an interim appropriations bill late in the evening of 16 October, suspending the debt limit until 7 February 2014.

Sequestration and the fiscal cliff

The Budget Control Act implied that automatic across-the-board reductions in the government spending were to come into force, known as 'sequestration'. 'Budget sequestration' means that across-the-board spending cuts are automatically imposed on all expenditure categories affecting all departments and all programmes by an equal percentage. In January 2013, a simultaneous decrease of expenditures and increase in tax rates was supposed to take place. The impending massive deficit reduction was called the 'fiscal cliff'.

The 'fiscal cliff' was avoided at the very last minute by Congress convening on New Year's Eve and New Year's Day. At 2:00 a.m. on 1 January 2013, the Senate passed a compromise bill. At 11:00 p.m. that evening, the House passed the same legislation. President Obama signed it the next day.

Source: Wikipedia: Budget sequestration, Fiscal cliff, accessed 6 June 2013

How Japan managed the global economic crisis

How did the third largest economy in the world, Japan, manage the global financial and economic fiscal crisis? As the current globally inflicted crisis is often compared to the major crisis that hit Japan in the early 1990s (European Central Bank 2012), which was followed by a 'lost decade' of economic stagnation, we first cast a brief look at that.

The global financial crisis of 2007–2008 left Japanese banks fairly unaffected. The financial system was resilient and much less severely hit than in the 1990s. The financial regulatory and supervisory framework had improved since the 1990s. Japanese banks were not strongly innovative and not exposed to exotic financial derivatives. The government took stabilisation measures. The Financial Services Agency, together with the Bank of Japan, coordinated the response.

The global economic crisis of 2008 hit Japan severely (Kawai and Takagi 2009). Decline in GDP between September 2008 and March 2009 in Japan was the highest among OECD countries. In terms of decline in its exports, Japan was clearly the worst affected. After a sharp GDP decline of 5.5 per cent in 2009, the Japanese economy began to recover in 2010 thanks to economic stimulus. However, in the wake of the great Eastern Japan earthquake in March 2011, the economy contracted again. In August 2011, the government announced a 19 trillion Yen (about 4 per cent of GDP) plan for recovery and reconstruction over five years. GDP declined 0.7 per cent in 2011. Fiscal deficit

'Lost decade' in Japan

Strong economic growth in the 1970s and 1980s led to an overheated economy, uncontrolled money supply and credit expansion, leading to highly inflated estate and stock prices. When the Bank of Japan realised the bubble was unsustainable and sharply raised interest rates in late 1989, the bubble burst. By August 1990, the stock prices had plummeted to half their peak, and the asset prices began to fall in late 1991, and had collapsed by early 1992. The bubble's collapse lasted for more than a decade, with plummeting asset prices resulting in huge non-performing loans, and hence banks and insurances loaded with bad debts, ultimately turning them into zombie banks. Many firms burdened with heavy debts, it became very difficult to obtain credit. Companies were cutting their debts for fear of deflation. Consumers deferred spending once prices started to fall, and were forced to cut spending once their wages started to fall. The government reformed labour laws to permit a large increase of the use of part-time and irregular workers, on lower wages and fewer employment benefits. The result was a continual decline in domestic demand. A long period of economic stagnation followed.

Source: Wikipedia: Lost decade (Japan), accessed 13 March 2014

also expanded again from 8.4 per cent of GDP in 2010 to 9.5 per cent in 2011. That was critical, as Japan, since 1993, had a budget deficit for eighteen consecutive years. Gross public debt had risen rapidly to above 200 per cent of GDP, the highest in the OECD area (OECD 2012: 168).

In 2012, the Japanese Noda government decided to balance the budget by means of revenue enhancement, a two-stage consumption tax increase from 5 per cent in 2012 to 10 per cent in 2015.

Japan hardly suffered from the global financial crisis, so extensive bank rescue packages were not necessary. Japan severely suffered from the global economic crisis, and because its economy had already endured a two-decades stagnation before, it is understandable that Japan therefore clearly chose for an explicit policy of economic and monetary stimulus.

As to the fiscal crisis, it is hard to see what fiscal consolidation Japan undertook except raising the consumption taxes. Due to the excessive state debt (230 per cent of GDP in 2011), an imminent danger is that international rating agencies might downgrade Japanese debt, resulting in increased interest costs. Interest rates increasing to just 2 per cent would imply interest payment on state debt amounting to 80 per cent of government revenue (*Forbes*, 10 August 2013). How the Japanese government is going to reduce its staggeringly high and still-climbing debt still remains to be seen.

Abenomics

After the December 2012 elections, the new Prime Minister Abe immediately announced his new economic policies – soon dubbed 'Abenomics' – consisting of fiscal stimulus, monetary easing and structural reforms. The fiscal spending was to be increased by 2 per cent of GDP, likely raising the budget deficit to 11.5 per cent in 2013. Within weeks of his election, Prime Minister Abe announced a 10.3 trillion Yen stimulus bill, and appointed a new head of the Bank of Japan with mandate to generate 2 per cent inflation through monetary easing.

'Abenomics' had immediate effects on the financial markets. By February 2013, a dramatic weakening of the Japanese Yen and a 22 per cent rise of the stock market index took place. The unemployment rate fell from 4.0 per cent in the final quarter of 2012 to 3.7 per cent in the first quarter of 2013. The Yen became about 25 per cent lower against the United States Dollar in the second quarter of 2013. By May 2013, the stock market had risen by 55 per cent, and consumer spending had pushed first quarter economic growth up 3.5 per cent annually. Japan's trade deficit worsened in 2013.

Prime Minister Abe's policy to alleviate Japan from the prolonged recession was widely praised in Japan. The IMF praised the programme as a unique opportunity to end decades-long deflation and sluggish growth and reverse the rise of public debt.

Source: The Economist, 18 May 2013 and Wikipedia: Abenomics, accessed 13 March 2014

How India managed the global economic crisis

During the 2000s, the Indian economy saw an enormous boost with annual GDP growth rates ranging from 8 to 10 per cent. The economic boom led to an overheating of the economy and rising inflation. As of 2004, the Reserve Bank of India (RBI) started tightening the monetary policy in order to maintain price stability. After the inflation in 2007 and 2008 initially declined, it climbed again, forcing the RBI to sharper monetary tightening. The economic growth began to slow in 2007–2008 (Mohan 2008).

The subprime mortgage crisis that broke out in the United States mid-2007 left the Indian banking sector more or less unaffected. Thanks to prudent regulations and active monitoring and control by the RBI, complex international finance structures, such as the subprime derivatives, were prohibited. As a whole, banks maintained sound balance sheets.

The global financial and economic crisis after the September 2008 Lehman Brothers collapse, however, seriously distressed the Indian financial markets and economy. The interbank loan market dried up, and the credit crunch, together with the loss of confidence, led Indian banks to drastically curtail their domestic lending. Foreign investors massively withdrew their capital from India. The stock markets panicked. The Bombay stock market lost more than 60 per cent. Exports of Indian products plummeted. Hundreds of thousands of workers suddenly became jobless. Unemployment sharply climbed. Furthermore, the Indian rupee came under pressure. In 2008–2009, the rupee lost about 25 per cent of its value compared to the United States Dollar. The foreign exchange reserves also considerably shrank.

The Indian economy, which was already being slowed down by the strict monetary policy measures of the RBI, was further slowed down by the global economic crisis. GDP growth dropped from 8.9 per cent in 2007–2008 to 5.3 per cent in 2008–2009 (Bajpai 2011; Kumar and Vashisht 2009).

The government had announced considerable fiscal stimulus measures in February 2008 at the presentation of its annual budget. That was, however, not in response to the global financial crisis, but only for electoral reasons. In India, general elections are habitually preceded by massive government spending programmes. This time, the pre-election spending spree primarily aimed at rural employment and reconstruction, fertiliser subsidies and electricity supplied to farmers. The February 2008 stimulus package amounted to a considerable 4 per cent of GDP.

This electoral voter-pleasing splurge left the government little room for another economic stimulus round when the global financial and economic crisis burst out after September 2008. Moreover, the government was slow in responding to that crisis. At first, it denied the severity of the crisis. As the Indian banking sector had remained unaffected by the crisis in 2007, the hopeful illusion was that the Indian economy would also remain unaffected.

The government announced three stimulus packages in December 2008, January 2009 and March 2009, in total amounting to 2 per cent of GDP. The three economic recovery packages mainly consisted of infrastructure spending, reduction of indirect taxes, and assistance for export industries.

The Reserve Bank of India (RBI) reacted upon the global economic crisis by shifting from tight monetary policy to monetary easing in order to stimulate the economy. Since October 2008, the RBI injected a considerable amount of liquidity into the economy, some $80 billion in total by April 2009.

In 2009, the government budget deficit rose to 11.4 per cent of GDP and the debt-to-GDP ratio to about 75 per cent (Kumar and Vashisht 2009).

Contrary to the wealthy countries in Europe, in India hundreds of millions suffer from poverty. Only large economic growth can create jobs and thus make the population escape from poverty, and that of course is the prime objective of India's leaders. The past decades have witnessed such an economic boom;

Indian economy

Economic growth dropped to about 5 per cent, nearly half what it once was. After the economy seemed to recover in 2009–2011, it again fell in 2011 and 2012. In 2011, the Indian stock market plummeted again. In 2013, the rupee plummeted again. The country faced the threat of a downgrade of its credit rating to 'junk' status. While the national debt as a proportion of GDP is running at about 70 per cent. India's overall (central plus state) budget deficit is running at 8–10 per cent of GDP.

Source: The Economist, 23 February 2013

---

keeping the economy growing as much as possible remains the main target. India's leaders cannot afford the European luxury of fiscal consolidation in a very prosperous economy. Decline of the economy would throw hundreds of millions back into unemployment and poverty. Government expenditure cutbacks are politically and socially inconceivable in India.

How China managed the global economic crisis

The single-party state of China has a highly centralised and hierarchical government's decision-making, which is fully politicised by the Communist Party. Such strong central power, residing in the Communist Party's central committee in Beijing, apparently was successful in swiftly and drastically managing the global financial and economic crisis.

Contrary to the widely held opinion that China's 'closed' capital account and insulated banking sector would leave it immune to the global financial crisis that emerged in the West, the crisis affected China. One of the reasons was the massive involvement of China in the American capital market. In June 2008, Chinese banks' holdings of Fannie Mae and Freddie Mac amounted to $25.3 billion. In the first quarter of 2009, China's foreign exchange reserves amounted to $2.1 trillion, of these some $1 trillion in the form of United States government securities. The global financial and economic crisis resulted in a dramatic fall in demand for Chinese export products. The Chinese government responded with an expansionary fiscal policy (Yu 2009).

In November 2008, the Chinese central government announced an economic stimulus package of 4 trillion Yuan ($568 billion, on a GDP of about 29 trillion Yuan that amounts to some 14 per cent of GDP).

Besides an increase in expenditures, the government also undertook tax reductions such as VAT, purchase tax cut and threshold of individual income taxes. Moreover, provincial governments were also encouraged to raise money

TABLE 8.1 Economic stimulus package in China

	2008–2010	By 2020
Railway	$44 billion spent in 2008 and $88 billion spent in 2009–2010	Expected investment: more than $725 billion Total operating railways: 75,000 miles
Road	186,000 miles of rural road paved or improved by 2009	53,000 additional miles of road, including twelve major highways
Air	$20 billion invested by 2010	97 new airports to be built, for a total of 244 airports Total of $64 billion invested
Water	$3 billion in hydraulic facilities	Over 100 seaports built Completion of water-saving facilities for large-scale irrigation areas across China
Energy and environment	Second West-East gas pipeline (5,600 miles), costing $20 billion, to be completed by 2011 $150 billion to be invested in environmental projects in next three years	10 more nuclear reactors; nuclear power increased to 5% of total power used Completion of more than 150 environmental projects

Source: Booz & Company (2009)

to launch their own stimulus packages. The total amount of planned stimulus announced by local governments stood at 18 trillion Yuan. The total (central plus local) government expenditure would go up 22.1 per cent of GDP. The total government deficit in 2009 would be 950 billion Yuan ($139 billion, 3.2 per cent of GDP), compared with 111 billion Yuan in 2008, which amounted to only 0.4 per cent of GDP.

China's fiscal and financial resources were affordable and sustainable. Over the past decades, the budget deficit was very low, and in 2007 China saw a budget surplus. At the end of 2008, state debt was only 18 per cent of GDP. Even after the adoption of the expansionary fiscal policy, by the end of 2009 state debt would still be lower than 20 per cent of GDP (Yu 2009).

What the Chinese government have completely abstained from doing is fiscal consolidation. Besides the lack of economic necessity to do so, political reasons seem paramount. China's leaders' prime objective is economic growth. As long as hundreds of millions of Chinese each year escape poverty and increase their income and material prosperity, the Communist Party state will continue to receive popular support. Decline of economic growth, let alone outright economic deterioration, would threaten the party's prime base of legitimacy. Government expenditure cutbacks and tax revenue increases are therefore politically inconceivable, although it is unofficially well known that local governments in Beijing, Shanghai and other major cities are confronted with gigantic debts and deficits, and hardly able to balance their books any longer.

Apparently, centralised and strong capabilities for swift and drastic decision-making are not the panacea.

Europe compared to Asia and the United States

Apparently, it is impossible to compare Europe with Asia with respect to fiscal consolidation for the simple reason that neither Japan, nor India, nor China is actually consolidating its public finances. Japan is struggling to overcome its two-decades-long period of economic stagnation by massive economic and monetary stimulus. In India and China, the governments' prime objective is to keep the economy growing and restore the pre-crisis GDP growth rate, in order to create jobs needed for its growing population to escape poverty. India does have a considerable budget deficit and state debt, but China does not. Despite its huge 2008 economic stimulus package, China still enjoys a modest deficit and debt. India and China are facing a fundamentally different problem than Europe regarding the global economic crisis.

In terms of the size and speed of fiscal consolidation decisions, and the capacity of governments to set political priorities in cutback decisions, Europe can be compared with the United States. The extreme political polarisation in American Congress seems to make it virtually impossible to reach substantial fiscal decisions and political priority-setting over cutbacks. As a result, across-the-board cuts seem to be the only feasible option. Taking targeted selective decisions based on political priority-setting is apparently not only difficult in Europe.

Future role of the European Union

In this book, we did not conduct a separate study of the multi-national joint European Union decision-making on managing the crisis. Our focus was on domestic governments' decision-making. The influence of the European Union on domestic fiscal consolidation, however, proved to be of utmost import-ance, as we clearly demonstrated. Despite the growing Eurosceptic public sentiments in many Western European countries, and the consequent tendency of politicians to oppose 'dictates from Brussels', it was apparent that the EU ceilings on budget deficits and debts played a prominent, and often decisive, role in domestic fiscal consolidation. The 'recommendations' that national governments received from the European Commission about what it considered proper fiscal measures to reduce the deficit to the required 3 per cent in time were most certainly taken quite seriously, to put it mildly.

Here, we now reflect upon a possible further role of the European Union in future fiscal decision-making: Europe not only as an important context and crucial input for domestic decision-making, but Europe in a more direct role, taking over domestic tasks and responsibilities. We draw a possible parallel with the increasing role of Europe in the banking crisis.

In 2008, the banking crisis, although worldwide and of apparent international origin, was basically handled domestically. The leaders of Western states convened to discuss a common international approach to the banking crisis, but in the end it came down to each national government independently saving its own domestic banks, at enormous costs that caused state debt to markedly increase, sometimes to a colossal extent. Then came the European sovereign debt crisis, with the European Central Bank as of 2009 buying up endangered state bonds of Southern European countries and Ireland in order to reduce further increases in bond yield spreads between these countries and other EU members, especially Germany. And in 2010, the bail-outs of Greece, Portugal and Ireland led to the establishment of the European Financial Stability Facility (EFSF) to provide the bail-outs. That was replaced in 2012 by the European Stability Mechanism (ESM) for support loans, recapitalisation and bail-outs of countries.

Meanwhile, Europe took over the regulatory task of banking supervision. In 2012, a European System of Financial Supervisors was established, with three European Authorities for banking, for insurances and pensions, and for securities and markets. The European Banking Authority started with the supervision of the 200 largest European banks with balances of over €30 billion, and Europe learned some lessons about saving banks without tax-payers having to pay the entire bill. The March 2013 Cypriot bail-out consisted of a guarantee of deposits up to €100,000, but introduced a bank deposit levy (haircut) of 6.7 per cent on deposits up to €100,000 and 9.9 per cent on higher deposits – chiefly held by wealthy clients, mainly from Russia, who were using Cyprus as a tax haven. In the European Commission's proposal for a 'European bank recovery and resolution Authority', European banks would be compelled to 'bail in' their creditors when they fail, and European banks would be obliged to reserve a percentage of their insured deposits for a special fund to finance the resolution of future banking crises. Thanks to European-level handling of future banking crises, national states (that is, tax-payers) no longer have to run huge bank rescue costs.

Is it conceivable that similar European institutions take over the domestic governments' tasks in economic and fiscal affairs? The European Commission is taking plenty initiatives to try to do so, but it is highly unlikely that in the current Eurosceptic climate, domestic politicians in Western Europe will let that happen. The European Central Bank already plays a central role in stimulating Europe-wide recovery. The European Structural Funds play a dominant role in the economic stimulus of new member states especially. But Western European governments, particularly Germany, will most probably strongly resist a collective take-over of the fiscal responsibilities of states that have run excessive deficits and debts. The prospects for a near-future European take-over of fiscal responsibilities therefore seem rather dim.

Basic dilemma

In the foreseeable future, fiscal consolidation in Europe will remain the task of domestic governments. And although some optimistic politicians are beginning to believe that the hard times of cutbacks and retrenchments are over, that the early signs of economic recovery can be trusted to indicate the final end of the crisis, we do not want to make an overly pessimistic impression, but sincerely doubt whether all is over and fine. After all, the previous worldwide crisis of the 1970s and 1980s was not over in a couple of years either. The decade of the 1980s was one long series of successive cutbacks rounds, with each successive spending cut deemed necessary, until at last, in the late 1980s, public budgets finally allowed for spending rises instead of eternal cuts. In the sad and unfortunate, but not improbable, case that, now, thirty years later, the fiscal crisis again festers longer than expected, European governments might once again be facing a decade-long succession of consolidation rounds.

This leads governments to a basic dilemma. The low-hanging fruit of apparent inefficiencies and organisational slack has been cut in the early consolidation rounds. In later consolidation rounds, sooner or later, there will be no major inefficiencies left to cut. So, politicians will no longer be able to escape their responsibilities, and will be obliged to set priorities about what public tasks to terminate and what tasks to continue, and how. Across-the-board and incremental cutback decisions will become deficient to turn the fiscal tide. The muddling through of successive rounds of small, slow and gradual cuts, which apparently is what most European governments are best at doing, will have to make way for fundamental political priority-setting, which is necessary to arrive at far-reaching and drastic spending cuts to really solve the mounting fiscal crisis.

As argued earlier by several authors (e.g. Levine 1980; Pandey 2010; Pollitt 2010), it is crucial not to limit crisis management to short-term budget cuts, but to handle it as the management of the organisational resources for the long term (also including the post-crisis period), as a short-sighted approach may lead to solving the wrong problem or making the current problems even worse. What is needed is a strategic approach towards Public Administration and rethinking the role of the state in recovery and in economic development at large. This requires a long-term vision, strategic thinking and explicit strategic action, as well as risk-taking, rather than incremental change and simply balancing the budget.

The basic dilemma is between the seeming incapability of governments to take drastic and targeted measures, and the ultimate inevitability of such decisions. Apparently, it is not enough for economists to derive from their theories and models what measures ought to be taken. It is also about political decision-making capabilities of governments. And that is what this book was about.

Country summaries of economic, fiscal and political data

BELGIUM

General information

Country surface (square km)	30,528
Total population in 2012 (million)	11.09
GDP per capita in PPS in 2012 (EU28 = 100)	120

Source: Eurostat

Economic and fiscal information

	2006	2007	2008	2009	2010	2011	2012
GDP growth rate (% of previous year)	2.7	2.9	1	−2.8	2.4	1.8	−0.3
Budget surplus/deficit (% of GDP)	0.4	−0.1	−1	−5.6	−3.8	−3.7	−3.9
Gross debt (% of GDP)	88	84	89.2	95.7	95.5	97.8	99.6

Source: Eurostat

Fiscal consolidation plans

	2009	2010	2011	2012	2013	2014	2015
Total accumulated volume (% of GDP)		0.4	0.8	3.4	3.8	4.3	

Source: OECD (2012)

List of political parties in federal parliament

Political party	Acronym	Political ideology
Christian Democratic and Flemish	CD&V	Christian democratic – Flemish
Centre Démocratic Humaniste	CDH	Christian democratic – French
Socialistische Partij Anders	SP.a	Centre-left social democratic – Flemish
Part Socialiste	PS	Centre-left social democratic – French

continued . . .

List of political parties in federal parliament *Continued*

Political party	Acronym	Political ideology
Vlaamse Liberalen en Democraten	VDL	Centre-right Liberal – Flemish
Mouvement Réformateur	MR	Centre-right Liberal – French
Green Flemish	Agalev	Left-wing ecologist – Flemish
Green French	Ecolo	Left-wing ecologist – French
Nieuw-Vlaamse Alliantie	N-VA	Social Liberal – Flemish
Vlaams Belang	VB	Extreme nationalist – Flemish – condemned and isolated by all other parties (cordon sanitaire)
Front National	FN	Extreme nationalist – French – idem

Note: German-language parties not in federal parliament.

Source: Wikipedia: list of political parties, accessed 9 June 2014

Elections and governments

Date general elections	Coalition government	Prime Minister	Explanations
June 2007	Christian Democrats Flemish (largest) and French (CDH), Socialist French (PS), Liberals French (MR) and Flemish (VLD)	Leterme (CD&V)	194 days negotiation about new coalition (December). December 2008 resignation of Leterme and replaced by van Rompuy. April 2010 coalition fell. Call for early elections.
June 2010	Socialist French (largest) and Flemish (SP.a), Christian Democrats French (CDH) and Flemish (CD&V), Liberals French (MR) and Flemish (VLD)	Di Rupo (PS)	N-VA won elections but off-side in coalition formation that lasted 541 days. New government – Di Rupo in December 2011.

Source: Wikipedia: list of governments, accessed 9 June 2014

ESTONIA

General information

Country surface (square km)	45,227
Total population in 2012 (million)	1.32
GDP per capita in PPS in 2012 (EU28 = 100)	71

Source: Eurostat

Economic and fiscal information

	2006	2007	2008	2009	2010	2011	2012
GDP growth rate (% of previous year)	10.1	7.5	−4.2	−14.1	3.3	8.3	3.2
Budget surplus/deficit (% of GDP)	2.5	2.4	−2.9	−2	0.2	1.2	−0.3
Gross debt (% of GDP)	4.4	3.7	4.5	7.2	6.7	6.2	10.1

Source: Eurostat

Fiscal consolidation plans

	2009	2010	2011	2012	2013	2014	2015
Total accumulated volume (% of GDP)	9.2	6.4	3.7	3.1	3.1	3.0	2.6

Source: OECD (2012)

List of political parties

Political party	Acronym	Political ideology
Estonian Reform Party	RE	Classical Liberalism
Estonian Centre Party	K	Centrism, social-Liberal
Union of Pro Patria and Res Publica	IRL	Conservative Liberals
Social Democratic Party	SDE	Centre-left social democratic

Source: Wikipedia: list of political parties, accessed 9 June 2014

Elections and governments

Date general elections	Coalition government	Prime Minister	Explanations
March 2007	Reform Party, Pro Patria Res Publica and Social Democrats	Ansip (Reform Party)	Right-centre-left coalition. In May 2009, Social Democrats left coalition. Centre-right cabinet

continued . . .

Elections and governments

Date general elections	Coalition government	Prime Minister	Explanations
			continued as minority (50 out of 101 seats).
March 2011	Reform Party and Pro Patria Res Publica	Ansip (Reform Party)	Centre-right minority cabinet won majority in elections.
March 2014	Reform Party and Social Democrats	Roivas (Reform Party)	Centre-left coalition.

Source: Wikipedia: list of governments, accessed 9 June 2014

FRANCE

General information

Country surface (square km)	643,801
Total population in 2012 (million)	65.28
GDP per capita in PPS in 2012 (EU28 = 100)	109

Source: Eurostat

Economic and fiscal information

	2006	2007	2008	2009	2010	2011	2012
GDP growth rate (% of previous year)	2.5	2.3	−0.1	−3.1	1.7	1.7	0
Budget surplus/deficit (% of GDP)	−2.3	−2.7	−3.3	−7.5	−7.1	−5.3	−4.8
Gross debt (% of GDP)	63.7	64.2	68.2	79.2	82.4	85.8	90.2

Source: Eurostat

Fiscal consolidation plans

	2009	2010	2011	2012	2013	2014	2015
Total accumulated volume (% of GDP)			1.1	2.5	3.2	3.7	4.2

Source: OECD (2012)

List of main political parties in Assemblée national

Political party	Acronym	Political ideology
Socialist Party	PS	Centre-left
Union for a Popular Movement	UMP	Centre-right
National Front	FN	Right-wing nationalist, did surprisingly well in presidential elections 2002 (see below)

Source: Wikipedia: list of political parties, accessed 9 June 2014

Elections and governments

Date presidential elections	One-party government	President	Explanations
April–May 2002	Centre-right (then RPR)	Cirac	Because Le Pen (FN) won against Jospin (divided Socialists) in first round, Chirac faced Le Pen (FN) in second round and won by 82%.
April–May 2007	UMP	Sarkozy	Sarkozy (UMP) won against Royal (PS).
April–May 2012	PS	Hollande	Hollande (PS) won against Sarkozy (UMP). June legislative elections PS 57% and UMP 39%.

Source: Wikipedia: list of governments, accessed 9 June 2014

GERMANY

General information

Country surface (square km)	357,121
Total population in 2012 (million)	80.32
GDP per capita in PPS in 2012 (EU28 = 100)	123

Source: Eurostat

Economic and fiscal information

	2006	2007	2008	2009	2010	2011	2012
GDP growth rate (% of previous year)	3.7	3.3	1.1	−5.1	4.2	3	0.7
Budget surplus/deficit (% of GDP)	−1.6	0.2	−0.1	−3.1	−4.1	−0.8	0.2
Gross debt (% of GDP)	68	65.2	66.8	74.5	82.4	80.4	81.9

Source: Eurostat

Fiscal consolidation plans

	2009	2010	2011	2012	2013	2014	2015
Total accumulated volume (% of GDP)			0.5	2.0	2.5	3.0	

Source: OECD (2012)

List of political parties in Bundestag

Political party	Acronym	Political ideology
Christian Democratic Union	CDU	Centre-right Christian democratic
Christian Social Union	CSU	Centre-right Christian democratic Bavarian sister-party
Social Democratic Party of Germany	SDP	Centre-left social democratic
Free Democratic Party	FDP	Centre-left Liberals
The Left	Die Linke	Left-wing former communists
The Greens	Grünen	Left-wing ecologist

Source: Wikipedia: list of political parties, accessed 9 June 2014

Elections and governments

Date general elections	Coalition government	Chancellor	Explanations
September 2005	Grand coalition between CDU/CSU and SPD	Merkel (CDU)	Grand coalition carried out constitutional reforms.
September 2009 and FDP	Coalition between CDU/CSU	Merkel (CDU)	Normal winning coalition. FDP smaller and weaker partner.
September 2013	Grand coalition between CDU/CSU and SPD	Merkel (CDU)	FDP no seats in Bundestag. Only opposition Left and Greens.

Source: Wikipedia: list of governments, accessed 9 June 2014

HUNGARY

General information

Country surface (square km)	93,027
Total population in 2012 (million)	9.93
GDP per capita in PPS in 2012 (EU28 = 100)	67

Source: Eurostat

Economic and fiscal information

	2006	2007	2008	2009	2010	2011	2012
GDP growth rate (% of previous year)	3.9	0.1	0.9	−6.8	1.3	1.6	−1.7
Budget surplus/deficit (% of GDP)	−9.4	−5.1	−3.7	−4.6	−4.3	4.3	−1.9
Gross debt (% of GDP)	65.9	67	73	79.8	81.8	81.4	79.2

Source: Eurostat

Fiscal consolidation plans

	2009	2010	2011	2012	2013	2014	2015
Total accumulated volume (% of GDP)		4.1	4.5	7.6	7.6	8.2	8.2

Source: OECD (2012)

List of political parties

Political party	Acronym	Political ideology
FIDESZ – Hungarian Civic Union	FIDESZ	Conservative; for 2006 elections, alliance with Christian Democratic People's Part (KDNP)
Hungarian Socialist Party	MSZP	Centre-left social democratic; for 2014 elections, alliance with others in 'Unity'
Alliance of Free Democrats – Hungarian Liberal Party	SZDSZ	Conservative Liberals
Politics Can Be Different	LMP	Green-Liberal, social progressive
Jobbik (Movement for a Better Hungary)	Jobbik	Extreme-right

Source: Wikipedia: list of political parties, accessed 9 June 2014

Elections and governments

Date general elections	Coalition government	Prime Minister	Explanations
April 2006	MSZP and SZDSZ	Gyurcsany (MSZP); replaced in 2009 by Bajnar (independent)	SZDSZ withdraw from coalition in May 2008. MSZP continued as minority government.
April 2010	FIDESZ	Orban (FIDESZ)	FIDESZ won two-thirds supermajority 68% of seats (227 out of 386). MSZP was wiped out. FIDESZ carried out constitutional reforms.
April 2014	FIDESZ	Orban (FIDESZ)	FIDESZ won again 66% of seats (117 out of 199 seats).

Source: Wikipedia: list of governments, accessed 9 June 2014

ICELAND

General information

Country surface (square km)	103,000
Total population in 2012 (million)	0.319
GDP per capita in PPS in 2012 (EU28 = 100)	115

Source: Eurostat

Economic and fiscal information

	2006	2007	2008	2009	2010	2011	2012
GDP growth rate (% of previous year)	4.7	6	1.2	−6.6	−4.1	2.9	6.6
Budget surplus/deficit (% of GDP)	6.3	5.4	−13.5	−10	−10.1	−5.4	
Gross debt (% of GDP)	27.9	28.5	70.4	87.9	93	101	

Source: Eurostat

Fiscal consolidation plans

	2009	2010	2011	2012	2013	2014	2015
Total accumulated volume (% of GDP)		3.6	6.2	7.9	8.5	8.9	9.1

Source: OECD (2012)

List of political parties in Albingi (total sixty-three seats)

Political party	Acronym	Political ideology
Social Democratic Alliance		Social democrats, pro-Europe
Independence Party		Conservative Liberals, Eurosceptic; always biggest; eighteen years in power; wiped out in 2009
Left-Green Movement		Left-wing, ecologist, Eurosceptic
Progressive Party		Liberal, agrarian, Eurosceptic

continued . . .

List of political parties in Albingi (total sixty-three seats) Continued

Political party	Acronym	Political ideology
Citizen's Movement		Democrats; renamed 'Dawn' in 2012
Liberal Party		Liberal
Democratic Movement		Democrats
Bright Future		New in 2012; Liberal MP plus social democrat MP
Rainbow Movement		New in 2013; two Left-Green MPs
Pirate Party		New in 2013; one MP

Source: Wikipedia: list of political parties, accessed 9 June 2014

Elections and governments

Date general elections	Coalition government	Prime Minister	Explanations
May 2007	Independence Party and Progressive Party	Haarde (Independence Party)	After massive protests, Haarde resigned in January 2009 and called early elections. Coalition collapsed. Minority government by Social Democratic Alliance.
April 2009	Social Democratic Alliance with Left-Green	Sigurdardottir (Social Democratic)	First ever left-wing majority cabinet.
April 2013	Independence Party with Progressive Party	Benediktsson (Independence Party)	Centre-right coalition regained power. Eurosceptic.

Source: Wikipedia: list of governments, accessed 9 June 2014

IRELAND

General information

Country surface (square km)	69,825
Total population in 2012 (million)	4.58
GDP per capita in PPS in 2012 (EU28 = 100)	129

Source: Eurostat

Economic and fiscal information

	2006	2007	2008	2009	2010	2011	2012
GDP growth rate (% of previous year)	5.4	5.4	–2.1	–5.5	–0.8	1.4	0.9
Budget surplus/deficit (% of GDP)	2.9	0.1	–7.4	–13.9	–30.8	–13.4	–7.6
Gross debt (% of GDP)	24.6	25.1	44.5	64.8	92.1	106.4	117.6

Source: Eurostat

Fiscal consolidation plans

	2009	2010	2011	2012	2013	2014	2015
Total accumulated volume (% of GDP)	5.9	8.8	12.8	14.8	16.5	17.6	17.9

Source: OECD (2012)

List of political parties

Political party	Acronym	Political ideology
Sinn Féin		Left-wing social democrats; Irish nationalist republican party with former links to IRA; leader Gerry Adams
Fianna Fáil		Centre-right conservative Liberals; Irish nationalist republican party
Fine Gael		Right-wing conservative Liberals
Labour Party		Left-wing social democrats
Progressive Democrats		Conservative Liberals; small but in coalition with Fianna Fáil since 1989
Irish Green Party		Left-wing ecologists

Source: Wikipedia: list of political parties, accessed 9 June 2014

Elections and governments

Date general elections	Coalition government	Prime Minister (Taoiseach)	Explanations
May 2007	Fianna Fáil (largest) with Green Party and Progressive Democrats	Cowen (Fianna Fáil); in 2008, replaced by Ahern	Fianna Fáil together with Progressive Democrats in power since 1989.
February 2011	Fine Gael (largest) with Labour Party	Kenny (Fine Gael)	Fianna Fáil was wiped out.

Source: Wikipedia: list of governments, accessed 9 June 2014

ITALY

General information

Country surface (square km)	301,336
Total population in 2012 (million)	59.39
GDP per capita in PPS in 2012 (EU28 = 100)	101

Source: Eurostat

Economic and fiscal information

	2006	2007	2008	2009	2010	2011	2012
GDP growth rate (% of previous year)	2.2	1.7	−1.2	−5.5	1.8	0.4	−2.4
Budget surplus/deficit (% of GDP)	−3.4	−1.6	−2.7	−5.5	−4.5	−3.8	−3
Gross debt (% of GDP)	106.3	103.3	116.4	116.1	119.3	120.8	127

Source: Eurostat

Fiscal consolidation plans

	2009	2010	2011	2012	2013	2014	2015
Total accumulated volume (% of GDP)			0.9	4.3	5.9	6.1	

Source: OECD (2012)

List of political parties

Political party	Acronym	Political ideology
People of Freedom	PdL	Centre-right alliance of parties; in 1994, Berlusconi created new centre-right party 'Forza Italia' out of the remainders of the wiped out old parties; later renamed 'Pole of Freedom', in 2000 'House of Freedom', and in 2008 'People of Freedom'; centre-right was in power 1994–1996, 2001–2006 and 2008–2011

continued . . .

List of political parties *Continued*

Political party	Acronym	Political ideology
Democratic Party	PD	Centre-left alliance of parties, originally named 'Olive Tree', changed in 2005 in broader alliance 'The Union'; in 2008, The Union broke with Communists and ceased to exist; new centre-left 'Democratic Party'; centre-left was in power 1996–2001 and 2006–2008.
Lega Nord (Northern League)	LN	Padanian separatist, conservative
National Alliance	AN	Former fascists, nationalist conservative
Five Star Movement	M5S	2013 anti-establishment protest party of Grillo
Civic Choice	SC	2013 conservative Liberal party of Monti
Union of the Centre	UdC	Christian democratic group of parties
New Centre-Right	NCD	2013 centre-right split-off from People of Freedom

Source: Wikipedia: list of political parties, accessed 9 June 2014

Elections and governments

Date general elections	Coalition government	Prime Minister	Explanations
April 2006	The Union	Prodi	Centre-left alliance of multitude of left-wing parties.
April 2008	People of Freedom, coalition between Forza Italia, National Alliance and Lega Nord	Berlusconi (PdL)	Centre-right alliance of parties won big majority against divided left-wing alliance.
November 2011 (no elections)	Berlusconi resigned and government was replaced by cabinet of technocrats	Monti	Due to Eurozone crisis, Berlusconi lost credit and had to resign. Replaced by independent economist Monti and supported by almost all parties.

continued . . .

Elections and governments *Continued*

Date general elections	Coalition government	Prime Minister	Explanations
February 2013	As of February 2014, coalition between Democratic Party (PD), New Centre-Right (NCD), independents, Civic Chice (SC) and Union of the Centre (UdC)	Renzi (PD)	In December 2012, Berlusconi withdrew support for Monti government. Call for elections. In 2013, general elections fragmented into four groups: Democratic Party, People of Freedom allied with Lega Nord, Five Star Movement (Grillo) and Civic Choice (Monti). Eelctions resulted in hung parliament. Coalition formation difficult.

Source: Wikipedia: list of governments, accessed 9 June 2014

LITHUANIA

General information

Country surface (square km)	65,300
Total population in 2012 (million)	3.00
GDP per capita in PPS in 2012 (EU28 = 100)	72

Source: Eurostat

Economic and fiscal information

	2006	2007	2008	2009	2010	2011	2012
GDP growth rate (% of previous year)	7.8	9.8	2.9	−14.8	1.5	5.9	3.7
Budget surplus/deficit (% of GDP)	−0.4	−1	−3.3	−9.4	−7.2	−5.5	−3.2
Gross debt (% of GDP)	17.9	16.8	15.5	29.3	37.9	38.5	40.7

Source: Eurostat

Fiscal consolidation plans

	2009	2010	2011	2012	2013	2014	2015
Total accumulated volume (% of GDP)			5.5				

Note: Lithuania is not an OECD member, hence it is not included in the OECD (2012) survey. Figure of 5.5% in 2011 based on Nakrosis *et al.* (2013).

List of political parties

Political party	Acronym	Political ideology
Homeland Union – Lithuanian Christian Democrats	TS-LKD	Conservative Christian democrats
Social Democratic Party Lithuania	LSDP	Social democrats
Labour Party	DP	Centrism, populism
Liberal Movement	LS	Liberalism

continued . . .

List of political parties *continued*

Political party	Acronym	Political ideology
Order and Justice	TT	National conservatism, populism
Electoral Action of Poles in Lithuania	LLRA	Polish minority, conservative
The Way of Courage	DK	Anti-corruption, populism
Lithuanian Peasant and Greens Union	LVZS	Agrarian

Source: Wikipedia: list of political parties, accessed 9 June 2014

Elections and governments

Date general elections	Coalition government	Prime Minister	Explanations
October 2008	Homeland Union (largest) with National Revival, Liberal Movement and Liberal and Centre Union	Kubilius	Centre-right coalition. In 2009, Liberal coalition parties left government. Early elections were not called.
October 2012	Social Democrat Party (largest) with Labour Party, Electoral Action Poles, Order and Justice	Butkevicius	Centre-left coalition.

Source: Wikipedia: list of governments, accessed 9 June 2014

NETHERLANDS

General information

Country surface (square km)	37,354
Total population in 2012 (million)	16.73
GDP per capita in PPS in 2012 (EU28 = 100)	128

Source: Eurostat

Economic and fiscal information

	2006	2007	2008	2009	2010	2011	2012
GDP growth rate (% of previous year)	3.4	3.9	1.8	−3.7	1.6	1	−1
Budget surplus/deficit (% of GDP)	0.5	0.2	0.5	−5.6	−5.1	−4.5	−4.1
Gross debt (% of GDP)	47.4	45.3	58.5	60.8	63.1	65.5	71.2

Source: Eurostat

Fiscal consolidation plans

	2009	2010	2011	2012	2013	2014	2015
Total accumulated volume (% of GDP)			0.3	1.0	1.7	2.4	2.9

Source: OECD (2012)

List of political parties

Political party	Acronym	Political ideology
Christian Democratic Appeal	CDA	Centre-right Christian democrats
Labour Party	PvdA	Centre-left social democrats
People's Party for Freedom and Democracy	VVD	Conservative Liberal
Democrats 66	D'66	Progressive social-Liberal
Party for Freedom	PVV	Anti-Muslim right-wing populist
Socialist Party	SP	Left-wing Socialist
Green Left	GL	Left-wing ecologist
Christian Union	CU	Orthodox Protestant
Political Reformed Party	SGP	Orthodox Protestant
Party for the Animals	PvdD	Single-issue animal rights

Source: Wikipedia: list of political parties, accessed 9 June 2014

Elections and governments

Date general elections	Coalition government	Prime Minister	Explanations
November 2006	Christian Democrats (largest) plus Labour Party (PvdA) and Christian Union (CU)	Balkenende (CDA)	Normal winning coalition. In February 2010, Labour left coalition. Call for early elections.
June 2010	Liberals (largest) plus Christian Democrats (CDA)	Rutte (VVD)	Minority coalition supported by right-populist PVV of Wilders. In April 2012, PVV withdrew support. Call for early elections.
September 2012	Liberals (largest) plus Labour (PvdA)	Rutte (VVD)	Normal winning coalition, but minority in Senate.

Source: Wikipedia: list of governments, accessed 9 June 2014

NORWAY

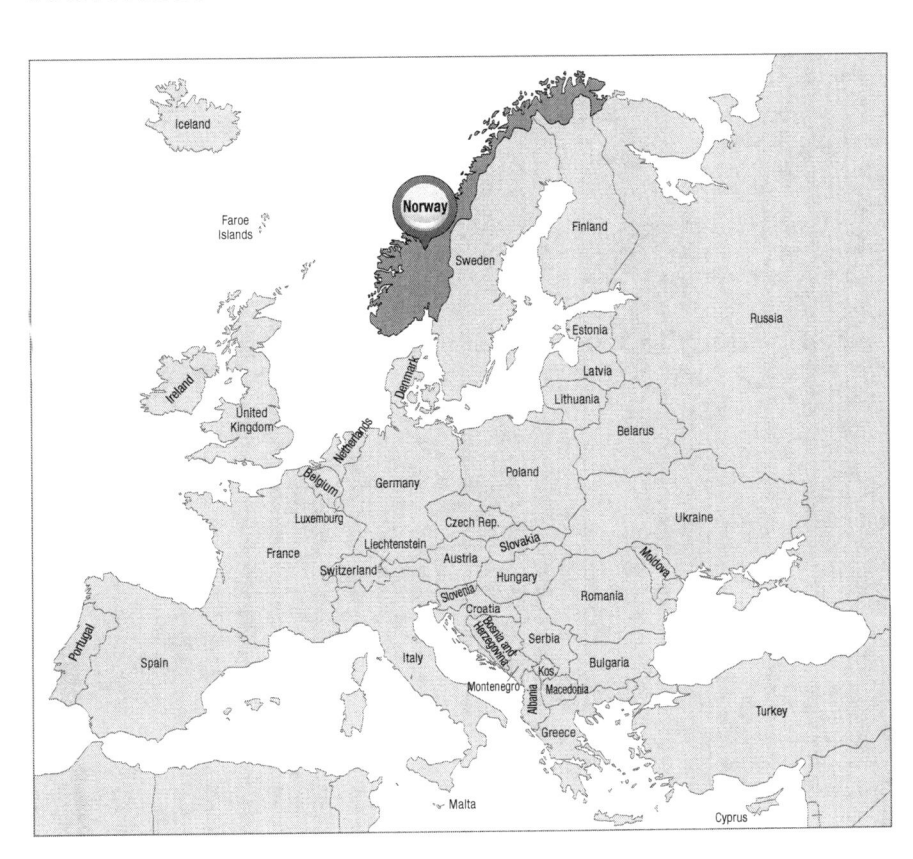

General information

Country surface (square km)	323,787
Total population in 2012 (million)	5.05
GDP per capita in PPS in 2012 (EU28 = 100)	195

Source: Eurostat

Economic and fiscal information

	2006	2007	2008	2009	2010	2011	2012
GDP growth rate (% of previous year)	2.3	2.7	0.1	−1.6	0.5	1.2	3.1
Budget surplus/deficit (% of GDP)	18.5	17.5	18.8	10.6	11.2	13.6	
Gross debt (% of GDP)	55.4	51.5	48.2	43.5	43.7	29	

Source: Eurostat

Fiscal consolidation plans

	2009	2010	2011	2012	2013	2014	2015
Total accumulated volume (% of GDP)							

Source: Not included in OECD (2012)

List of political parties in 'Storting'

Political party	Acronym	Political ideology
Labour Party	Ap	Centre-left social democrats
Conservative Party	H	Conservative
Progress Party	FrP	Conservative Liberalism
Christian Democratic Party	KrF	Centre-right Christian democrats
Centre Party	Sp	Centrist, agrarian
Liberal Party (Venstre)	V	Social Liberal, centrist
Socialist Left Party	SV	Left-wing Socialist
Green Party	Mp	Left-wing ecologist

Source: Wikipedia: list of political parties, accessed 9 June 2014

Elections and governments

Date general elections	Coalition government	Prime Minister	Explanations
September 2005	Labour Party (largest) with Socialist Left Party and Centre Party	Stoltenberg (Labour)	Red-green coalition on 87 out of 169 seats in 'Storting'.
September 2009	Labour Party (largest) with Socialist Left Party and Centre Party	Stoltenberg (Labour)	Red-green coalition continued in power (86 out of 169 seats).
September 2013	Conservative Party (largest) with Progress Party	Solberg (Conservative)	Minority coalition supported by Liberal Party and Christian Democratic Party (four parties together 96 out of 169 seats).

Source: Wikipedia: list of governments, accessed 9 June 2014

SLOVENIA

General information

Country surface (square km)	20,373
Total population in 2012 (million)	2.05
GDP per capita in PPS in 2012 (EU28 = 100)	84

Source: Eurostat

Economic and fiscal information

	2006	2007	2008	2009	2010	2011	2012
GDP growth rate (% of previous year)	5.8	7	3.4	−7.8	1.2	0.6	−2.3
Budget surplus/deficit (% of GDP)	−1.4	0	−1.9	−6.2	−5.9	−6.4	−4
Gross debt (% of GDP)	26.4	23.1	22	35	38.6	46.9	54.1

Source: Eurostat

Fiscal consolidation plans

	2009	2010	2011	2012	2013	2014	2015
Total accumulated volume (% of GDP)		2.6	3.8	4.5	5.3	6.0	

Source: OECD (2012)

List of political parties

Political party	Acronym	Political ideology
Positive Slovenia	PS	Centre-left social Liberalism
Slovenian Democratic Party	SDS	Conservative Liberalism
Social Democrats	SD	Centre-left social democrats
Civic List	DL	Classical Liberalism
Slovenian People's Party	SLS	Christian democrat, agrarian
Democratic Party of Pensioners of Slovenia	DeSUS	Single-issue: pensions
New Slovenia – Christian People's Party	NSi	Christian democrat, social conservatism

Source: Wikipedia: list of political parties, accessed 9 June 2014

Elections and governments

Date general elections	Coalition government	Prime Minister	Explanations
September 2008	Social Democrats (SD) with Zares (Social Liberals), Liberal Democracy of Slovenia (LDS) and Democratic Party Pensioners (DeSUS)	Pahor (SD)	Centre-left coalition.
December 2011	Social Democrats (SD) with Slovenian Democractic Party (SDS) and Democratic Party Pensioners (DeSUS)	Jansa (SDS)	Positibe Slovenia (PS) won elections but failed to form coalition. PS in opposition.

Source: Wikipedia: list of governments, accessed 9 June 2014

SPAIN

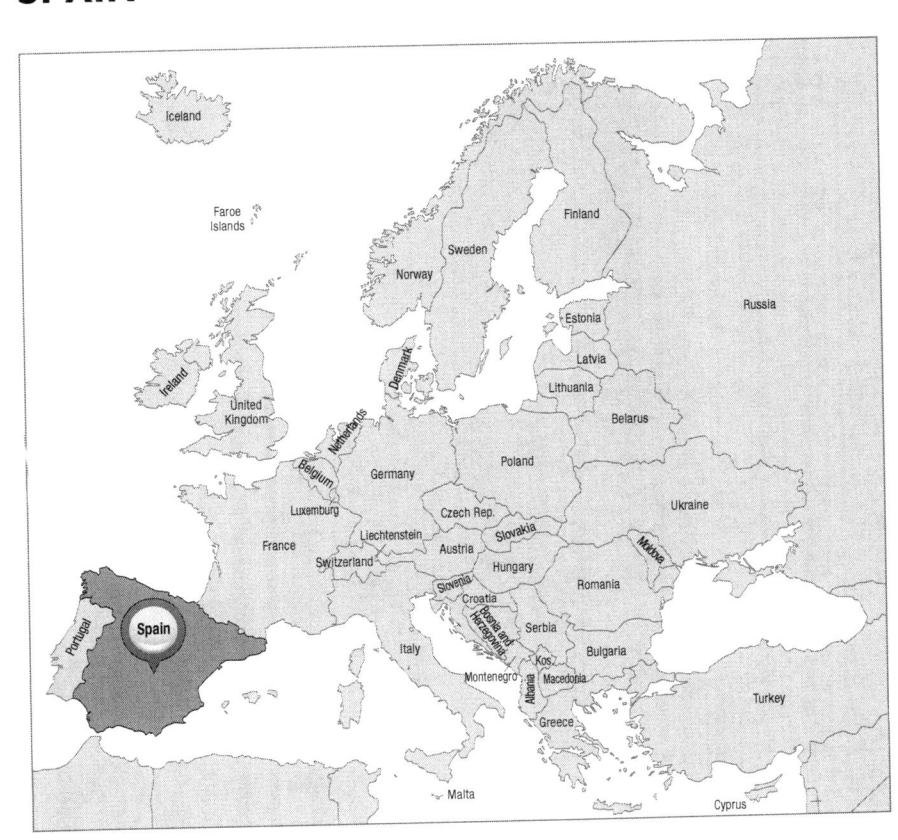

General information

Country surface (square km)	505,992
Total population in 2012 (million)	46.81
GDP per capita in PPS in 2012 (EU28 = 100)	96

Source: Eurostat

Economic and fiscal information

	2006	2007	2008	2009	2010	2011	2012
GDP growth rate (% of previous year)	4.1	3.5	0.9	−3.7	−0.3	0.4	−1.4
Budget surplus/deficit (% of GDP)	2.4	1.9	−4.5	−11.2	−9.7	−9.4	−10.6
Gross debt (% of GDP)	39.7	36.3	40.2	53.9	61.5	69.3	84.2

Source: Eurostat

Fiscal consolidation plans

	2009	2010	2011	2012	2013	2014	2015
Total accumulated volume (% of GDP)		2.7		5.7	7.1	7.3	

Source: OECD (2012)

List of political parties

Political party	Acronym	Political ideology
People's Party	PP	Mainstream centre-right
Spanish Socialist Workers Party	PSOE	Mainstream centre-left social democrats
Union, Progress and Democracy	UPyD	Recently established progressive Liberal party
United Left	IU	Alliance of minor left-wing, republican and green parties, led by Communist Party of Spain

Source: Wikipedia: list of political parties, accessed 9 June 2014

Elections and governments

Date general elections	One-party government	Prime Minister	Explanations
March 2004	PSOE	Zapatero	Supported by IU and ERC.
March 2008	PSOE	Zapatero	Minority government. In July 2011, Zapatero stepped down and called early elections.
November 2011	PP	Rajoy	Majority of 10 seats.

Source: Wikipedia: list of governments, accessed 9 June 2014

UNITED KINGDOM

General information

Country surface (square km)	242,495
Total population in 2012 (million)	63.49
GDP per capita in PPS in 2012 (EU28 = 100)	106

Source: Eurostat

Economic and fiscal information

	2006	2007	2008	2009	2010	2011	2012
GDP growth rate (% of previous year)	2.6	3.6	−1	−4	1.8	0.8	0.3
Budget surplus/deficit (% of GDP)	−2.7	−2.8	−5.1	−11.5	−10.2	−7.8	−6.3
Gross debt (% of GDP)	43.3	44.2	52.7	67.8	79.4	85.5	90

Source: Eurostat

Fiscal consolidation plans

	2009	2010	2011	2012	2013	2014	2015
Total accumulated volume (% of GDP)		0.6	2.8	3.8	5.1	6.1	7.1

Source: OECD (2012)

List of political parties

Political party	Acronym	Political ideology
Conservative Party	Tory	Mainstream centre-right
Labour Party	Labour	Mainstream centre-left
Liberal Democrat Party	Lib Dem	Recently (1988) established progressive Liberal party

Source: Wikipedia: list of political parties, accessed 9 June 2014

Elections and governments

Date general elections	Government	Prime Minister	Explanations
May 2005	Labour one-party government	Blair	Lowest majority ever. Blair stepped down as party leader in 2007, and was replaced by Brown.
May 2010	Coalition between Conservatives and Liberal Democrats	Cameron (Tory)	Elections resulted in hung parliament (last time 1974). Coalition necessary.

Source: Wikipedia: list of governments, accessed 9 June 2014

References

Agostino, D. and Lapsley, I. (2013) City-charity partnerships and the financial crisis: Case study evidence, *Public Management Review*, 15(5): 633–56.

Algemene Rekenkamer (2009) *Kredietcrisis 2008/2009*, TK 2009–2010, 31 941, The Hague.

Amabile, T. M. and Conti, R. (1999) Change in the work environment for creativity during downsizing, *Academy of Management Journal*, 42(6): 630–40.

Armenakis, A. A. and Bedeian, A. G. (1999) Organizational change: A review of theory and research in the 1990s, *Journal of Management*, 25(3): 293–315.

Austin, M. J. (1984) Managing cutbacks in the 1980s, *Social Work*, 29(5): 428–34.

Bajpai, N. (2011) *Global Financial Crisis, its Impact on India and the Policy Response*, Columbia University, Columbia Global Centers South Asia, Working Paper no. 5, July.

Banner, G. (1985) Budgetary imbalance and the politics of cutback management in German local government, *Local Government Studies*, 11(4): 43–61.

Bartle, J. (1996) Coping with cutbacks: City response to aid cuts in New York State, *State and Local Government Review*, 28(1): 38–48.

Behn, R. D. (1980) Leadership for cut-back management: The use of corporate strategy. *Public Administration Review*, 40(6): 613–20.

Behn, R. D. (1985) Cutback budgeting, *Journal of Policy Analysis and Management*, 4(2): 155–77.

Béland, D. and Cox, R. H. (eds) (2011) *Ideas and Politics in Social Science Research*, New York: Oxford University Press.

Bernstein, N. (2010) *The Danish Krone During the Crisis*, Speech by the Governor of the Danish National Bank at Copenhagen Business School, 22 March.

Beynet, P., Fuentes, A., Gillingham, R. and Hageman, R. (2011) *Restoring Fiscal Sustainability in Spain*, OECD Economics Department Working Paper no. 850, March.

Bezes, P. and LeLidec, P. (2013) The French politics of retrenchment 'à la carte' (2007–2012): COCOPS country case-study, submitted for publication to *International Review of Administrative Sciences*.

Bideleux, R. (2011) Contrasting responses to the international economic crisis of 2008–2010 in the 11 CIS countries and in the 10 post-communist EU member countries, *Journal of Communist Studies and Transition Politics*, 27(3/4): 338–63.

Biller, R. P. (1980) Leadership tactics for retrenchment, *Public Administration Review*, 40(6): 604–9.

Blondel, J. (1990) *Comparative Government: An Introduction*, Hempstead: Simon & Schuster.

Boin, A., Hart't, P. Stern, E. and Sundelius, B. (2008) *The Politics of Crisis Management: Public Leadership Under Pressure*, Cambridge: Cambridge University Press.

Booz & Company (2009) *Asia and the Global Economic Crisis: Accelerating Transitions, Expanded Opportunities*, available at: www.strategyand.pwc.com/media/file/asia_and_the_global_economic_crisis.pdf.

Bouvard, F., Dohrmann, T. and Lovegrove, N. (2009) The case for government reform now, *McKinsey Quarterly*, 3: 1–13.

Bozeman, B. (2010) Hard lessons from hard times: Reconsidering and reorienting the 'managing decline' literature, *Public Administration Review*, 42(6): 509–15.

Bozeman, B. and Straussman, J. D. (1990) *Public Management Strategies*, San Fransisco, CA: Jossey-Bass.

Burnes, B. (2009) *Managing Change*, London: Prentice Hall.

Carnall, C. A. (2003) *Managing Change in Organizations*, London: Prentice Hall.

Carstensen, M. B. (2011) New financial regulation after the crisis, *Danish Foreign Policy Yearbook*, 106–10.

Castles, F. (1981) How does politics matter? Structure or agency in the determination of public policy outcomes, *European Journal of Political Research*, 9: 119–32.

Castles, F. (1982) *The Impact of Parties*, London: Sage.

Castles, F. and McKinlay, R. D. (1979) Does politics matter? An analysis of the public welfare commitment in advanced democratic states, *European Journal of Political Research*, 7: 160–86.

Castles, F. and McKinlay, R. D. (1997) Does politics matter? *European Journal of Political Research*, 31: 99–107.

Cayer, N. J. (1986) Management implications of reduction in force, *Public Administration Quarterly*, 10(1): 36–49.

Cepiku, D. and Savignon, A. B. (2012) Governing cutback management: Is there a global strategy for Public Administrations? *International Journal of Public Sector Management*, 25(6/7): 428–36.

Clifton, J. and Alonso, J. M. (2013) The global financial crisis in the public sector: Spain, COCOPS short country report.

Connolly, R. (2012) The determinants of the economic crisis in post-socialist Europe, *Europe-Asia Studies*, 64(1): 35–67.

Contijoch, J. (2012) The end of the Spanish banking system's golden era, *Catalan International View*, 12: 12–15.

Corry, D. (2011) Power at the centre: Is the National Economic Council a mode for a new way of organizing things? *The Political Quarterly*, 82(3): 459–68.

Cusack, T. R. (1999) Partisan politics and fiscal policy, *Comparative Political Studies*, 32(4): 464–86.

Cusack, T. R. (2001) Partisanship in the setting and coordination of fiscal and monetary policies, *European Journal of Political Research*, 40(1): 93–115.

Daalder, H. (1971) On building consociational nations: The cases of the Netherlands and Switzerland, *International Social Science Journal*, 23(3): 355–71.

Daalder, H. (ed.) (1987) *Party Systems in Denmark, Austria, Switzerland, the Netherlands and Belgium*, New York: St. Martin's Press.

Dabrowski, M. (2009) *The Global Financial Crisis: Lessons for European Integration*, CASE Network Studies & Analyses No. 384.

Darling, A. (2011) *Back from the Brink: 1,000 Days at Number 11*, London: Atlantic Books.

De Nederlandse Bank (2009) *Jaarverslag 2008*, Amsterdam: DNB.

Dellepiane, S. (2012) *The Political Power of Economic Ideas: The Case of Expansionary Fiscal Contraction*, ECPR Joint Sessions, Antwerp.

Di Mascio, F. and Natalini, A. (2015) Fiscal retrenchment in Southern Europe: Changing patterns of governance in Greece, Italy, Portugal and Spain, *Public Management Review*, 17(1): 129–48.

Downs, G. W. and Rocke, D. M. (1984) Theories of budgetary decision-making and revenue decline, *Policy Sciences*, 16: 329–47.

Dunsire, A. and Hood, C. (1989) *Cutback Management in Public Bureaucracies: Popular Theories and Observed Outcomes in Whitehall*. Cambridge: Cambridge University Press.

Drazen, A. and Grilli, V. (1993) Do crises induce reform? Simple empirical tests of conventional wisdom, *Economics and Politics*, 13(2): 129–57.

Elder, N., Thomas, A. H. and Arter, D. (1982) *The Consensual Democracies: The Government and Politics of the Scandinavian States*, Oxford: Martin Robertson.

European Central Bank (2012) Comparing the recent financial crisis in the United States and the euro area with the experience of Japan in the 1990s, *ECB Bulletin*, May 2012.

European Commission (2009a) *Economic Crises in Europe: Causes, Consequences and Responses*, European Economy 7/2009.

European Commission (2009b) *DG Competitions Review of Guarantee & Recapitalisation Schemes in the Financial Sector in Current Crisis*, August 2009.

Fernandez, S. and Rainey, H. G. (2006) Managing successful organizational change in the public sector, *Public Administration Review*, 66(2): 1–22.

Flynn, N. (1990) *Public Sector Management*, London: Harvester Wheatsheaf.

Gieve, J. and Provost, C. (2012) Ideas and coordination in policymaking: The financial crisis of 2007–2009, *Governance*, 25(1): 61–77.

Glennerster, H. (1981) Social service spending in a hostile environment, in C. Hood and M. Wright (eds), *Big Governments in Hard Times*, Oxford: Martin Robertson, 174–96.

Goul. A. J. (2011) From the edge of the abyss to bonanza – and beyond: Danish economy and economic politics 1980–2011, *Comparative Social Research*, 28: 89–165.

Green, R. T. (2012) Plutocracy, Bureaucracy, and the End of Public Trust, *Administration & Society*, 44(1): 109–43.

Greenhalgh, L. and McKersie, R. (1980) Cost-effectiveness of alternative strategies for cutback management, *Public Administration Review*, 40(6): 575–84.

Hague, R., Harrop, M. and Breslin, S. (1993) *Comparative Government and Politics: An Introduction*, Houndmills: Macmillan.

Hajnal, G. (2013) Fiscal consolidation in Hungary, COCOPS country case study.

Hancock, M. D., Conradt, D. P., Peters, B. G., Safran, W. and Zariski, R. (1993) *Politics in Western Europe*, Houndmills: Macmillan.

Hammerschmidt, G., Oprisor, A. and Stimac, V. (2013) *COCOPS Executive Survey on Public Sector Reform in Europe*, COCOPS deliverable 3.1, May 2013.

Hendrick, R. (1989) Top-down budgeting, fiscal stress and budgeting theory, *The American Review of Public Administration*, 19(1): 29–48.

Hood, C. (1991) A public management for all seasons, *Public Administration*, 69(1): 3–19.

Hood, C. and Wright, M. (1981) From decrementalism to quantum cuts? in C. Hood and M. Wright (eds), *Big Governments in Hard Times*, Oxford: Martin Robertson, 199–227.

Hood, C., Dunsire, A. and Huby, M. (1988) Bureaucracies in retrenchment: Vulnerability theory and the case of U.K. central government departments 1975–85, *Administration & Society*, 20(3): 275–312.

Hughes, O. E. (1994) *Public Management and Administration*, Houndmills: Palgrave Macmillan.

Huyse, L. (1970) *Passiviteit, Pacificatie en Verzuiling in de Belgische Politiek*, Antwerp: Standaard Wetenschappelijke Uitgeverij.

Huyse, L. (1986) *De Gewapende Vrede: Politiek in België na 1945*, Leuven: Kritak.

International Labour Organisation (2013) *World of Work Report 2013: Repairing the Economic and Social Fabric*, Geneva: ILO.

International Herald Tribune (2008) China unveils sweeping plan for economy, 12 November.

International Monetary Fund (IMF) (2010) *Strategies for Fiscal Consolidation in the Post-Crisis World*, IMF Policy Paper, 4 February.

James, O. and Nakamura, A. (2013) The global financial crisis in the public sector: United Kingdom, COCOPS short country report.

Jick, T. D. and Murray, V. V. (1982) The management of hard times: Budget cutbacks in public sector organizations, *Organization Studies*, 3(2): 141–69.

Kanter, R. M. (1983) *The Change Masters: Corporate Entrepreneurs at Work*, London: Unwin Hyman.

Kattel, R. and Raudla, R. (2013) The Baltic republics and the crisis 2009–2011, *Europe-Asia Studies*, 65(3): 426–49.

Kawai, M. and Takagi, S. (2009) *Why was Japan Hit so Hard by the Global Economic Crisis?* Asia Development Bank Institute, Working Paper no. 153, October.

Kelman, S. (2006) Downsizing, competition, and organizational change in government: Is necessity the mother of invention? *Journal of Policy Analysis and Management* 25(4): 875–95.

Khademian, A. M. (2012) How to make the motivational, operational: A response to Rick Green, *Administration & Society*, 44(3): 374–7.

Kickert, W. (2000) *Public Management Reforms in the Netherlands*, Delft: Eburon.

Kickert, W. (2012a) State responses to the fiscal crisis in Britain, Germany and the Netherlands, *Public Management Review*, 14(3): 299–309.

Kickert, W. (2012b) How the UK government responded to the fiscal crisis: An outsider's view, *Public Money and Management*, 32(3): 169–76.

Kickert, W. (2012c) State responses to the fiscal crisis: Belgium, *Public Money and Management*, 32(4): 303–310.

Kickert, W. (2012d) How the Dutch government responded to financial, economic and fiscal crisis, *Public Money and Management*, 32(6): 439–444.

Kickert, W. (2013a) How the Danish government responded to the financial crisis, *Public Money and Management*, 33(1): 55–62.

Kickert, W. (2013b) How the German government responded to the fiscal crisis, *Public Money and Management*, 33(4): 291–296.

Kickert, W. (2013c) The politics of fiscal consolidation in the Netherlands in 2008–2013, COCOPS, submitted for publication to *International Review of Administrative Sciences*.

Kickert, W. (2014) Specificity of change management in public organisations, *American Review of Public Administration*, 44(6): 693–717.

Kickert, W. and Ysa, T. (2014) New development: How the Spanish government responded to the global banking crisis, *Public Money and Management*, 34(6): 453–458.

Kickert, W., Randma-Liiv, T. and Savi, R. (2013) Fiscal consolidation in Europe: A comparative analysis, COCOPS deliverable 7.2, September 2013, submitted for publication to *International Review of Administrative Sciences*.

Kogan, M. (1981) Education in 'hard times', in C. Hood and M. Wright (eds), *Big Governments in Hard Times*, Oxford: Martin Robertson, 152–73.

Kotter, J. (1996) *Leading Change*, Boston, MA: Harvard Business School Press.

Kristinsson, G. H. (2013) Iceland after the revolution: The impact of crisis on governance, COCOPS country case study, submitted for publication to *International Public Management Journal*.

Krugman, P. (2009) *The Return of Depression Economics and the Crisis of 2008*. New York: Norton & Company.

Kumar, R. and Vashisht, P. (2009) *The Global Economic Crisis: Impact on India and Policy Responses*, Asian Development Bank Institute, Working Paper no. 164, November.

Lægreid, P. (2013) Impact of the global financial crisis that started in 2008 in Norway: No fiscal crisis and cutback management, COCOPS country report.

Laswell, H. D. (1936) *Politics: Who Gets What When How?* New York: Whittlesey House.

Lehmbruch, G. (1967) *Proporz Demokratie: Politische Systeme und Politische Kultur in der Schweiz und in Österreich*, Tübingen: Mohr.

Levine, C. H. (1978) Organizational decline and cutback management, *Public Administration Review*, 38(4): 316–25.

Levine, C. H. (1979) More on cutback management: Hard questions for hard times, *Public Administration Review*, 39(2): 179–83.

Levine, C. H. (1980) *Managing Fiscal Stress*, Chatham, NJ: Chatham Press.

Levine, C. H. (1984) Retrenchment, human resource erosion, and the role of the personnel manager, *Public Personnel Management Journal*, 13(3): 249–63.

Levine, C. H. (1985) Police management in the 1980s. From decrementalism to strategic thinking, *Public Administration Review*, 45: 691–700.

Levine, C. H., Rubin, I. and Wolohojian, G. G. (1981) Resource scarcity and the reform model: The management of retrenchment in Cincinnati and Oakland, *Public Administration Review*, 41(6): 619–28.

Lewin, K. (1951) *Field Theory in Social Science*, New York: Harper & Row.

Lewis, C. and Logalbo, A. (1980) Cutback principles and practices: A checklist for managers, *Public Administration Review*, 40(2): 184–8.

Lijphart, A. (1968) Typologies of democratic systems, *Comparative Political Studies*, 1(1): 3–44.

Lijphart, A. (1969) Consociational democracy, *World Politics*, 21(2): 207–25.

Lijphart, A. (1977) *Democracies in Plural Societies: A Comparative Exploration*, New Haven, CT: Yale University Press.

Lijphart, A. (1984) *Democracies: Patterns of Majoritarian and Consensus Government in Twenty-One Countries*, New Haven, CT: Yale University Press.

Lindblom, C. E. (1959) The science of 'muddling through', *Public Administration Review*, 19(2): 79–88.

Lo, A. W. (2011) Reading about the financial crisis: A 21-book review, *Journal of Economic Literature*, 50(1): 151–78.

Lodge, M. and Hood, C. (2012) Into an age of multiple austerities? Public management and public service bargains across OECD countries, *Governance*, 25(1): 79–101.

Lynn, L. E. (1996) *Public Management as Art, Science and Profession*, Chatham, NJ: Chatham House.

MacCarthaigh, M. and Hardiman, N. (2013) State retrenchment and fiscal consolidation in Ireland, COCOPS country case study, submitted for publication to *International Public Management Journal*.

MacManus, S. A., Rattley, J. M., Ungaro, P. J., Brown, W. R., Jr, O'Donnell, S., Shalmy, D. L., Hickey, N. and Jubell, D. (1989) A decade of decline: A longitudinal look at big city and big county strategies to cope with declining revenues, *International Journal of Public Administration*, 12(5): 749–96.

McTighe, J. J. (1979) Management strategies to deal with shrinking resources, *Public Administration Review*, 39(1): 86–90.

Marando, V. L. (1990) General revenue sharing: Termination and city responses, *State and Local Government Review*, 22: 98–107.

Marer, P. (2010) The global economic crises: Impacts on Eastern Europe, *Acta Oeconomica*, 60(1): 3–33.

Massey, A. (2011) Nonsense on stilts: United Kingdom perspectives on the global financial crisis and governance, *Public Organization Review*, 11: 61–75.

Mohan, R. (2008) *Global Financial Crisis and Key Risks: Impact on India and Asia*, remarks by the deputy governor Reserve Bank of India at IMF-FSF meeting, Washington, DC, October 2008.

Moulton, S. and Wise, C. (2010) Shifting boundaries between the public and private sectors, *Public Administration Review*, 70(3): 349–60.

Müller, W. and Strom, K. (2003) *Coalition Government in Western Europe*, Oxford: Oxford University Press.

Myant, M. and Drahokoupil, J. (2012) International integration, varieties of capitalism and resilience to crisis in transition economies, *Europe-Asia Studies*, 64(1): 1–33.

Nakrosis, V., Vilpisauskas, R. and Kuokstis, V. (2013) Fiscal consolidation in Lithuania in the period 2008–2012, COCOPS, submitted for publication to *International Review of Administrative Sciences*.

OECD (2009) *Economic Outlook 85*, Paris: OECD.

OECD (2011) Restoring public finances, Special Issue of the *OECD Journal on Budgeting*.

OECD (2012) *Restoring Public Finances, 2012 Update*, Paris: OECD.

Ongaro, E., Di Mascio, F., Galli, D., Natalini, A. and Stolfi, F. (2013) The impact of the crisis on administrative reform in a 'context of motion': Italy 2007–2012, COCOPS country case study, submitted for publication to *International Public Management Journal*.

Osterheld, M., Fiedler, J., Görnitz, A. and Hammerschmidt, G. (2013) Public sector cutback management in Germany, COCOPS country case study.

Overmans, T. and Noordegraaf, M. (2014) Managing austerity: Rhetorical and real responses to fiscal stress in local government. *Public Money & Management*, 34(2): 99–106.

Page, E. C. (1992) *Political Authority and Bureaucratic Power: A Comparative Analysis*, London: Harvester Wheatsheaf.

Pandey, S. K. (2010) Cutback management and the paradox of publicness, *Public Administration Review*, 70(4): 564–71.

Peters, B. G. (2011) Governance responses to the fiscal crisis: Comparative perspectives, *Public Money and Management*, 31(1): 75–80.

Peters, B. G. and Pierre, J. (2004) *Politicization of the Civil Service in Comparative Perspective: The Quest for Control*, London: Routledge.

Peters, B. G., Pierre, J. and Randma-Liiv, T. (2011) Global financial crisis, Public Administration and governance: Do new problems require new solutions? *Public Organization Review*, 11: 13–27.

Pevcin, P. (2013) Fiscal balance and public sector downsizing in Slovenia, COCOPS country study.

Pisani-Ferry, J. (2007) Foreword, in J. Henriksson (ed.), *Ten Lessons About Fiscal Consolidation*, Brussels: Bruegel Lecture and Essay Series, 3–4.

Pollitt, C. (1990) *Managerialism and the Public Services*, Cambridge: Blackwell.

Pollitt, C. (2010) Cuts and reforms: Public services as we move into a new era, *Society and Economy*, 32(1): 17–31.

Pollitt, C. and Bouckaert, G. (2000) *Public Management Reform: A Comparative Analysis*, Oxford: Oxford University Press.

Ponticello, J. and Voth, J. (2011) *Austerity and Anarchy: Budget Cuts and Social Unrest in Europe, 1919–2008*, Work Document, Barcelona: University Pompeu Fabra.

Posner, P. and Blöndal, J. (2012) Democracies and deficits: Prospects for fiscal responsibility in democratic nations, *Governance*, 25(1): 11–34.

Posner, P. and Sommerfeld, M. (2013) The politics of fiscal austerity, *OECD Journal of Budgeting*, 13(1): 141–74.

Potter, M. (2012) Still learning to speak and still not being heard: Public Administration and the latest financial crisis, *Administration & Society*, 44(3): 367–73.

Raudla, R. (2013) Fiscal retrenchment in Estonia during the financial crisis: The role of institutional factors, *Public Administration*, 91(1): 32–50.

Raudla, R., Savi, R. and Randma-Liiv, T. (2013) Cutback management literature in the 1970s and 1980s: Taking stock, accepted for publication to *International Review of Administrative Sciences*.

Rekenhof (2009) *Impact van de Financiële Crisis and de genomen Maatregelen op het Beheer van de Staatsschuld en de Evolutie van de Staatsfinanciën*, Brussels: December 2009.

Rodrik, D. (1996) Understanding economic policy reform, *Journal of Economic Literature*, 34: 9–41.

Rubin, I. (1980) Universities in stress: Decision making under conditions of reduced resources, in C. H. Levine (ed.), *Managing Fiscal Stress: The Crisis in the Public Sector*, Chatham, NJ: Chatham House Publishers, 167–79.

Rubin, I. (1985) *Shrinking the Federal Government: The Effect of Cutbacks on Five Federal Agencies*, New York: Longman.

Savi, R. and Cepilovs, A. (forthcoming) The impact of crisis time central cutback strategies in public agencies: Comparing the cases of Estonia and Latvia, *Journal of Comparative Policy Analysis*.

Savi, R. and Randma-Liiv, T. (2013) Public policy making in time of crisis: Cutback management in Estonia, COCOPS country case-study, submitted for publication to *International Review of Administrative Sciences*.

Schick, A. (1980) Budgetary adaptations to resource scarcity, in C. H. Levine and I. Rubin (eds), *Fiscal Stress and Public Policy*, London: Sage, 113–34.

Schick, A. (1983) Incremental budgeting in a decremental cge, *Policy Sciences*, 16(1): 1–25.

Schick, A. (1988) Micro-budgetary adaptations to fiscal stress in industrialized democracies, *Public Administration Review*, 48(1): 523–33.

Schick, A. (2009) Crisis budgeting, *OECD Journal on Budgeting*, 3: 1–14.

Seldon, A. and Lodge, G. (2011) *Brown at 10*, London: Biteback Publishing.

Senior, B. (1997) *Organisational Change*, London: Pitman Publishing.

Sharpe, L. J. and Newton, K. (1984) *Does Politics Matter? The Determinants of Public Policy*, Oxford: Clarendon Press.

Starke, P. (2006) The politics of welfare state retrenchment: A literature review, *Social Policy and Administration*, 40(1): 104–20.

Steiner, J. (1974) *Amicable Agreement versus Majority Rule: Conflict Resolution in Switzerland*, Chapel Hill, NC: University of North Carolina Press.

Stern, E. and Sundelius, B. (1997) Sweden's twin monetary crises of 1992: Rigidity and learning in crisis decision making, *Journal of Contingencies and Crisis Management*, 5: 32–48.

Stiglitz, J. E. and Heymann, D. (2014) *Life After Debt*. Basingstoke: Palgrave Macmillan.

Strom, K. (1990) *Minority Government and Majority Rule*, Cambridge: Cambridge University Press.

Tarschys, D. (1981) Rational decremental budgeting: Elements of an expenditure policy for the 1980s, *Policy Sciences*, 14(1): 49–58.

Tarschys, D. (1985) Curbing public expenditure: Current trends, *Journal of Public Policy*, 5(1): 23–67.

Thelen, K. (1999) Historical institutionalism in comparative politics, *Annual Review of Political Science*, 2: 369–404.

Thynne, I. (2011) Symposium introduction: The global financial crisis, governance and institutional dynamics, *Public Organization Review*, 11: 1–12.

Tompson, W. (2010) Reform beyond the crisis, in *Making Reform Happen: Lessons from OECD Countries*, Paris: OECD Publishing, 11–38.

Treasury Committee (2009a) *Banking Crisis: Dealing with the Failure of the UK Banks*, HC 416, London: The Stationary Office.

Treasury Committee (2009b) *Budget 2009*, HC 438-I, London: The Stationary Office.

Treasury Committee (2010) *Spending Review 2010*, HC 544-I, London: The Stationary Office.

Troupin, S., Stroobants, J. and Steen, T. (2013) The impact of the fiscal crisis on Belgian federal government, COCOPS country case study, submitted for publication to *International Review of Administrative Sciences*.

Van de Walle, S. and Jilke, S. (2014) Saving in public services: A multilevel analysis of public preferences in the EU27, International Review of Administrative Sciences, 80(3): 597–618.

van den Noord, P. (2011) Turning the page: EU fiscal consolidation in the wake of the crisis, *Empirica*, 38: 19–51.

Verick, S. and Islam, I. (2010) *The Great Recession of 2008–2009: Causes, Consequences and Policy Responses*, Institute for the Study of Labor, Discussion Paper No. 4934.

Vis, B., van Kersbergen, K. and Hylands, T. (2011) To what extent did the financial crisis intensify the pressure to reform the welfare state? *Social Policy & Administration*, 45(4): 338–53.

Wildavsky, A. (2001) *Budgeting and Governing*, New Brunswick, NJ: Transaction Publishers.

Wolman, H. (1983) Understanding local government responses to fiscal pressure: A cross national analysis, *Journal of Public Policy*, 3(3): 245–63.

Wolman, H. and Davis, B. (1980) Local government strategies to cope with fiscal pressure, in C. H. Levine and I. Rubin (eds), *Fiscal Stress and Public Policy*, London: Sage, 231–48.

World Bank (2008) *Lessons from World Bank Research on Financial Crises*, Policy Research Working Paper 4779.

World Bank (2012) *World Bank Database of Political Institutions*, DPI2012, December 2012.

World Health Organization (2009) *The Financial Crisis and Global Health: Report of a High-Level Consultation*, 19 January.

Wright, M. (1981) Big governments in hard times: The restraint of public expenditure, in C. Hood and M. Wright (eds), *Big Governments in Hard Times*, Oxford: Martin Robertson, 3–31.

Ysa, T., Giné, M., Esteve, M. and Sierra, V. (2012) Public corporate governance of state-owned enterprises: Evidence from the Spanish banking industry, *Public Money and Management*, 32(4): 265–72.

Yu, Y. (2010) *The Impact of the Global Financial Crisis on the Chinese Economy and China's Policy Responses*, Malaysia: Third World Network.

Ziller, J. (1993) *Administrations Comparées: Les Systèmes Politico-Administratifs de l'Europe des Douze*, Paris: Montchrestien.

Index